# THE ULTIMATE PREPPER'S SURVIVAL GUIDE

**Thunder Bay Press**
An imprint of Printers Row Publishing Group
10350 Barnes Canyon Road, Suite 100, San Diego, CA 92121
www.thunderbaybooks.com • mail@thunderbaybooks.com



Printers Row Publishing Group is a division of Readerlink Distribution Services, LLC.
Thunder Bay Press is a registered trademark of Readerlink Distribution Services, LLC.

Correspondence regarding the content of this book should be sent to Thunder Bay Press, Editorial Department, at the above address. Rights, permissions, and author inquiries should be addressed to Welbeck Publishing, 20 Mortimer Street, London, W1T 3JW, United Kingdom.

**Thunder Bay Press**
Publisher: Peter Norton • Associate Publisher: Ana Parker
Editor: Dan Mansfield
Senior Product Manager: Kathryn C. Dalby

**Welbeck Publishing Group**
Editorial: Chris Mitchell
Design Manager: Stephen Cary

Library of Congress Cataloging-in-Publication data available on request.

ISBN: 978-1-64517-377-9

Printed in China

24 23 22 21 20 1 2 3 4 5

# THE ULTIMATE PREPPER'S SURVIVAL GUIDE

## SURVIVE THE END OF THE WORLD AS WE KNOW IT

**JAMES WESLEY, RAWLES**

Founder and Senior Editor of SurvivalBlog.com

THUNDER BAY
P·R·E·S·S
San Diego, California

# PUBLISHER'S NOTE

Please read the following provisos and disclaimers:

## Not a Doctor or Attorney

The author, James Wesley, Rawles (JWR), is not a physician, and doesn't give medical advice. JWR and Welbeck Publishing Group are not responsible for the use or misuse of any drug, medical device, supplement, or other product mentioned in this book.

JWR is not a lawyer, and doesn't give legal advice. Any laws, regulations, or case citations contained within this book do not constitute legal advice. Laws change frequently and vary by territory. Consult a lawyer if you have legal questions. If you choose to act upon the details cited in the book without doing your own research, then you do so at your own risk.

## Not a Financial Adviser

Per the SEC Investment Advisers Act of 1940 (as amended): JWR is not a paid investment counselor or adviser. JWR is not a stockholder of any company, nor employed by or a contractor with any company. JWR does not make specific stock or bond buying recommendations. Make all investments at your own risk.

## No Seditious Intent

Nothing herein is intended, in any way to be seditious (per 18 U.S. Code § 2384). JWR and the publisher are not making a call to arms, nor any threats to a government or to any individual, agency, or group. This book is for educational/informational purposes only, with presumptions and conjecture about the future.

## Accuracy, Safety, and Legality

The content of this book is not guaranteed for accuracy, reliability, safety, timeliness, or legality in all jurisdictions. It is presented for educational and informational purposes only. You are responsible for your own actions. This includes your stupidity or carelessness. Refer to manufacturer documentation for product safety and dosing information.

Consult a locally licensed attorney to check on the legality in your area of the tools, weapons, devices, formulas, and practices mentioned. JWR and Welbeck Publishing Group are not responsible for the use, misuse, or failure to use any information or product mentioned in this book.

# ACKNOWLEDGMENTS


This book is dedicated to my wonderful wife, Avalanche Lily. She is my partner in prepping. If every family in the world had a bountiful and well-tended garden like hers, then hunger would become just a memory.

My sincere thanks to the many readers of SurvivalBlog.com. Your collective knowledge and hard-earned wisdom are tremendous. You've added greatly to my knowledge, and now I'm sharing that with readers of this book. I am profoundly grateful!

Special thanks to SurvivalBlog readers C.Y., Charles K., J.S.F., "John and Abigail Adams," P.R., and "Tona" for their input to this book.

Thanks also to my fellow blog editors Pat Cascio, Michael Z. Williamson, and Hugh Latimer for their regular posts to SurvivalBlog, and their suggestions for topics to cover in this text.

I'd also like to acknowledge the sage influence of Craig DeLuz, Alan Gottlieb, Bill Buppert, Alan Korwin, the late Col. Jeff Cooper, the late Mel Tappan, and the late Jerry Pournelle—all of whom inspired this book and many of my other writings.

A tip of the hat to my agent Robert Gottlieb, for securing the contract that made publication of this book possible.

Lastly, my thanks to the skilled editors and graphic designers of Welbeck Publishing Group. You are truly masters at your craft.

**– JWR**

# CONTENTS

# FOREWORD BY MICHAEL Z. WILLIAMSON

Mr. Rawles begins his introduction with "We live in a fragile world..." after lengthy disclaimers earlier in the book that prove it. It's a complex world where laws, customs, wants, needs, and agendas all overlap, interlock, and interact with each other, sometimes disastrously.

One often thinks of disasters both as something that happens to others, and as apocalyptically newsworthy. Certainly, earthquakes, volcanoes, and climate shifts are these, and are documented throughout history. Less well-documented—until recently—are smaller events like tornadoes, regional fires, and local floods (or even major ones). Who now remembers the Mississippi Flood of 1993? I was there fighting it for six weeks, so I certainly remember it. We've also had meteor strikes within human history, some even caught on camera.

Then there are the minor calamities. "Minor" unless one is directly affected, of course. A couple of years back, within the course of ten days my family experienced: a near miss with a tornado that knocked down trees, a lightning strike that took out some of our electronics, and a deluge of rain that caused our house to flood (we live on the slope of a hill, not in the valley). A house fire is a disaster for those involved. People have died on the roadside in blizzards or deserts. And unemployment can cause upheaval for any family.

Mundane people will often snicker and mock those who are prepared. In my experience, such comments stop the moment that an actual emergency occurs, and resume again shortly afterward. They say things like, "If the end of the world happens, I'm coming to your place." I suppose they can. But please bring useful skills, people willing to work, food, tools, and a means of defense. I'm charitable, but there are limits.

This book is an excellent introduction to the mindset of being prepared, or a good reminder to those who are already on the path, but distracted by real-world matters like jobs, bills, and family. There really is no end to preparedness. One can certainly be educated, but as with any pursuit, there is always more knowledge. You may find yourself observing the tiniest of incidents and analyzing how they could be handled better. While hindsight is easy, it's also the key to foresight. This doesn't solely relate to mistakes, of course—if one survives an event relatively unscathed, one did it right. But is it possible to do even better next time? This thought process is key. The prepared mind has no guarantees, but certainly better odds of surviving any particular disaster than those that aren't.

Nor does it take a fortune to prepare, as Mr. Rawles will explain. A few dollars on food here, some basic reliable tools there, soundly planned emergency kits in vehicles and the house built a piece at a time. The modern economy allows for the poorest among us to be ready to face the worst the universe can throw at us. With a solid mindset, and a faith in your God or guiding philosophy, one can be ready to face any disaster with a cool head, tools in hand, and, if not a solution in mind, then at least the methodology to formulate one.

When it is all over (for the time being, at least), the goal is to be intact and healthy, ideally with one's family, friends, community, nation, and world all moving forward. Our species has survived any number of events that could have meant our end. Every nation, most cities, and many people have faced historic events, local troubles, and personal emergencies, and come through stronger afterward.

As in any field, there are few people who truly qualify as experts, and many who will humbly deny the charge, admitting only to being "learned" or "having studied." After thirty-five years dealing with various disasters as a military engineer and in the civilian world, and having known Mr. Rawles for twenty of those, I can confidently call him an expert, even if he is always continuing to hone his craft—as we all should.

If you are new to the concept of preparedness, then welcome. We're mostly friendly, eager to share, and sometimes a bit odd. If you're seeking a refresher or more structure to your existing plans, then this is also the place to be.

**Biographical Note:** Michael Z. Williamson is a prolific and award-winning science-fiction author. Born in Birkenhead, England, he emigrated first to Canada and then to the United States. He retired as a member of the U.S. military, serving in active and reserve components with both the U.S. Army and U.S. Air Force, for twenty-five years. He deployed overseas for Operation Guarded Skies in support of Operation Desert Fox, and for Operation Iraqi Freedom (OIF). Mike is also an accomplished bladesmith and hobby gunsmith. He volunteers as SurvivalBlog's Editor-at-Large.

# INTRODUCTION

We live in a fragile world.

Modern societies are complex and surprisingly dependent on liquid fuels, power grids, telecommunications, and electronic funds transfers. Globe-spanning supply chains provide our necessities of life. It doesn't take much to disrupt any of those. If several of them went missing for an extended period, then the world would be plunged into a deep economic depression, and it is easy to see how this could descend into a full-scale collapse.

Preparedness for disasters is not alarmist. Rather, given the many existential threats we face, it is wise and prudent. In *The Ultimate Prepper's Survival Guide,* I will describe how you can prepare yourself and your family to be ready for disaster—whether it is localized and short-term or a multigenerational "worst-case" Malthusian societal implosion.

For more than thirty years, I've watched the complexity and interdependency of modern society steadily increase, and warned my readers of the inimical risks. Since 2005, I have described ways to mitigate those risks in my daily blog, at SurvivalBlog.com. This blog relates much more than just my own knowledge. It also imparts the collective knowledge and hard-earned wisdom of readers in more than 100 countries. To them, I am truly thankful.

As you read this book, I urge you to take it seriously. Whether you are a youthful tyro or a wizened veteran, there will be something herein that will boost your chances of survival, no matter what hazardous situations arise.

I have not written this book at the "beginner level." I am assuming that you have common sense and know the basics of everyday living, such as cooking, cleaning, and how to use hand tools. In general, my intent with this book is for it to cover the topics that all of the extant survival and preparedness books gloss over or skip entirely.

Unless you have read my blog regularly, you will most likely find yourself flipping back often to refer to the glossary; I tend to use a lot of acronyms. There is a steep learning curve to prepping. Challenge yourself to learn quickly. In *The Ultimate Prepper's Survival Guide*, you will be drinking from a fire hose.

With competence comes confidence. With dedicated study comes deep understanding. With practice comes skill and speed. With faith comes assurance and peace of mind.

This book goes to press in the year 2020, with the benefit of "20/20 hindsight" on the past two centuries. The world has changed tremendously since 1820. The vast majority of citizens of Western nations are now almost completely detached from agrarian living. Back in 1820, 95 percent of the world's population lived off the land. But today, just 2 percent of the population of First World nations either farms or fishes to feed the other ninety-eight. A disruption of supply chains could very easily lead to a monumental catastrophe with an unprecedented loss of life.

Therefore, be ready.

I wish you God's blessings and the love of Christ in the dark days that may come in our lifetimes.

**James Wesley, Rawles**
The Rawles Ranch
Somewhere west of the Rockies

CHAPTER 1

# A WORLD OF RISK

- Too Little for Too Many
- Economic Collapse
- Fire, Flood, and Earthquake Risks
- A Little Ice Age?
- Famine Stalks the Land
- Invasion, Evasion, and Resistance Warfare
- Fearful Masters?
- The Nukes
- Calculated Control (AI and Sovereign E-currencies)
- Pandemics and Biological Warfare

# TOO LITTLE FOR TOO MANY

**"'Be Prepared'... the meaning of the motto is that a Scout must prepare himself by previous thinking out and practicing how to act on any accident or emergency so that he is never taken by surprise."**

Gen. Robert Baden Powell

Historians may someday characterize the twenty-first century as both a century of plenty and one of shortages. We are presently living in the time of plenty, with technological advances driving unprecedented economic growth, urbanization, innovation, and prosperity. But simultaneously, global debt is rising, the population is increasing, and crop failures are looming. Therefore, there is the possible threat of economic collapse and famine, followed by massive displacement of refugee populations worldwide. In this chapter, I will describe a variety of scenarios that could lead to economic displacement, depopulation, and societal collapse.

The world's population has grown from 2.5 billion in 1950 to 7.8 billion in 2020. Recently, the rate of increase has slowed substantially, but even the current growth is alarming. Even with the slower rate of increase, the population is theoretically projected to exceed 9.7 billion by 2050. I say "theoretically" because I consider a die-off event in the interim far more likely. There are simply too many people scrambling after too few resources.

A pandemic, a massive famine, or a large-scale war will probably prevent the world population reaching 9.7 billion by 2050.

Other threats abound wherever you look. The oceans of the world have already seen their fish populations substantially depleted by overfishing. Desertification is harmfully affecting sub-Saharan Africa. Elsewhere, other climate effects of change are ongoing, but the world's climate scientists have divided into camps. Some claim that the climate is warming, while others claim that we could be headed into a profound solar-activity minimum and hence global cooling.

For the past three decades, the politics of Western nations have been dominated by a view that the Earth is undergoing "global warming." In recent years, the advocates of this view have shifted their rhetoric, to instead use the terms "climate change" and "climate emergency." In November 2019, the European Parliament received a climate declaration from Professor Guus Berkhout, the spokesman of a Dutch group called Climate Intelligence Foundation (CLINTEL). They had collected signatures from more than 700 prominent scientists, academics, and industrialists in support of the core statement: "There is no climate emergency." Signatories to the CLINTEL declaration included Nobel laureate and professor Ivar Giaever and the influential mathematician and physicist Professor Freeman Dyson.

The "climate change" issue is both unsettled science, and deeply divisive, and it remains to be seen just how the climate is changing. However, because it shapes national and supranational policies and taxation, climate-change politics have some profound and far-reaching consequences. Whatever happens, it is already cause for concern and strategic planning. If the climate is indeed warming, then relocation to higher latitudes, and up in elevation from seashores would be wise. But if the climate is instead cooling, then relocation to lower latitudes—and perhaps lower elevations—would be prudent.

**WORLD'S POPULATION IN 2020**

**7.8 BILLION**

## Triggers to a Die-Off

The most likely triggers for a global die-off would be an economic collapse, a blight of one or more principal crops, or famine caused by weather extremes. With any of these, the risk exists that both globalized and local chains of supply would break down and that power grids would collapse. Once the grids go down, the essential structure of modern technologically driven societies will crumble. Modern technological infrastructures are now so intertwined with power grids and the global Internet that losing grid power would be completely devastating. Sans grid power, a breakdown of law and order could come within a few days, a massive dislocation of refugees within two weeks, and a die-off of population perhaps within six months.

# ECONOMIC COLLAPSE

Modern nations have currencies built on mountains of debt, and most governments are accustomed to chronically overspending. Overspending from national treasuries often leads to gradual debasement of currencies. This, in turn, typically leads to mass inflation and then revaluation or even outright repudiation of national currencies. This seemingly endless cycle of debt and currency inflation seen in dozens of nations has meant that the average period between currency reforms for national currencies is around seventy-five years. Currency swaps usually take place only after destabilizing bouts of high inflation, or even hyperinflation. Sometimes an inflated currency can be somewhat salvaged by simply lopping off a zero or two. In more extreme cases, such as was seen in Weimar Germany or more recently in Zimbabwe, an old currency is completely repudiated, making any savings absolutely worthless.

In the case of the United States, it has had a currency managed by a private banking cartel since 1913. Since the Federal Reserve was established in the United States, we have seen: gradual inflation of the currency (Federal Reserve Notes), one major economic depression, a series of economic recessions, and full debasement of our coinage. This debasement deserves particular mention: Gold coins were seized and replaced with paper notes in 1934, and silver coins were

phased out between 1964 and 1970. All the coins that are issued now are nearly worthless copper and zinc tokens. Only the U.S. nickel coin has any real value.

Since 1913, the U.S. dollar has lost 97 percent of its purchasing power.

## End of the Gold Standard

This same pattern of inflation and currency debasement has been repeated all around the world. In fact, there is no longer any national currency that is redeemable for gold or silver. This is a huge change from eighty years ago. (Before World War II, the majority of national currencies were redeemable, and most nations still issued silver coins for general circulation.)

Since 1913, the U.S. dollar has also lost 97 percent of its purchasing power, with the majority of that loss occurring after circulating silver coinage was no longer minted. Our currency is now entirely debt-based with inflation relentlessly driven by fractional reserve banking. In contrast, up until the early twentieth century, currencies were based on specie (gold and/or silver) and issued independently by national mints. But today, money comes into circulation by a coordination of national treasuries and central bankers handling the monetization of sovereign debt. Thus, money is now "loaned" into circulation, and the volume of money is controlled by manipulation of interest rates by central banks. What's more, today the vast majority of "currency" is electronic-ledger entries, rather than printed bills.

The inflation of the U.S. dollar has benefited the government, as it works as a hidden form of taxation. Since it is gradual, inflation is not plainly noticeable to most citizens. But it constitutes an ongoing erosion of any cash on hand, and of any savings. In effect, we are being robbed in slow motion. The key benefit to the government is that all debts (including government debts) are paid off in inflated dollars.

Another benefit to the government is that taxpayers experience "bracket creep," as their wages and salaries increase. This gradually pushes more of the middle class into higher income-tax brackets. And with more households needing to have both adults working long hours outside the home to "keep up" and pay ever-increasing taxes, it has had the unintended consequence of fostering a myriad of social problems created by stress, anxiety, and lack of parental supervision for children.

Since inflation discourages saving, it conversely encourages consumerism and indebtedness. It has also put residential housing at a premium. Most Americans look at tangible home ownership as one of their few safe refuges from the ravages of inflation. But now, for much of Generation X (and later generations), house-price inflation has put home ownership beyond their reach.

In the final analysis, the era of inflation, big government, and high taxes is slowly destroying the middle class, while real wealth is being concentrated in only the upper echelons of society, particularly in banking, finance, and corporate management. This has been occurring all around the world for much of the twentieth and twenty-first centuries. The modern world has always had "haves" and "have-nots," but never before has this income stratification been so stark.

## Destructive Debt

The mountains of debt that have been created are nearly impossible to repay. It would only be in a period of mass inflation or hyperinflation that there would be any opportunity to completely repay public and private debts. The global debt goes on and on, with various national currencies falling into disfavor in succession. But virtually all of the world's currencies are debt-based and inflating

As Venezuelan society collapsed in the late 2010s, hyperinflation bit hard. At one point, one U.S. dollar was worth 250,000 bolivars.

at various rates, and inevitably they are all doomed. These currencies are in a race to the bottom. There are no winners, only losers. Some "strong" currencies will resist going to zero longer than others, but they are still losing, albeit more slowly than most others.

Having both debt-based currencies and profligate-spending governments locks the various national economies into repeated boom–and–bust business cycles. The busts are rarely enough to force governments out of power or to bankrupt the "banksters." But they certainly cause plenty of grief and hardship for small businesses. Large corporations and commercial banks have learned how to lobby for special tax status, legal perquisites, and taxpayer-funded bailouts that seem to make them less vulnerable to the boom–and–bust business cycle.

Despite all of this, the United States has fared relatively well since the end of World War II, in part because we are the dominant player in global trade. Because of this, the U.S. dollar has held international Reserve Currency status. Having most international transactions settled in U.S. dollars has been a huge benefit for the country politically, militarily, and economically.

There is, however, a downside to this, which is that a strong dollar has indirectly caused a steep decline in U.S. exports and U.S. manufacturing. Dollar dominance and global peacekeeper status has also made the United States a key target for transnational terrorism.

At some point, the debt balloon generated by all of these actions will become unsustainable, and even the almighty dollar will meet its demise. What's more, the longer that this is forestalled through central-bank trickery, the deeper and longer the inevitable resultant depression will be. Someday, the piper must be paid, and he will demand a lot! By then, the only relative safety will be for those living on productive land with no debt, and holding true tangible wealth that is not in U.S. dollars. When the end comes, nearly every dollar-denominated investment will be wiped out, along with the dollar itself.

The hyperinflation orchestrated by Zimbabwe's central bank created currency that literally was not worth the paper it was printed on. Before they capitulated, the highest denomination note was 100 trillion Zimbabwean dollars.

**DOLLAR WIPEOUT: ON DECEMBER 7, 2018, ALMOST $1 TRILLION WAS WIPED FROM THE VALUE OF STOCKS IN JUST FOUR DAYS OF TRADING.**

# FIRE, FLOOD, AND EARTHQUAKE RISKS

Economic collapse is the most likely major man-made disaster in the next two decades, but natural disasters can be counted on, year in, year out. In the past ten years, the average number of deaths from catastrophes averaged 60,000 per year. Fires, floods, and earthquakes were some of the top contributors. The extensive bushfires in Australia in 2020 illustrated just how extensive, fast moving, and devastating fires can be. Wildfires in Siberia in the summer of 2019 burned more than 15,000 square miles. Notably, there had also been large fires in Siberia in 2017 and 2018. Though not directly affected by the flames, residents of major cities that were downwind found themselves choking on dense smoke, and it was not just those nearby that had to worry. The 2019 Siberian fires were so huge that their smoke plumes reached the western United States.

Floods tend to be short-term events, but their costs can be enormous, especially when they occur in well-developed urban areas. And in terms of personal risk, major floods, weather-triggered landslides, and tsunamis can be some of the greatest risks to human life. The Boxing Day tsunami of 2004 off the cost of Indonesiea took nearly 228,000 lives, and was the sixth-largest disaster in recorded history.

More recently, in 2017, the largest catastrophic loss of life was in Sierra Leone, with 1,141 deaths caused by landslides triggered by heavy rains.

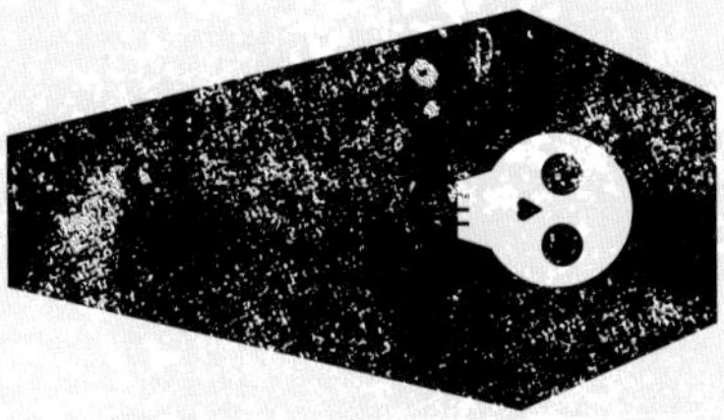

**60,000**

**AVERAGE NUMBER OF DEATHS FROM CATASTROPHES IN THE PAST TEN YEARS.**

The Eagle Creek wildfire burned for three months in 2017 in Columbia River Gorge, Oregon. Roughly 50,000 acres were consumed.

Flooding all across the American Midwest in 2019 caused hundreds of millions of dollars in damages. Pictured is a photo of deluged Davenport, Iowa.

Vehicles try to drive through a flooded street in Dhaka, Bangladesh, in July 2018. Bangladesh has been repeatedly plagued by flooding, often with huge loss of life and property.

A flooded shopping street in Walmgate, England, after the river Ouse left its banks in December 2015.

In that same year, an earthquake on the Iran-Iraq border took 630 lives. Also in 2017, monsoon flooding in India killed 514 people. These are just a few examples taken from one single year. As population increases and more of the earth is covered by human sprawl, these instances will grow more frequent and worsen.

Regular summer monsoon season flooding in Bangladesh illustrates just how precarious life can be in a flood zone. Bangladesh sits on a low river delta, and India has dammed all the delta's major source rivers. With the rivers' water levels and silt-deposition rates dropping, the land is eroding away into the sea, and every storm and seasonal rain floods what is left. Thus, every monsoon season tends to be a "disaster season" in Bangladesh. The most memorable flood there occurred in 1970 and took an unimaginable 300,000 lives. In 1991, a tropical cyclone took another 138,000 lives. Calling Bangladesh "disaster prone" is an understatement. I will discuss some of the personal-preparedness implications of floods in chapter 3.

## Preparing for Earthquakes

Major earthquakes are difficult to predict and their effects can be profound. The 1976

**SEA LEVELS COULD RISE AS MUCH AS 19 INCHES (48 CM) BY 2050, ACCORDING TO WHAT A REPORT CALLS "MID-RANGE PROJECTIONS."**

earthquake in China was estimated to have killed 255,000 people, for example. More recently, the 2010 earthquake in Haiti took 222,570 lives.

Thankfully, I live in a country with modern building standards. This is not so in the case of many third world nations, where unreinforced masonry construction is the norm. In the third world, builders tend to be very parsimonious with reinforcing bar ("rebar"). As a consequence, nearly every time there is a large earthquake in those regions, there are multiple building collapses with large loss of life.

By far the safest houses for earthquakes are of wood-frame construction. This is because such structures can flex and sway when an earthquake rolls through. Take the recent history of relatively large earthquakes in California as an example. You will see that the three things that suffer the most are: (1) bridges and overpasses; (2) brick fireplace chimneys attached to wood-frame houses; and (3) water mains. Residents there can be thankful that wood-frame construction is the norm, and that most masonry buildings in the U.S. and Canada have sufficient rebar for reinforcement. However, even reinforced concrete and brick is inherently more vulnerable than wood frame in the most severe earthquakes, such as magnitude 7 or higher on the Richter scale. Incidentally, the Richter scale is logarithmic (base 100). This means that a magnitude 7 is ten times more powerful than a magnitude 6.

For those of you reading this who live in a wood-frame house or apartment in an area prone to earthquakes, you should have two concerns: (1) seismic retrofitting, if needed; and (2) securing furniture, water heaters, wall hangings, and fragile items from falling.

**IN 2010, THE NUMBER OF PEOPLE THAT DIED BY EARTHQUAKES WORLDWIDE WAS**

# 320,120

Tangshan City, China, was devastated by an earthquake in 1976. It was reported that up to 500,000 people died. The event was hushed up by Chinese Communist Party officials, who feared loss of face over substandard building practices that had put lives at risk.

**NOTE**

Unless you already own a large, high-torque 90-degree masonry drill and have the requisite experience to use it, then you should probably hire a contractor to handle the job of retrofitting sill bolts. According to the 2008 FEMA advisory on seismic retrofitting:

"Having a contractor bolt the sill plates to the foundation will cost approximately $50 to $75 per bolt, depending on the type of foundation you have. For example, a structure measuring 60 feet by 30 feet would have a perimeter of 180 feet and would therefore require a minimum of thirty bolts (if the bolts are placed no more than 6 feet apart). So the cost for that structure would be about $1,500 to $2,250."

Also see: FEMA 232, Homebuilders' Guide to Earthquake-Resistant Design and Construction, dated June 2006.

## Seismic Retrofitting Standards

To become earthquake-safe, many wood-frame houses that were built on typical concrete "ring and pier" foundations before the 1980s may require additional sill bolts. These are the large bolts that attach the wooden bottom sill plate (also known as the "sole plate") of your house frame to the concrete foundation. To be safe from most earthquakes under magnitude 7, your house should have sill lag bolts spaced at no smaller than six-foot intervals. To check, simply grab a flashlight and check your house!

## Strap That!

After you have made sure that your house structure itself is earthquake-safe, you should look closely at the contents of your house. Walk through, room-by-room, and perform a mental exercise: Imagine a magnitude 6+ earthquake hitting your house. What items are vulnerable to tipping or coming loose? Look particularly at attachments for shelves, lockers, tall cabinets, televisions, aquariums, and armoires. Ditto for any large-framed pictures or mirrors. Examine their current attachments (or lack thereof), and beef them up. When you consider the potential risk of injury and the high cost of replacing damaged items in your house, then the time

Inexpensive retrofits of sill bolts and hot-water heater strapping could prevent some very expensive damage in the event of an earthquake.

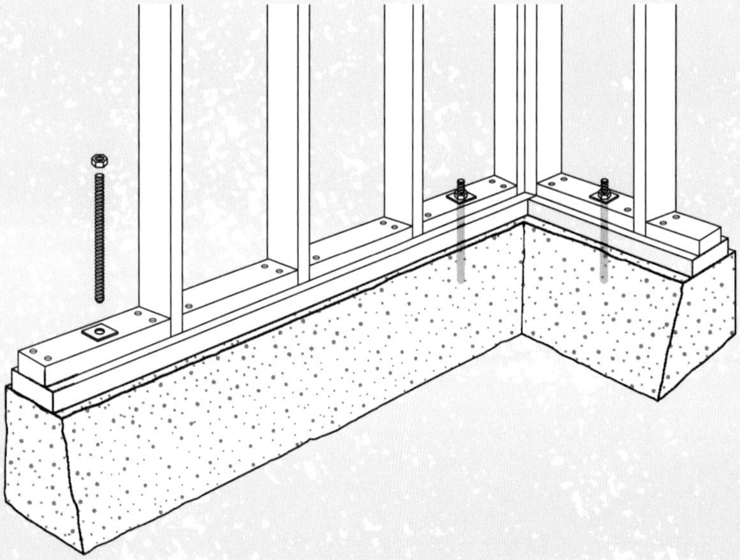

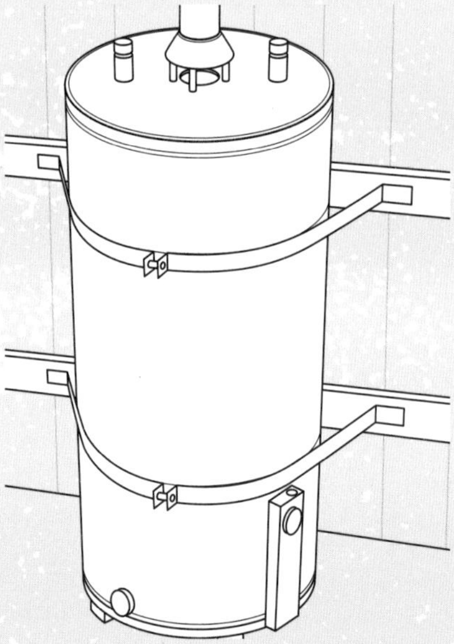

required and cost of adding protective straps is negligible.

I want to make special mention of flat-screen televisions and computer monitors. These have become ubiquitous in the past fifteen years. Not only are they inherently more prone to tipping than traditional "box" CRTs, but both their number and their sizes have steadily grown as their price has quickly decreased. The good news is that most televisions and monitors have one or more threaded holes in the back. You can use these to insert an appropriate-size eyebolt. This bolt can be chained, roped, or cable-tied to a wall anchor bolt. Don't leave more than two inches of free play in that attachment.

## Preventing Huge Messes

Retaining straps for shelf contents are also important, but an essential is installing a hot-water heater retaining strap if you have a traditional freestanding water tank heater. It could be a considerable risk to your household if it were to tip over in an earthquake. Not only would it dump its contents, but it is also very likely to break the inlet water line, and break its natural gas, propane, or electric service line. Those are huge risks that could badly damage or destroy your house by either flooding or fire. However, there is a simple solution: attaching a galvanized steel retaining strap to the nearest wall(s). These straps will stop a hot-water heater from tipping over in all but the most severe earthquakes. Their cost is quite low: under $25, assuming that you do the installation yourself.

## Plan B: Evacuation

No matter how well you plan, prepare, construct, and retrofit to be ready for an earthquake, there is always that dreaded "worst case." Here, I'm talking about an earthquake of such great magnitude that it makes even stout wood-frame houses uninhabitable. One "plan B" fallback would be to preposition clothing, bedding, tentage, fuel, weapons, field gear, first-aid supplies, a fire extinguisher, and so forth in a freestanding shed, in a car trunk, or in a camping trailer that will survive even a high-magnitude earthquake. Obviously, the trunk of a car is only an option if the car is parked out in a safe location away from large trees and buildings.

In a severe earthquake, many windows will be broken, so I also recommend buying some rolls of 6 mm (or thicker) translucent sheet plastic to keep on hand. A house with broken windows would be at least habitable, with ersatz plastic windows tacked up in place, while you await the availability of proper replacements. Window-glass shops will surely be very busy for weeks or months afterward.

All of the preceding advice is, of course, primarily of great concern to folks living along the Pacific Rim and in the New Madrid Seismic Zone. The regions along the edges of western North America are also at considerable risk. But everyone in America needs to prepare for earthquakes. Earthquakes can occur in places where they have never been reported before. In August 2019, there was a magnitude 6.4 earthquake in a locale where quakes were not even expected, on Alaska's North Slope. Luckily, that is a very lightly populated region. In my opinion, this illustrates that the earthquakes in the "diverse places" mentioned in the Bible really are a possibility:

> **For many shall come in my name, saying, I am Christ; and shall deceive many. And ye shall hear of wars and rumors of wars: see that ye be not troubled: for all these things must come to pass, but the end is not yet. For nation shall rise against nation, and kingdom against kingdom: and there shall be famines, and pestilences, and earthquakes, in diverse places. All these are the beginning of sorrows.**
>
> Matthew 24:5-8

Be ready, folks.

**6.4**

**IN AUGUST 2019, THERE WAS A MAGNITUDE 6.4 EARTHQUAKE IN A LOCALE WHERE QUAKES WERE NOT EVEN EXPECTED, ON ALASKA'S NORTH SLOPE.**

# A LITTLE ICE AGE?

The Earth's weather, climate, and all biological systems are driven by the Sun. With the exception of fungi, life on Earth is directly or indirectly solar powered. The Sun experiences a regular cycle of solar activity that runs on average over eleven years, and this cycle is believed to affect the temperatures on Earth. The most recent cycle has been unusually weak, with an extremely low number of sunspots. In comparison with previous cycles, the face of the Sun has been nearly blank. This has been dubbed the Eddy Minimum, after the astronomer John A. Eddy; Eddy's work in solar astronomy has some enormous implications for global weather, climate, agriculture, the economy, and even global demographics. Solar minimums seem to occur roughly once every 400 years, and this timescale has led some climatologists to predict that we are now entering a prolonged solar minimum.

During the winter months of many years in the period from 1650 to 1700, the planet experienced cold weather far beyond the normal range. The Mississippi River, for example, froze nearly all the way to the Gulf of Mexico while, across the Atlantic, parts of the river Thames froze thick enough to allow ice-skating. An early English astronomer, Edward Walter Maunder, was the first to notice and publish evidence of an extreme lack of sunspots between 1645 and 1715.

"Black" sunspots are still very hot (3,800°F) but look darker, because the rest of the surface is over 5,000°F. Sunspots have been very uncommon in the last two 11-year solar cycles.

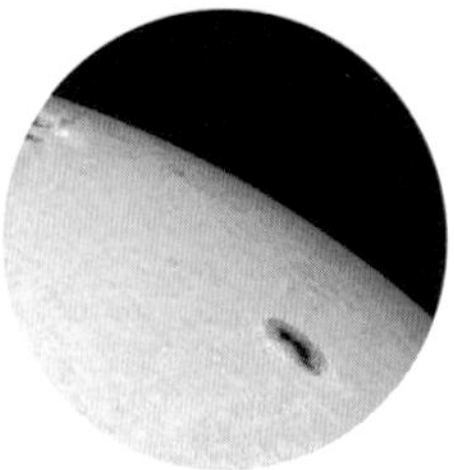

The "deep Maunder minimum," as Eddy has named this global cold snap, is a worrying example of what could occur if we are now reentering a lengthy solar minimum phase.

Some of the most outspoken advocates of the global cooling theory are Russian climatologists. The following is a quote from a 2019 article published by the Russian Novosti news service:

> **Khabibullo Abdusamatov of the Pulkovo Astronomic Observatory in St. Petersburg said Monday that temperatures will begin falling six or seven years from now, when global warming caused by increased solar activity in the twentieth century reaches its peak, RIA Novosti reported. The coldest period will occur 15 to 20 years after a major solar output decline between 2035 and 2045, Abdusamatov said. Dramatic changes in the earth's surface temperatures are an ordinary phenomenon, not an anomaly, he said, and result from variations in the sun's energy output and ultraviolet radiation.**

*Le Paiement de la Dime* by Pieter Brueghel the Younger. (On display at the Lille Palace of Fine Arts.) There was plenty of time for ice-skating during the "Little Ice Age."

Brian Fagan argues in *The Little Ice Age: How Climate Made History 1300–1850* that the severe impact of the Maunder minimum caused crop failures, which in turn created famines, and those in turn generated both refugee displacements and triggered local and regional wars.

Imagine if we were to witness a climate shift comparable to the Maunder Minimum in the twenty-first century. With a global population several times larger, with much longer chains of supply, and with a profoundly more urban population, the societal impact of another "Mini Ice Age" would be genuinely catastrophic.

**A "MINI ICE AGE" COULD BE COMING IN THE NEXT**

# 15 YEARS

**A NEW MODEL THAT PREDICTS THE SOLAR CYCLES MORE ACCURATELY THAN EVER BEFORE SUGGESTS THAT SOLAR MAGNETIC ACTIVITY WILL DROP BY 60 PERCENT BETWEEN 2030 AND 2040. AS A RESULT, EARTH COULD SINK INTO WHAT RESEARCHERS ARE CALLING A "MINI ICE AGE."**

# FAMINE STALKS THE LAND

Dead and dying horses during the Holodomor famine in Soviet Ukraine in 1934.

Human history is replete with famines, stretching back to the very earliest written records. For most citizens—even in Western industrialized nations—the effects of a famine are difficult to escape. Historically, the same story has been played out, over and over again: one year there is food in abundant supply, the next there are shortages, and then the year after that, there is genuine famine.

The worst famines in human history have been created by governments, rather than by weather or plant diseases. The Ukrainian famine-genocide of 1932–33, often referred to as the Holodomor, took *five million lives.* (The Ukrainian word *Holodomor* is most often translated as "to kill by starvation.") This famine was also known as the Famine-Genocide, the Terror-Famine, or the Great Famine.

The Holodomor famine was orchestrated by Soviet dictator Joseph Stalin, reportedly because he viewed the independent spirit displayed by the Ukranian *kulaks* as "counter-revolutionary." By diverting 90 percent of their crop production by force of arms, the Soviets starved the Ukrainians into submission.

In contrast, the Irish Potato Famine (1845–49) was caused by a potato blight, which is a plant fungus. Over 1 million of Ireland's 8 million people died from disease and starvation. Later, and partly through forced emigration, the population of Ireland was reduced by nearly 2 million more people.

These are just two examples, but there are many others to choose from. The repeated famines seen throughout history should be inducement enough for you and your family to stock up on long-term storage food. I strongly encourage my readers to reprioritize their budgets so that they can lay in a large supply of these provisions. Second in priority only to water filtration, food storage could make a crucial difference between your family thriving or perishing. In chapter 5, I will discuss food storage in detail.

An engraving of a peasant's hut during the Irish Potato Famine. Ireland's demographics and economy were dramatically changed, the effects of which we are still feeling today.

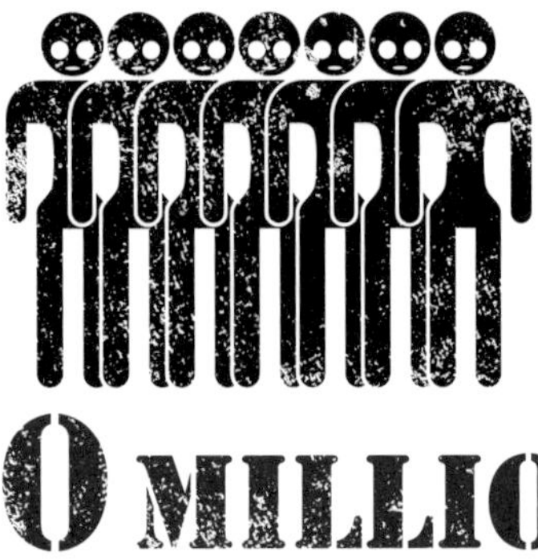

**70 MILLION**

**HAVE FALLEN TO FAMINE IN THE PREVIOUS CENTURY.**

# INVASION, EVASION, AND RESISTANCE WARFARE

Though the risk in any given year is low, the threat of foreign invasion or a civil insurrection cannot be overlooked. Either of those situations might require you to flee your current abode, evade—and possibly resist—those who would seek to destroy your way of life.

A new paradigm has become evident in both the demographics and the political landscape of twenty-first-century America, which is reflected in societies throughout the world, particularly in what were previously seen as stable Western nations. Our nation's major political camps are becoming increasingly polarized. The differences between the more populous and liberal coastal regions versus the lightly populated and conservative inland regions are growing sharper with every passing year.

This divide is most starkly seen in states like Oregon and Washington. In both of these, the lightly populated portions east of the Cascade Mountain Range are broadly conservative and religious, while the residents west of the Cascades are broadly liberal and secular. In the long term, a clash of wills between the red (Republicans) and the blue (Democrats) across America is almost inevitable. Whether this will result in conflict or in eventual partition and accommodation remains to be seen.

A full red/blue split might occur in just a few years, or it might still be a full generation away. But sooner or later, I can see it coming. This rift might even result in a second civil war. If and when it comes, this war will not

The American Civil War (as depicted here at the Atlanta Cyclorama) had repercussions that are still apparent. Most notably, the outcome of the war cemented the position of the federal government over the states, and set the stage for federal taxation, state-run schools, police forces, and regulation of nearly every aspect of the daily lives of Americans.

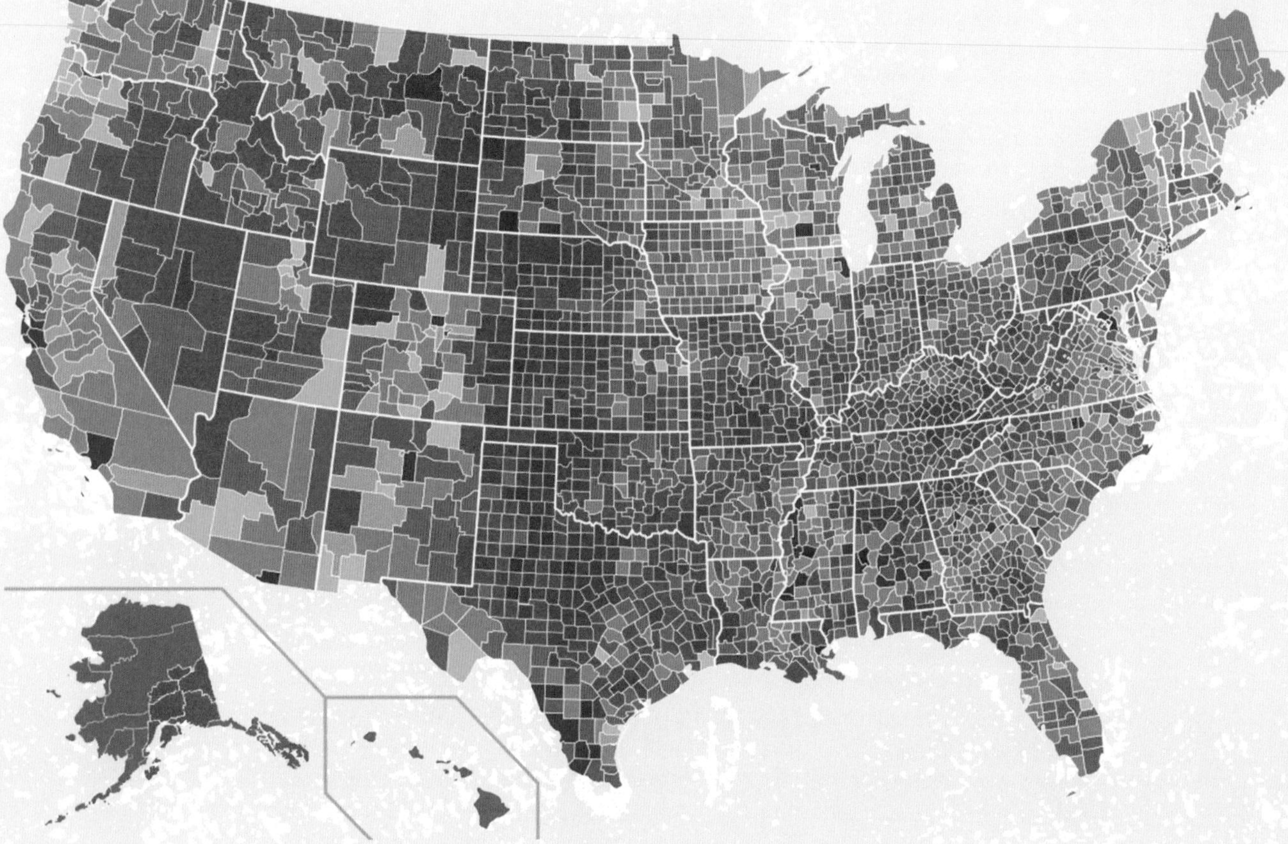

A map showing voting patterns (by county) in the 2016 U.S. presidential election. The red/blue divide is growing ever more pronounced with ongoing urbanization and centralization of power.

be on racial lines or on economic lines per se. Rather, it will be a war of worldviews.

Another troubling change is the overt politicization of government agencies. Recently, the FBI—once considered an unassailable paragon of the even-handed rule of law—came under fire for harboring political schemers. These conspirators formed a secret group within the FBI that maneuvered the agency to selectively soften investigations on their friends, while ramrodding investigations on their political opponents.

There are now competing camps within the FBI, the CIA, the Pentagon, and even the Department of the Interior. No state or federal agency or subdivision of government can now be trusted to conform to the Constitution and its strictures. All of that became passé, back around the turn of the century (the twenty-first century, that is).

## The Third Gulf War

The issues explored in this section currently apply to many countries across the Western world, where democracy is becoming increasingly fraught. Insert the relevant color scheme for other countries, and you will find the problems and results are much the same.

I am predicting a third Gulf War, but it won't be fought in the Middle East. It will be the second Civil War, here in America, and caused by the gulf between the right and left—or between the religious and the secular, or between the libertarians and the statists, or between the individualists and the collectivists.

Individualism and collectivism exist in diametric opposition. Nationalism and globalism are both inherently collectivist constructs. Therefore, I believe that nationalism must be tempered and

**Striking a balance between these competing societal forces over the long term is very difficult.**

restrained, lest it destroy individual liberty. The logical brake on any excesses of nationalism is a strong constitution, with carefully crafted checks and balances.

Although I am a libertarian (that is, with a lowercase "l"), I have doubts about full anarchism. Any truly anarchist state is simply too vulnerable when surrounded by other countries with natural expansionist tendencies. The lack of any national identity opens the door for foreign invaders (arriving piecemeal or in wholesale numbers) to overwhelm an undefended territory. So some semblance of national identity must be maintained (that is: defined borders, a common cultural framework, and a common language).

Striking a balance between these competing societal forces over the long term is very difficult. Indeed, some pundits contend that it is impossible. Once too much government creeps in, it tends to consolidate power and institute mass surveillance. And surveillance is a key tool of tyrants. I personally believe the goal should be a constitutional republic with an underlying strong anarchist streak. Perhaps H. L. Mencken said it best: "Every normal man must be tempted, at times, to spit on his hands, hoist the black flag, and begin slitting throats." (That was written by a socialist, but you can see his point.) The constant tensions and battles between conflicting ideologies can result in isolated sectarian violence and even civil war.

Striking a balance between personal liberty and the need to have a governable state with practicable commerce is something that no nation has yet achieved perfectly. Governments always have a tendency to expand. Taxes have a corresponding tendency to increase, to the point of outright revulsion—and then revolution. Sadly, the end results tend to be more totalitarian than libertarian. This perhaps explains why there are massive flows of emigration, immigration, and outcries for border partition, as people always yearn for more freedom and more economic opportunity for their progeny.

**THE THIRD GULF WAR WILL BE BETWEEN THE POLITICAL LEFT AND RIGHT.**

Two Chinese men kneeling prior to execution. In the Sino-Japanese War (1937–1945), the fight against the Japanese occupation was concurrent with a civil war between Nationalist and Communist forces, further complicating the violence.

## War When?

The outbreak of actual fighting between red and blue regions will probably begin with street riots during a heated political campaign, or perhaps immediately following a contested election. The most recent national election (in November 2018) was marred by allegations of vote tallying "irregularities," particularly in Florida and a few other eastern states. With trust in politics being so low, if this is repeated in 2020 with enough vote-counting manipulation to flip a presidential election—or even just the suggestion that votes had been tampered with—there could be huge riots. This might be the trigger for skirmishing and, for some states, demanding partition or even secession.

Regardless of where it begins, I predict that the second Civil War will break out piecemeal, and almost unexpectedly. It might be something as simple as one state declaring a boycott of goods from another state. Or it might be a revolt of a group of counties in one part of a state being denied pleas for partition by state legislators in a state capitol in another, more populous part of the same state. Again, the situations described in both Oregon and Washington are prime examples.

## Preserving Life and Limb

With a civil war now on the horizon, you may have questions:

- Will my family be involved?
- Will we *want* to be involved?
- What regions of the country will be safe?

Supporters of an opposition coalition try to overturn a burned bus to block the road from riot police accessing it, in Mathare North, Nairobi, Kenya, November 2017. These riots occurred after a court upheld President Uhuru Kenyatta's victory in the October 26 presidential election.

**IN THE 1992 LOS ANGELES RIOTS, THE NUMBER OF PEOPLE REPORTED INJURED:**

# 2,383

The answers to these questions may not be immediately clear. But some places definitely won't be safe. Take a look at the state or region you live in. Is it largely uniform in its political beliefs? If so, then you will probably be safe. But if there is a large amount of local regional variation, and especially if the majority does not align with your beliefs, then you might want to seriously consider relocating.

My advice is simple: vote with your feet. The threat of a future civil war is a reason to permanently relocate to a less populous inland state in the United States. If you are living away from the conflict, then you will have the option to become involved—either directly or indirectly. But if you are living right in the thick of it, then you are more likely to be tossed about by events. Many situations will be determined by simple geography, rather than by volition. So pick your locale wisely. This advice is not just for Americans. It applies in every country around the world.

## A Second Civil War

Of all of the "worst-case" possibilities that we prepare for, near the top of my "most dreaded" list is the second Civil War. This falls in the category of being highly unlikely, but profoundly lethal if it were to occur. However, it is important to note that there is a full spectrum of threats—such as large-scale riots or terrorist attacks—that require preparation, even if events never reach a full-scale civil war.

I believe that the United States—and the wider world—has entered a period of great instability, born of political divisiveness. The sharp differences between liberals and conservatives are now profoundly felt. Virtually every topic and issue has become heavily politicized. This polarization has grown worse since around the turn of the century.

Pundits across the political spectrum, from Alex Barron to Carl Bernstein, have dubbed the current era a "cold civil war." The question is, will this cold civil war ever turn hot?

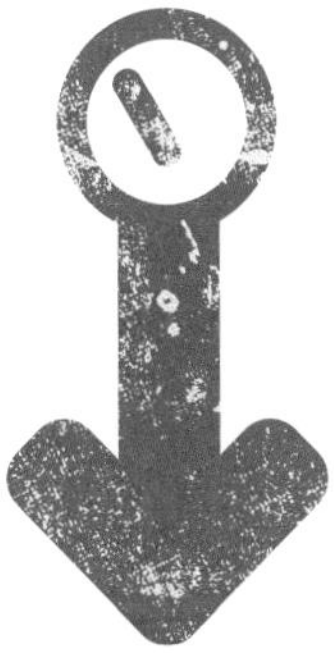

**RISK OF SECOND CIVIL WAR IS LOW—AT THE MOMENT.**

In today's politicized environment, even peaceful protests can swiftly escalate, as here in Milan during a student march in 2015.

"The Troubles": a British soldier armed with an L1A1 SLR on the Shankill Road in Belfast, Northern Ireland, circa 1970.

**IN 2016, POLICE DEPARTMENTS SERVING CITIES WITH POPULATIONS EXCEEDING 25,000 EMPLOYED AN AVERAGE OF 16.8 OFFICERS AND 21.4 TOTAL PERSONNEL FOR EVERY 10,000 RESIDENTS.**

## "Troubles" of Our Own?

The situation that develops in the next few years will most likely be characterized by riots and isolated terrorist attacks, although there is a small chance that it could morph into an outright civil war. Whatever happens, these events would not have sharp geographic dividing lines. It will not be a war between states, or other large and easily identifiable bodies. It will be a war between worldviews. History is clear: worldviews have clashed and will continue to clash.

With no sharp dividing lines, large-scale riots or a twenty-first-century civil war will inherently be very messy conflicts. I can posit two parallels for a near-future U.S. civil war:

- First, a similarity to the domestic terrorism in the U.S. of the late 1960s and early 1970s
- Second, a similarity in the level of violence and profound ambiguity of the Troubles in Northern Ireland in the 1970s

In the Troubles, there were lots of double agents, uncertain allegiances, large-scale infiltrations, wiretappings, false-flag attacks, internecine fighting, kneecappings (mostly of alleged informants or collaborators), bribed (or extorted) officials, conveniently "missing" police guns, stolen explosives, arms-smuggling operations, and robberies. All of that was in addition to the expected riots, bombings, kidnappings, assassinations, sniper attacks, and arson attacks of a modern civil war.

Not surprisingly, the Irish "civil" guerrilla war reached all the way to London and Boston. And although officially "disarmed," some of the IRA old-timers are still at it. In my estimation, that war isn't truly over yet, just as any violence in the United States would likely rumble on for decades.

## What We Might See

If a "hot" civil war breaks out in the United States, then the initial battlegrounds will probably be on city streets. These will be street protests on steroids. The fighting will not be just with batons, rocks, and pepper spray. At some point, the street brawls will evolve into gunfights.

We are also likely to see a larger number of mass shootings of soft (disarmed) targets. Schools, amusement parks, public memorial sites, churches, synagogues, and any public events that have security searches of hand baggage will all be targets. Public meetings of political and religious groups are at the top of the potential list of targets.

The other likely development is of domestic kidnapping teams. So if you are a high-profile or wealthy individual, then take note! You may end up on target lists, even if you don't live in a coastal state. Take appropriate security precautions. For further information, I would advise exploring "executive protection" services. Strategize through all of the possibilities in your particular region. Forewarned is forearmed.

## Study Up, Stock Up, Team Up, Train Up

Regardless of the potential range of severity or likelihood of riots, terrorist attacks, or a future civil war, it is wise to prepare. There are many existential threats. As I've written before, it is wise to study up, stock up, team up, and train up. The same preparations that you make for an economic collapse will look a lot like preparing for surviving a civil war. Think in terms of location, logistics, training, communications, operational security (OPSEC), and force multipliers. These will all be explored more fully later in the book.

## Pick Your Fights Wisely

The risk of a second civil war is low. But if it does come, then its implications will be huge. So be ready. Most importantly, be ready to make big decisions. I have mentioned it before, but the most important thing you can do, unless you want to willingly put yourself and your family in the line of fire, is relocate. Where? To a lightly populated region that is well removed from major cities.

No matter where you are, you will need to decide what your role will be. Every adult has to know how to pick their fights. For those with families, we have to recognize that our first and foremost responsibility is to protect those that we love. But beyond that initial decision, the big decisions become very difficult. If the worst does occur, should you be an active participant? Or act in a support role, such as a medical or safe-house provider? Become a financial supporter? Or an armorer, or logistician? Should you even be involved at all?

It may be fiction, but as an example you could do worse than to look at the choices made by my character Ben Fielding in my third novel, *Founders*. Such big decisions are sometimes simultaneously both simple and complex. Ultimately, you must follow what you know to be right. In the emotional heat of the day, never let anyone convince you to do something that you know is immoral.

Remember that participating in a civil war can be optional, at least for some of us. However, even if you survive it, *it is sure to change you*, and not necessarily for the better. Civil war is never pretty. We need to be honest with ourselves about our ability to be combatants versus support troops, or just financial or logistic supporters. Please pray about being on the right side of history. And again, pick your fights wisely.

Three Republican fighters take aim with rifles behind a barricade made up of dead horses in Barcelona in 1937, during the Spanish Civil War.

## Your Threat Matrix

Intelligence analysts in many Western nations have a common saying: "Threat equals intention plus capability." In analyzing the myriad threats that we face in the modern world, it is important to evaluate both likelihood and consequences. I suggest that you put pen to paper and create your own threat-matrix worksheet. In such a matrix, you would divide the sheet into four quadrants. You then mark "high probability" at the top, and "low probability" at the bottom, and in the left-right axis, you write "lethal consequence" on one side of the page, and "trivial consequence" on the other. Hence, you would probably position "global nuclear war" in the corner that is both "low probability" and "lethal consequence." However, your entries for "automobile engine trouble" and "brief power outage" would be closer to the opposite corner of the page, namely "high probability" and "trivial consequence."

When determining the probability of occurrence of a threat, you will need to weigh both intention and capability. This applies to evaluating both grouchy neighbors and transnational terrorist groups. The same principles apply. Again, threat equals intention plus capability.

By creating your *own* threat matrix, you can tailor it to your particular age, locale, physical health, and so forth. I hope that you find this a valuable *gedenken* (thought experiment).

Listing every conceivable threat would of course go far beyond the scope of this book. It is my hope that you create a threat matrix worksheet that is grounded in truth and tailored to suit your needs. Once you have your draft worksheet completed, then start creating your "mitigation lists." The highest priority for those mitigation tasks/training/purchases would be to counter the threats in the "lethal consequence" and "high probability" quadrant of your threat worksheet. Logic dictates that it is *those* mitigations that should receive your top priority.

The Bielski brothers led a resistance to the German occupation of Belarus. In remote forest camps, they sheltered more than 1,200 fellow Jews from death.

### YOUR THREAT MATRIX

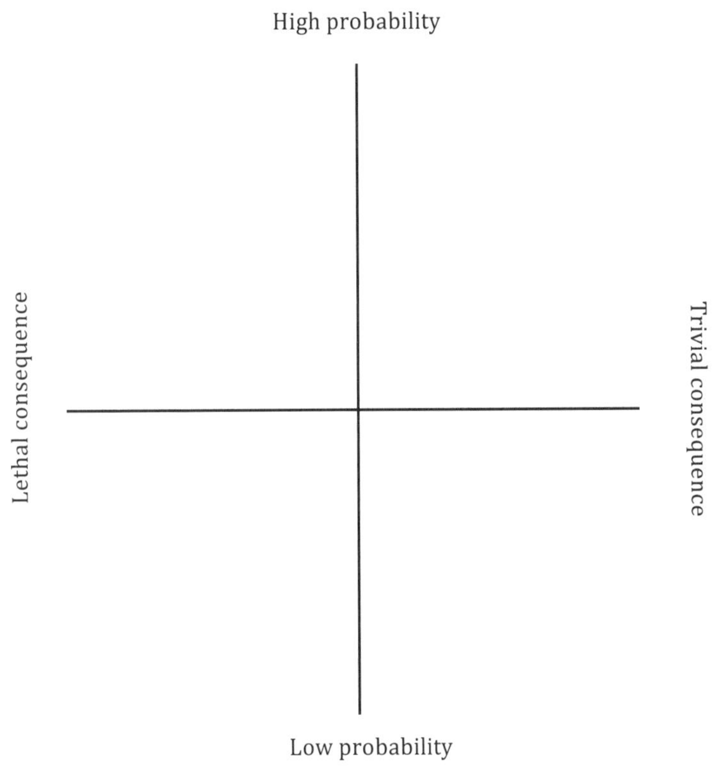

# FEARFUL MASTERS?

Modern armies equipped with tanks and APCs are more than a deterrent to invading armies. They can also strike fear into the hearts of anyone who stands in opposition to the often arbitrary and capricious power wielded by ostensibly "democratic" governments.

Governments in the twentieth and twenty-first centuries have become fearful masters. The size, budget, and sheer power of many governments is frightening. They hold what is often arbitrary power over nearly every aspect of our lives. With their taxes, regulations, and licensing schemes, they make earning a living or even traveling almost impossible without seeking their permission. In his 1952 book *Remember These Things*, commentator Paul Harvey wisely wrote, "Any government that is big enough to give you anything that you need is also big enough to take everything that you have."

Since the 1940s, the governments of many Western nations have been co-opted by corporate interests. In my lifetime, this was first illustrated by the slap on the wrist that Union Carbide Corporation received for the Bhopal disaster. On December 2, 1984, an industrial accident at the Union Carbide plant in Bhopal, India, released at least thirty tons of methyl isocyanate, an extremely toxic gas. The company's pesticide plant was surrounded by shantytowns. It is estimated that more than 600,000 people were exposed to the deadly gas cloud. The gases caused throats and eyes to burn, induced nausea, and caused many deaths. Estimates of the number of deaths range from 3,800 to as many as 16,000. Official figures from the Indian government estimated that 15,000 were killed, including delayed deaths due to chronic lung conditions. Thousands of others who survived suffered permanent disabilities such as blindness and asthmatic conditions.

Before being acquired by Dow Chemical, Union Carbide settled its liabilities to the Indian government in 1989 by paying only $470 million. That is about $31,300 per person killed, or $780 for each person exposed to the gases.

Unfortunately, corporate manslaughter events such as these, albeit on a smaller scale, are all too common around the world, and you must be prepared for whatever dangers lurk in your area. These could be sudden disasters like mining-dam collapses, such as the Brumadinho dam disaster that killed 250 people in Brazil in January 2019.

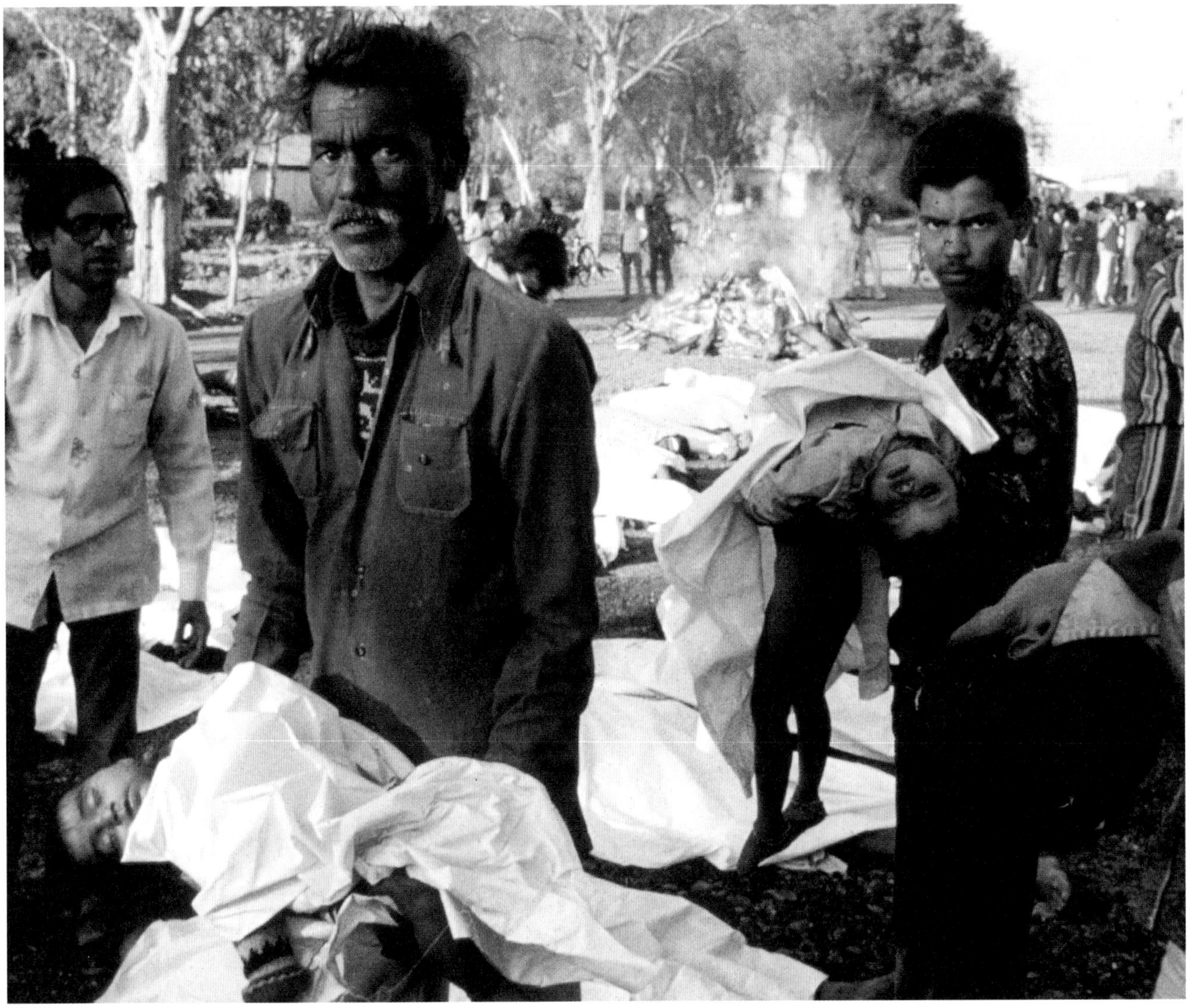

But they could just as easily be long-term dangers, such as the contaminated water in Flint, Michigan (this is a common issue in communities around the world) that will cause health issues for decades.

Take stock of the local government or corporate installations, and make sure you plan accordingly.

**Corporate manslaughter events such as these, albeit on a smaller scale, are all too common around the world.**

**15,000**

**IS THE OFFICIAL INDIAN GOVERNMENT FIGURE FOR THE NUMBER OF PEOPLE KILLED BY THE BHOPAL GAS LEAK.**

The Bhopal chemical disaster, India, 1984.

# THE NUKES

The world profoundly changed on August 6, 1945, with the nuclear bomb that was dropped on Hiroshima, Japan. Since then, the global nuclear threat has grown rapidly. Nuclear weapons have created the risk for loss of life a full order of magnitude larger than conventional warfare. As I see it, in the twenty-first century, the nuclear threat is fourfold:

- Global thermonuclear war with fusion H-bombs; or
- Terrorist use of fission A-bombs; or
- Terrorist use of subcritical mass-radioactive dirty bombs; or
- Nuclear power plant meltdowns or fuel-rod storage-pond meltdowns (either intentional or accidental).

The risk of nuclear war is now actually greater than during the bad old days of the Cold War. Back then, there were just a handful of nuclear powers that were divided into two or three camps. But, today, there are umpteen factions and even terrorist groups with potential access to nukes. Face the facts: we live in a dangerous world. Someday, one or more of those nukes is going to go *boom*!

If at all possible, I recommend relocating to a lightly populated region, and soon. Ideally, that would be an area that is not downwind of major nuclear targets. But at the very least, move out beyond the expected blast, thermal, and overpressure radii (these vary depending on bomb size, of course).

It makes sense for every family to have a nuclear-fallout shelter. A lot of your preps to survive fallout will also double up with being prepared for the ash fall from a major volcanic eruption. As a bonus, your shelter can also be a cool-storage room. The storage food in your shelter can of course be used in other disasters—or even just surviving an extended period of unemployment.

The general advice that I've given my consulting clients is: for an existing property, buy a house with a full dry basement and then retrofit half or all of it into a walk-in gun vault/fallout shelter with a vault door that opens inward. If you are going to the expense of adding a walk-in vault, then it is worth spending a bit more to have it double as a fallout shelter. For a new construction, I suggest that you have a cased well drilled in one corner of the planned footprint of your shelter before you excavate your basement.

## Time

Once the nuclear missile's reentry vehicles (RVs) start to drop, unless you are within the blast radius, you will likely have an hour or more to get your family safely into your fallout shelter. As soon as the fallout from the ground bursts begins to settle, you need to have your shelter buttoned up, and importantly you need to be breathing filtered air, as anything that comes from outside could be deadly. Obviously, the better built and stocked your shelter is, the more ready you are, and the less time you will waste after any nuclear detonations. Those first couple of hours are critical and should not be spent in a frantic rush to get most of your food and water into your shelter, as those should already be stored there! Rather, the pre-fallout interval should be spent going though a *very* short prepared checklist, to shift perishable food, batteries, medicines, and crucial "one-off" items down to your shelter.

## Mass

First and foremost, you need to put a lot of mass between your family and the fallout. Concrete and soil thickness are your friends. See the box on the next page to learn about gamma-stopping "halving thicknesses." A shelter with two halving thickness is good. But three or four halving thicknesses is better!

**HOW MANY TIMES WE CAN AFFORD TO DESTROY THE WORLD.**

The Ark Two Underground Nuclear Shelter, constructed from forty-two buried school buses. It is located near Hornings Mills, Ontario, Canada.

## GAMMA RADIATION HALVING THICKNESSES

A halving thickness is the amount of material that will block half of the gamma rays passing through it. Any mass will block gamma, whether lead or feathers, sand or chocolate bars, as long as you have enough mass. You can use all of your survival foods, water containers, and other stored items for extra shielding.

| A list of materials and their approximate halving thicknesses (Note: Some sources differ slightly from the below figures): | |
|---|---|
| 2.2" | concrete |
| 3.5" | sand or dirt |
| 4.4" | water |
| 8.8" | wood |
| 0.7" | steel |
| 7" | books or magazines |
| 4" | hollow concrete blocks |
| 3.2" | standard red bricks |
| 5" | broken anthracite coal |
| 5" | wet peat moss |

| Some examples of stored items that can contribute to shielding: | |
|---|---|
| 7" | sugar |
| 7" | navy or soy beans |
| 7" | butter or oil |
| 7" | shelled corn |
| 7" | wheat |
| 7" | potatoes |
| 7" | rice |
| 12" | coffee beans |
| 9" | apples |

**Note:** If in sealed containers stacked above a basement shelter, these foodstuffs will still be safe to consume after shelter emergence if any residual fallout dust is first washed off the exterior of the container.

One layer of any item listed above will block *half* the gamma rays. (That is $\frac{1}{2}$, which is called a protection factor [PF] of 2). Thus, $\frac{1}{2}$ of the rays are piercing you, while $\frac{1}{2}$ are blocked. By adding one more halving thickness, you block half of the remaining gamma rays, so now only $\frac{1}{4}$ are hitting you, and you have a PF of 4. Another layer blocks $\frac{1}{2}$ of that remaining $\frac{1}{2}$ of the radiation, so that means only $\frac{1}{8}$ of the original total of outside radiation is hitting you, and you have a PF of 8.

This all works additively: A fourth layer of anything listed above blocks half of that $\frac{1}{8}$ radiation still entering, so now we only have $\frac{1}{16}$ of the outside gamma rays hitting our body (PF 16), and so on:

| | | |
|---|---|---|
| **5 layers = PF 32** | **7 layers = PF 128** | **9 layers = PF 512** |
| **6 layers = PF 64** | **8 layers = PF 256** | **10 layers = PF 1024** |

Now, how much of a PF do you need? The answer involves how much gamma radiation—or Roentgens (R)—the fallout outside of your house is emitting. The less R, the better. Fifty R in one day is considered the most you can safely handle, or 10 R a day for a week, or 100 R over the course of two weeks. So the walls/earth-berming/whatever your shelter has must be thick enough to not let you get more than 100 R in two weeks. It is best, of course, to get as few R as possible.

**JUST 7 INCHES (18 CM) OF BOOKS OR MAGAZINES CAN GIVE YOU TWICE THE AMOUNT OF PROTECTION AGAINST GAMMA RADIATION THAN NONE AT ALL.**

## Air Filtration

You can build yourself a dandy fallout shelter with much halving-thickness mass between you and the gamma emitters, but without proper air filtration, it could all be for nothing. You would face the risk of having irradiated fallout dust enter your shelter, which would result in beta and gamma emitters entering your lungs, your digestive tract, or contacting your skin. True high-efficiency particulate air (HEPA) filters and commercially made hand, treadle, or electric-powered pumps are best, but they are expensive. Homemade substitute air pumps and filters can be fabricated. For those who want more detail, the excellent *Nuclear War Survival Skills* by Cresson H. Kearny is the seminal guide.

An important design consideration for your shelter is that you need to provide an airlock vestibule. This is your decontamination and clothing-shedding room, for anyone who is coming in from the fallout-contaminated outdoors. And, needless to say, this vestibule space must be outside of your shielding wall and outside of your filtered air space. Also, it would be best for this vestibule to have a shower for decontamination. You might need some empty trash barrels with trash-bag liners to hold contaminated clothing. Those containers must also be outside of your shielding walls.

## Water

Ideally, a shelter should be constructed in a basement that is served by either gravity-fed spring water (with a cover to protect it from fallout contamination) or a hand-pumped well. However, I recognize that less than 1 percent of those reading this have a shallow well casing inside their basement! Instead, for most of us comes the daunting task of storing enough water to provide a scant one gallon of water per person, per day for three months. That is a lot of water—both in terms of weight and volume. For a family of four, that equates to 365 gallons. If stored in seven-gallon food-grade super pails, then that means you would need 53 pails of lightly chlorinated water. Assuming that they are stacked three pails high, that equates to about 3,100 pounds in a 25-square-foot footprint. Using the more commonly available five-gallon pails would take up even more space. See chapter 3 for more about water treatment and storage.

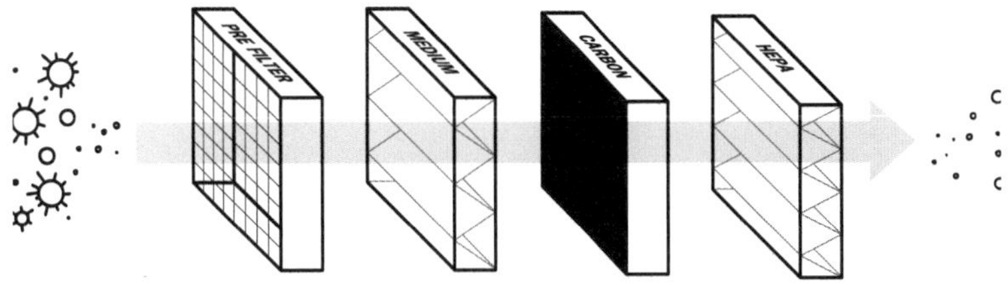


The layers of filters needed for an HVAC (heating, ventilation and air conditioning) cleanroom. HEPA filters are a key component, and could be a life-saver for you.

## Potassium Iodate

For anyone who will be occupying your shelter, it is important to lay in a supply of potassium iodate ($KIO_3$), to prevent thyroid damage after a nuclear attack. This is a thyroid blocker, so it should be used for radiological emergencies only, and, to prevent thyroid damage, it is not to be used at any other time. Potassium iodate is widely available from Internet vendors.

**Note:** One recent scientific paper suggested that KI or $KIO_3$ is best for people *under the age of fifty.* Apparently, for those *over* fifty, the risks outweigh the reward.

## Provisions, in Depth

A deep larder of stored foods will be crucial. If you don't have a sufficient food stockpile, then you will be forced to emerge from your shelter early. Early emergence will both increase the gamma dose of those who exit and also increase the risk of contaminating your shelter with the inevitable in-and-out foot traffic.

An example of a prepared basement larder of stored foods.

Food storage is also crucial for another reason: every calorie of food that you have stored represents one less calorie that must be purchased, grown, raised, fished, or hunted after you emerge from your shelter. That equates to more time in your shelter and less time outdoors kicking up fallout dust (and possibly inhaling or ingesting it), as well as that much less time having your body penetrated by hard gamma rays.

Storing several months of food will also mean that your family will be one less family that is putting a demand on the retail-food supply chain. With extra food stored, you will thus be part of the solution instead of contributing to the very likely food-shortage problem. And, yes, it will be a big problem. A famine following a nuclear war could kill as many people, if not more, than the preceding nuclear-weapons effects.

## Sanitation

Don't overlook the importance of sanitation. At the very minimum, buy several big bundles of toilet rolls, diaper wipes, and a couple of rolls of heavy-duty black-plastic trash bags.

It is noteworthy that as each five-gallon bucket of stored food and water is consumed, it can be reused as a commode bucket—with black trash bags as liners. Also, be sure to get a couple of snap-on toilet seats. (These are sold under the brand name Luggable Loo, and fit standard five- or seven-gallon plastic buckets.)

## Lighting

I recommend white LEDs, powered by a deep-cycle battery bank, for lights inside your shelter. This is because LEDs draw less than one tenth of the current of traditional filament light bulbs. Even though the spectrum that they throw is not very healthy, living with that for three months certainly beats living in pitch darkness. To provide minimal lighting for three months without any charging, you should plan on a bank for four to six golf-cart/marine deep-cycle 6-volt batteries. They should be wired in series/parallel, so that the output voltage is just over 12 volts.

An illustrated example of a Luggable Loo bucket toilet.

A Uniden handheld trunk scanner.

## Communications and Monitoring

Don't overlook having a few radios in your shelter protected by a Faraday enclosure. Being cooped up in a shelter is bad enough, but to be cooped up and cut off from news of the outside world would be terrifying. Test them first, to see if you need an external antenna. After you have rigged that, be sure to leave your radio *disconnected* until needed—both from power and from the antenna—since *both* can couple EMP to your equipment.

I would recommend a "DC to daylight" multiband scanner as a critical radio to have on hand for monitoring. This should be stored in a Faraday cage inside your shelter, at all times. The Icom R6 Sport Wide Band Handheld Communications Receiver is really good value for the money. If you live in a major metro area with trunked traffic, then you should think about investing in a more expensive Uniden TrunkTracker scanner. If you can afford it, it is worth the additional expense to buy a trunking-enabled scanner.

This is because without it, you will miss out on hearing a huge volume of traffic, especially in urban and suburban areas. That traffic would be essentially invisible to you. Of course, no commercially made scanner can demodulate military frequency-hopping/spread-spectrum or other forms of encryption. However, the Icom R6 Handheld is a great portable scanner that covers AM and FM broadcast, police, fire, weather, air-traffic control, shortwave broadcast, various amateur bands, MURS, commercial, CB, Marine Band, and much more.

## Radiation Monitoring

Radiation dose, rate, and survey metering (three distinct measurements) are fairly complex subjects that would double the length of this book to discuss in detail. However, to summarize briefly:

- A **dosimeter** measures your total dose of radiation received, from the onset of an event, when you zero the meter.
- A **rate meter** measures the level of radiation that you are receiving *per hour*.
- A **survey meter** (aka "Geiger counter") measures the amount of radiation emitted by a contaminated item or other discrete/point source.

My advice is to buy the best modern equipment you can find, starting with a Nuk-Alert. Also, build in some redundancy by getting a surplus set of "PEN" dosimeters, rate meters, and chargers. These are available from several companies, but most notably Ready Made Resources. Of all these instruments, the rate meter is the most important. (If you keep a daily logbook of radiation readings, then just a rate meter can also let you know your total dose.) The aforementioned *Nuclear War Survival Skills* describes how to make an improvised fallout rate meter in a pinch, but that is a poor substitute for a good set of modern instruments.

Recently, the U.S. Air Force surplussed their Canberra combination survey/rate/dosimeters, because they decided to standardize with meters that use size AA batteries; the surplussed units are a slightly older model that use 9 VDC batteries. These are currently available on eBay, and can be found using the search phrase "Canberra NRC ADM-300." They originally cost taxpayers around $3,000 each, but can now be found for less than $200 each. They are a tremendous bargain. By the year 2021 or 2022, they should all still be within calibration specifications.

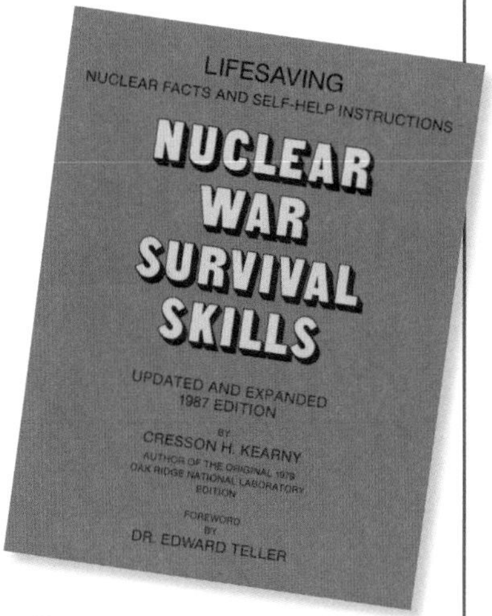


*Nuclear War Survival Skills* is a must for your bookshelf.

## Sanity

Having a family and perhaps a pet or two all cooped up in a 200-square-foot shelter for three months (or more) is undoubtedly going to cause stress and frayed nerves. To prevent mental breakdowns, my suggested list to pass the time would be a Bible (or religious book of your faith), lots of paperback novels, numerous board games, a chess and checkers set, a chess-strategy book, musical instruments, an iPod (preloaded with the family's favorite audiobooks, hymns, songs, and calming music), several new decks of playing cards, a cribbage board, and a book of card-game rules. Value items that can be played, read, or listened to multiple times without taking up too much space.

You will need both a radiation dosimeter and a rate meter, or a combination meter (shown).

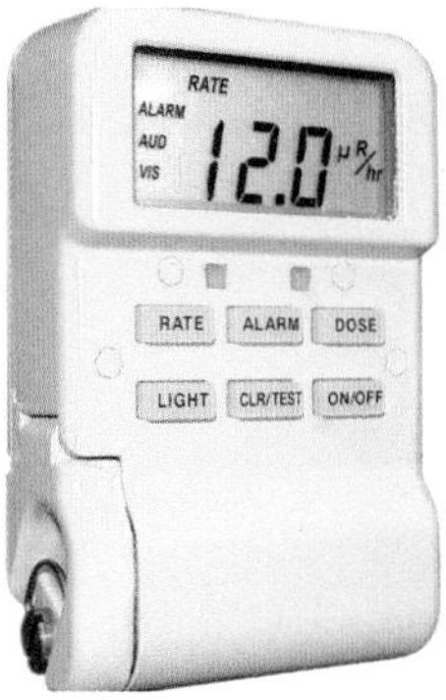


## Patience

I suggest that you hunker in your bunker even longer than authorities will recommend. Here is some truth to ponder: government officials have more interest in reestablishing a functional economy than they do in assuring your health and longevity.

I should mention that *I've already been lied to once this way*. I was stationed in Stuttgart, West Germany, with the 2nd M.I. Battalion in the spring of 1986. I was then partially downwind of the Chernobyl reactor meltdown. The USSR governments lied about the risks, as they later admitted, because they wanted to prevent any panic and dislocation. We were falsely told that it was safe to be outdoors.

Meanwhile, officials in West Germany issued a warning on milk, but, otherwise, there

**WHEN IS IT SAFE TO GO OUTSIDE? GOVERNMENT OFFICIALS HAVE MORE INTEREST IN REESTABLISHING A FUNCTIONAL ECONOMY THAN THEY DO IN ASSURING YOUR HEALTH AND LONGEVITY.**

were no warnings or special precautions taken for fresh produce. They also didn't issue an advisory about wearing dust masks, reportedly because there were *insufficient supplies* of them on hand for the entire population. So, again, public health was compromised to prevent panic.

More recently, following the Fukushima meltdown, the government of Japan intentionally downplayed risks to the public. My conclusion: to expect genuine altruism and sincerity by government officials in any radiological emergency is naïve.

## Safe Emergence

Your family's emergence from your shelter should be gradual. Plan on sleeping every night in the shelter for the next six months. (This is dubbed "partial emergence.") Remember: radiation damage to the human body is *cumulative*. If you can spend half of your time in the shelter after the announced "safe emergence" date, then you will greatly reduce your exposure to any residual radiation.

During the first year of emergence, it will be important to wear at least a paper mask—preferably an N95 mask—as much as possible. Whenever returning from outdoors, footwear must be removed and hands washed in a vestibule. Any unpackaged foods that are purchased, grown, or gathered from the wild must be washed before bringing them indoors.

## A Shattered World

In the aftermath of a full-scale nuclear exchange, life will never be the same as it was before: There will surely be massive depopulation of the northern hemisphere; the global economy might take a century or more to fully recover; cancer rates will be higher for at least several decades; average life expectancy will probably drop down into the mid-50s and possibly even lower for both men and women for a few decades.

But the bottom line is that nuclear war is indeed survivable!

There is obviously a lot more to consider in fully stocking a shelter. But that is largely common sense: first aid, sleeping bags, privacy screens, fire extinguishers, intruder security measures, cooking implements, spill cleanup, pet care, etc. There is one important note on first aid that differs from preparing for many other disasters: if you are close to a nuclear target, then expect to have to treat lots of lacerations and flash burns. And if anyone gets a blast of gamma through their body before entering your shelter, then also expect to have to treat both vomiting and diarrhea.

If you don't already have one, then I again recommend getting a copy of *Nuclear War Survival Skills*. It was developed by nuclear physicists at Oak Ridge National Laboratory, and it is in the public domain, so PDFs are available via the Internet. However, because this is such a key reference, I strongly recommend buying a hard copy.

Dead forest near Chernobyl in the former Soviet Union.

# CALCULATED CONTROL

Far in the future, as historians describe the past three centuries, they will most likely focus on the waves of societal change created by increasingly powerful national governments, and later by supranational governments. The key word in all of their descriptions will be *control*—control of lives, labor, and livelihood; control of population numbers; control of population movement; control of small-arms ownership; control of the means of production; control of information; control of water; control of disease; control of transport; and, ultimately, control of free will.

The calculated control sought by socialists and globalists can only be achieved with twenty-first-century technology. The twentieth century was largely analog, whereas the twenty-first century is almost entirely digital. Digital communications can be fully archived, cataloged, and parsed into dossiers on every man, woman, and child. It is only in the present-day era of smartphones and Internet video chats that there is the requisite digital stream for artificial intelligence (AI) to analyze nearly all citizens. And when at least 90 percent of the population carries a smartphone, the possibility to fully implement a "social credit score" or similar apparatus of calculated societal control will exist.

It pains me to say that calculated control of the masses by just a few technocrats is now achievable. This is a truly frightening prospect. With this level of control, were the Nazi genocide to take place in the twenty-first century rather than as it had in the twentieth century, there would have been virtually no Jewish survivors to serve as post facto witnesses to that horror. Instead of 80 percent extermination, there would be 99 percent extermination. Frightening, indeed.

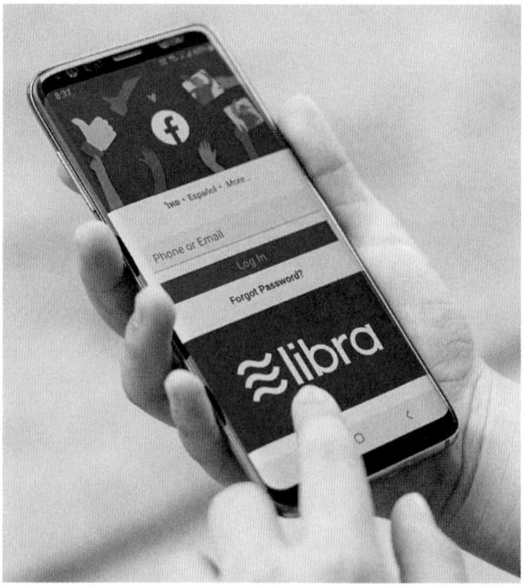

**245 MILLION**

**CCTV CAMERAS AROUND THE WORLD.**

The only good news today is that some new technologies may create a counterbalance to governmental overreach. These include private cryptocurrencies, consumer-level strong encryption, digital flash-mobbing (as recently seen in the mass Hong Kong protests), and untraceable 3-D-printed firearms made without serial numbers.

## Cryptocurrencies: Theirs and Ours

Fully distributed private cryptocurrencies are inherently confidential, and their transactions are opaque to all but the two parties making a trade. In contrast, government-issued ("sovereign") e-currencies are public and the transactions are transparent to government officials—including taxing and law-enforcement authorities. I predict that

A Boston Dynamics Inc. Spot robot on display in November 2017. Increasingly, our data is being used to create seemingly dystopian versions of our future.

sovereign cryptos will be introduced as both a tax-revenue source and as a calculated method of societal control.

Forcing everyone into a state-managed cryptocurrency will create both a big carrot and a big stick. The carrot will be the convenience of going cashless and the lowered risk of street-crime risk that comes with this. The stick will be the ability to track and tax every transaction, as well as the ability of the government to levy e-currency accounts. Presumably, this would mean that they could "zero out" the accounts or stop all transactions of anyone who runs afoul of the law. And with 100 percent transparency of transactions, there would be no way that someone could live entirely "off the grid." Sovereign e-currencies will be a totalitarian's dream come true.

The mega-corporation cryptos that are soon to be launched (such as Libra, which Facebook is currently attempting to create) will similarly offer no transaction privacy. As currently envisioned, every user and even every transaction will be fully transparent to both the issuing corporation and to government authorities. If transactions can be tracked and attributed, then they can be taxed or proscribed. Thus, any mega-corporation cryptos will be almost indistinguishable from sovereign e-currencies.

## Artificial Intelligence

The rise of AI in the past ten years is alarming. AI now works in the background at Google, Amazon, and dozens of other major websites. Unlike simple transactional databases, AI-driven databases use predictive algorithms, for customer-profile and marketing purposes. For example, if a woman were to buy a pregnancy test and then a baby-name book, she might soon see e-mails and web pages offering cribs and diapers. But it could get much more nefarious than that. Governments are now seeking predictive AI to indicate future behavior and criminal intent. So, for example, simply doing a "how to" web search on firearms cleaning in a locale with restrictive gun laws could result in a visit from the authorities.

It is noteworthy that the government of mainland China has instituted a "social credit score" for every Chinese citizen. I believe that this is just a precursor for similar schemes in many other nations—even the much-touted "free" nations of the West. High-technology communications, databases, and artificial intelligence can act as two-edged swords. While they can bring both prosperity and lightning-fast communications, they can also be used as instruments of segregation, evil, and oppression. So beware!

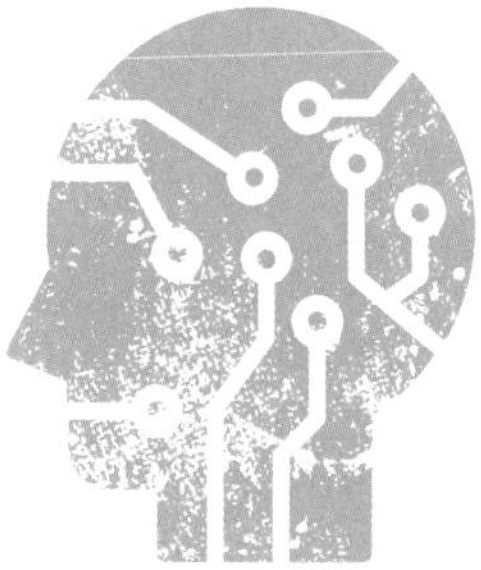

**RISE OF THE MACHINES: "DEEP FAKES" CAN BE USED TO CONTROL THE MASSES.**

# PANDEMICS AND BIOLOGICAL WARFARE

The threat of expanding government power may be the least of your concerns if there is a major pandemic in your lifetime. Modern passenger airplanes now crisscross the globe. More than 4.1 billion travelers fly each year, on more than 110,000 scheduled flights. Together, the United States and China account for over a third of all passenger traffic in the world. It has been estimated that an average of 9,728 planes carrying 1,270,406 passengers are in the sky at any given time, worldwide. This means that rather than it taking months or years for a future pandemic to sweep the globe, it could happen in a matter of *days*.

## Good Immune Health

As with any infectious agent spread by contact with other people, living in a remote, lightly populated region will greatly decrease your chance of becoming ill. But geographic isolation won't help protect you from biological agents carried by the wind. In a "worst-case" pandemic or biological-warfare event, where there is a casual-contact-spread pathogen with a high mortality rate, your best chance for survival will be to completely isolate your family for six months or longer, waiting for a population die-off—or, ideally, a cure.

A modern epidemic can take many forms. In the past forty years, we have witnessed:

- The HIV/AIDS epidemic, which is transmitted sexually and through blood transfusions.
- The SARS epidemic, which was transmitted by coughing or sneezing.
- Several outbreaks of various strains of Ebola, which is transmitted through contact with blood, secretions, and contact with uncooked animal organs or meat. The 2014–16 outbreak in West Africa was the most severe to date. While some progress has been made on developing a cure, there are concerns that a new, more easily transmissible strain could develop.
- Zika, which is transmitted by mosquito bites. In addition to acute affects, it also reportedly causes severe birth defects.
- Middle East respiratory syndrome (MERS), a coronavirus that was first reported in 2012. It is transmitted by coughing or sneezing.
- The Wuhan coronavirus—Covid-19—starting in late 2019. The scope of the eventual loss of life from this pandemic is difficult to predict. But at the time of writing in March 2020, the global economy has already felt shockwaves, particularly in the commodities markets.

However, we have yet to see something as widespread and lethal as the 1918 Spanish flu pandemic, which killed 50 to 100 million people—roughly 3 percent of the world's population! It is staggering to consider that this figure was three times more than the total number of people who died in combat in World War I.

**THE SPANISH FLU PANDEMIC KILLED**

**3%**

**OF THE WORLD'S POPULATION.**

Health workers preparing to bury an eleven-month-old child during an Ebola outbreak in Bunzi, North Kivu province, Democratic Republic of the Congo in May 2019.

"GOD, GIVE US MEN!
A TIME LIKE THIS DEMANDS
STRONG MINDS, GREAT HEARTS, TRUE FAITH AND READY HANDS;
MEN WHOM THE LUST OF OFFICE DOES NOT KILL;
MEN WHOM THE SPOILS OF OFFICE CAN NOT BUY;
MEN WHO POSSESS OPINIONS AND A WILL;
MEN WHO HAVE HONOR; MEN WHO WILL NOT LIE;
MEN WHO CAN STAND BEFORE A DEMAGOGUE
AND DAMN HIS TREACHEROUS FLATTERIES WITHOUT WINKING!
TALL MEN, SUN-CROWNED, WHO LIVE ABOVE THE FOG
IN PUBLIC DUTY, AND IN PRIVATE THINKING;
FOR WHILE THE RABBLE, WITH THEIR THUMB-WORN CREEDS,
THEIR LARGE PROFESSIONS AND THEIR LITTLE DEEDS,
MINGLE IN SELFISH STRIFE, LO! FREEDOM WEEPS,
WRONG RULES THE LAND AND WAITING JUSTICE SLEEPS."

JOSIAH GILBERT HOLLAND

CHAPTER 2

# THE PREPARED MIND

- A Place of Safety
- A Viable Occupation
- A Store of Wealth
- A Level Head

# A PLACE OF SAFETY

Given the manifold threats—some of which have just been explored—that we face in the twenty-first century, prudence dictates that prepared families have plans to relocate to a place of refuge. A key focus of my writings is the concept of relocating to lightly populated farming or ranching country to establish retreats. Ideally, you should live at your retreat year-round. That is just what I did with my family, starting in the early 1990s.

While I realize that owning a retreat property is not affordable for many, it is still a worthy goal. Even if you feel stuck in the suburbs—bound by family obligations, proximity to your work, or proximity to medical care for chronic ailments—you can still accomplish some of what a retreat would provide, while living on a ¼-acre house lot.

"Safety," of course, is a relative term. Property crimes can happen anywhere. But, statistically, they happen the most in large cities and the least in less-populated areas. From a dispassionate actuarial viewpoint, your chances of surviving a societal collapse with your life and property intact are best in a lightly populated farming or ranching region that has plentiful water. Proximity to hydroelectric power generation is also a huge plus. These factors make the "American Redoubt" region a particularly good choice for relocation.

The American Redoubt relocation strategy ties in closely with my general philosophy and outlook on life. Although this movement is particular to the United States of America, the philosophies that lie behind it are global. No matter where you live, a rural location with neighbors that share your mindset—forming a strong community—is your best bet for safety.

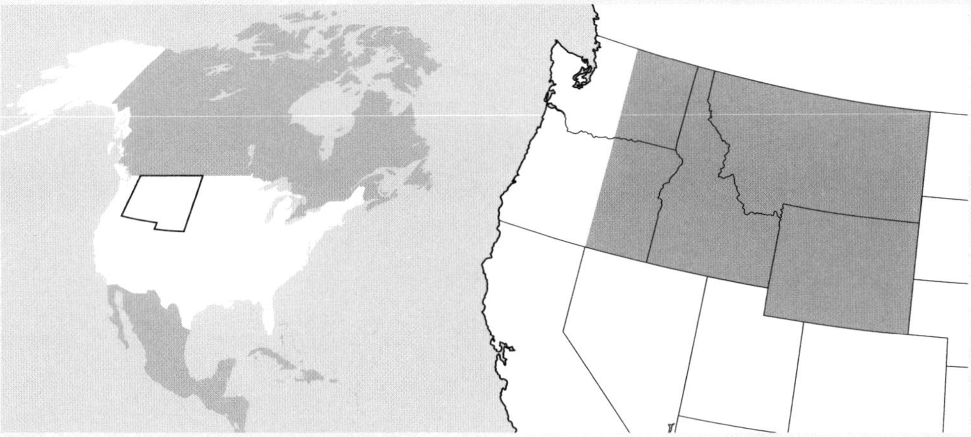

## THE AMERICAN REDOUBT

I originated the term "American Redoubt" in 2011, to refer to the multistate area consisting of Idaho, Montana, Wyoming, eastern Oregon and eastern Washington. This soon developed into a political migration movement that garnered considerable press coverage. The movement encourages citizens to pull up stakes and move to a region that is intended to be a safe haven similar to Ayn Rand's fictional Galt's Gulch. I've encouraged like-minded Americans to thereby vote with their feet. Demographics are destiny.

I've been pleased to see great success with the American Redoubt movement. Tens of thousands of people have moved to the Redoubt states since 2011. And, as societal fracturing increases in the coastal states, I expect the influx to only increase in the 2020s.

**35%**

**OF VEGETABLES CONSUMED IN THE U.S. IN 2018 WERE IMPORTED, UP FROM**

**5.8%**

**IN 1975.**

**Your chances of surviving a societal collapse with your life and property intact are best in a lightly populated farming or ranching region that has plentiful water.**

## The Rawlesian Survivalist Philosophy

With each passing year, technology progresses and chains of interdependency lengthen. In the past thirty years, chains of retail supply have grown longer and longer. The food on your supermarket shelf does not come from local farmers. It often comes from hundreds or even thousands of miles away. This has created an alarming vulnerability to disruption. Simultaneously, global population is still increasing in a near-geometrical progression. At some point, that must end—most likely with a sudden and sharp drop in population. The linchpin is the grid. Without functioning power grids, modern industrial societies will collapse within weeks.

## Civilization is just a thin veneer

In the absence of law and order, men quickly revert to savagery. As has been illustrated by the rioting and looting that accompanied disasters in the past three decades, the transition from tranquility to absolute barbarism can occur overnight. People expect tomorrow to be just like today, and they act accordingly. But then comes an unpredictable disaster that catches the vast majority unprepared. The average American family has four days' worth of food on hand. When that food is gone, we soon see the thin veneer stripped away.

## People move in herds and packs but both follow natural lines of drift

Most people are sheep ("sheeple"). A few are wolves that prey on others. But just a few of us are more like sheepdogs—we think independently, and instead of predation, we are geared toward protecting and helping others. People naturally follow lines of drift, or the path of least resistance. When the end arrives, 99 percent of urbanites will try to leave the cities on freeways. The highways and freeways will soon resemble parking lots. This means that you need to be prepared to both get out of town ahead of the rush and to use lightly traveled back roads. Plan, study, and practice.

## Lightly populated areas are safer than high-density areas

With a few exceptions, a smaller population means fewer problems. When society collapses, there will be a mass exodus from the cities. Think of it as if it is an army that is spreading out across a battlefield: the wider that they are spread, the less effective that they are. The inverse square law hasn't been repealed.

## Show restraint, but always have recourse to lethal force

My father often told me, "It is better to have a gun and not need it than need a gun and not have it." I urge readers to use non-lethal means when safe and practicable, but at times, there is not a satisfactory substitute for well-aimed lead going downrange at high velocity.

## There is strength in numbers

Rugged individualism is all well and good, but it takes more than one man to defend a retreat. Effective retreat defense necessitates

Homeowners in Gulfport, Mississippi, posted warnings to looters in the aftermath of Hurricane Katrina.

A looter makes off with merchandise in the quake-devastated Concepción, Chile, after a magnitude 8.8 earthquake hit on February 28, 2010.

having at least two families to provide 24/7 perimeter security. Of course, every individual added means another mouth to feed. Absent having an unlimited budget and an infinite larder, this necessitates striking a balance when deciding the size of a retreat group.

### There *are* moral absolutes

I believe that the foundational morality of the Western civilized world is best summarized in the Ten Commandments. Moral relativism and secular humanism are slippery slopes. The terminal moraine at the base of these slopes is a rubble pile consisting of either despotism and pillage, or anarchy and the depths of depravity. I believe that it takes both faith and friends to survive perilous times.

### Racism ignores reason

People should be judged as individuals. Anyone who makes blanket statements about other races is ignorant to the idea that there are both good and bad individuals in all groups. I have accepted the Great Commission to spread the teachings of the Bible with sincerity. "Go forth into all nations" means exactly that: all nations.

### Skills beat gadgets and practicality beats style

The modern world is full of pundits, poseurs and "mall ninjas," who mistake purchasing the latest tools and gadgets for actual knowledge and readiness. Preparedness is not just about accumulating a pile of stuff. You need practical skills, and those only come with study, training, and practice. Any armchair survivalist can buy a set of stylish camouflage fatigues and an M4gery Carbine adorned with umpteen accessories. Style points should not be mistaken for genuine skills and practicality.

Isolated rural land with a mix of pasture, cultivable land for row crops, and timber is ideal for retreats.

### Plentiful water and good soil are crucial

Modern mechanized farming, electrically pumped irrigation, chemical fertilizers, and pesticides can make deserts bloom. But when the grid goes down, deserts and marginal farmland will revert to their natural states. In my estimation, the most viable places to survive in the midst of a long-term societal collapse will be those areas with reliable summer rains and rich topsoil.

### Tangibles trump conceptuals

Modern fiat currencies are generally accepted, but have essentially no backing. Because they are largely a byproduct of interest-bearing debt, modern currencies are destined to inflation. As previously explored, in the long run, inflation dooms fiat currencies to collapse. The majority of your assets should be invested in productive farmland and other tangibles such as useful hand tools. Only after you have your key logistics squared away, invest anything extra in silver and gold.

### Governments tend to expand their power to the point that they do harm

In the SurvivalBlog, I often warn of the insidious tyranny of the "Nanny State." If the state where you live becomes oppressive, then don't hesitate to relocate. I have said it before, but it bears repeating: vote with your feet!

### There is value in redundancy

A common saying of my blog readers is: "Two is one, and one is none." You must be prepared to provide for your family in a protracted period of societal disruption. That means storing up all of the essential "beans, bullets, and Band-Aids" in *quantity*. If commerce is disrupted by a disaster, then at least in the short term you will only have your own logistics to fall back on. The more that you have stored, the more that you will have available for barter and charity.

Just as important as redundancy are the attributes of versatility and flexibility. A Rawlesian survivalist likely owns as many as four vehicles: one powered by gasoline, one by diesel, one by propane, and one that is electric. The same individual should also own a tri-fuel backup power generator that can run on gasoline, propane, or utility-piped natural gas.

### A deep larder is essential

Food storage is one of the key preparations that I recommend. Even if you have a fantastic self-sufficient garden and pasture ground, you must always have food storage that you can fall back on in the event that your crops fail due to drought, disease, contamination, or infestation.

### Tools without training are almost useless

Owning a gun doesn't make someone a "shooter" any more than owning a surfboard makes someone a surfer. With proper training and practice, you will be miles ahead of the average citizen. Get advanced medical training. Get the best firearms training that you can afford. Learn about amateur radio from your local affiliated ARRL club, or a similar organization if you are based outside of the United States. Practice raising a vegetable garden each summer. Learn how to weld and buy your own oxyacetylene rig. Some skills are only perfected over a period of years.

### Old technologies are appropriate technologies

In the event of a societal collapse, ninth-century (or earlier) technologies such as the blacksmith's forge, the treadle sewing machine, and the horse-drawn plow will be far easier to reconstruct than modern technologies.

### Charity is a moral imperative

As a Christian, I feel morally obligated to assist others who are less fortunate. Following the Old Testament laws of Tzedakah (charity and tithing), I believe that my responsibility begins with my immediate family and expands in successive rings to supporting my immediate neighborhood and church, to my community, and beyond, as resources allow. In short, my philosophy is to "give until it hurts" in times of disaster.

### Buy life *assurance*, not life insurance

Self-sufficiency and self-reliance are multifaceted. You need to systematically provide for water, food, shelter, fuel, first aid, communication, and, if need be, the tools to enforce Rule 308 (*see Glossary*), potentially with a .308 Winchester.

A nineteenth-century level of technology would be appropriate for rebuilding society in the event of an EMP, solar flare, or another disaster that wipes out modern technology.

Blacksmithing is just one of many traditional skills that may prove to be important in coming years.

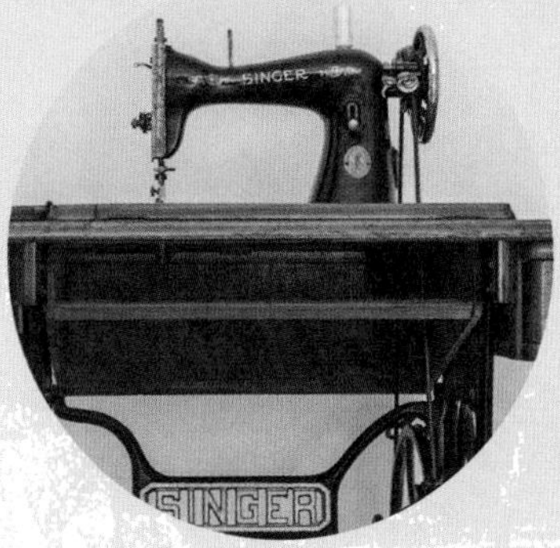


An antique treadle sewing machine. Hand-powered and foot-powered machinery does not require electricity.

## A REDUNDANCY OF VEHICLES IS IMPORTANT.

**IDEALLY, YOU WOULD HAVE ACCESS TO ONE OF EACH POWERED BY GASOLINE, DIESEL, PROPANE, AND ELECTRICITY.**

Be prepared to heat your home and cook with firewood.

### Live at your retreat year-round

If your financial and family circumstances allow it, then I strongly recommend that you relocate to a safe area and live there year-round. This has several advantages, most notably that it will prevent burglary of your retreat logistics and allow you to regularly tend to gardens, orchards, and livestock. It will also remove the stress of timing a "Get Out of Dodge" (G.O.O.D.) trip at the eleventh hour. However, if circumstances dictate that you can't live at your retreat year-round, then at least have a caretaker and stock the vast majority of your logistics in advance, since you may only have *one trip* there before roads are impassable.

### Exploit force multipliers

Night-vision gear, intrusion detection sensors, and radio communications equipment are key force multipliers. As these use high technology, they cannot be depended upon in a long-term collapse, but in the short term, they can provide a big advantage. Some low-technology defenses, such as barbed wire and defensive road cables, also provide advantages and can last for several decades.

### Invest your sweat equity

Even if you have a millionaire's budget, you need to learn how to do things for yourself, and be willing to get your hands dirty. In a societal collapse, the division of labor will be reduced tremendously. Odds are that the only "skilled craftsmen" available to build a shed, mend a fence, shuck corn, repair an engine, or pitch manure will be you and your family. A byproduct of sweat equity is muscle tone and proper body weight. Hiring someone to deliver three cords of firewood

**THINK MEDIEVAL CASTLE. ALMOST EVERY THREAT CAN BE STOPPED OR DELAYED BY PUTTING MASS IN BETWEEN YOU AND WHATEVER IS TRYING TO GET AT YOU.**

is a far cry from felling, cutting, hauling, splitting and stacking it all yourself.

### Choose your friends wisely

Associate yourself with skilled doers, not "talkers." Seek out people who share your outlook and morality. Living in close confines with other families is sure to cause friction, but that will be minimized if you share a common religion and norms of behavior. You can't learn every skill yourself. Assemble a team that includes members with medical knowledge, tactical skills, electronics experience, and traditional practical skills.

### There is no substitute for mass

Mass stops bullets. Mass stops gamma radiation. Mass stops (or at least slows down) bad guys from entering a home and depriving its residents of life and property. Sandbags are cheap, so buy plenty of them. When planning your retreat house, think: medieval castle.

### Always have a plan B and a plan C

Regardless of your pet scenario and your personal grand plan of survival, you need to be flexible and adaptable. Situations and circumstances change. Always keep a G.O.O.D. kit handy, even if you are fortunate enough to live at your retreat year-round.

### Be frugal

I grew up in a family that still remembered both our pioneer history and the more recent lessons of the Great Depression. One of our family mottos is: "Use it up, wear it out, make do, or do without." I thank my mother for passing that wisdom along to my generation, and I am doing the same with my children.

### Survivalism is most compatible with the libertarian mindset

Survivalists value being left alone to be self-sufficient. Collectivism is contrary to libertarian ideals. I am opposed to socialism, fascism, communism, and any other "-ism" that uses force to deny anyone else of their life, liberty, or property.

### Some things are worth fighting for

I encourage my readers to avoid trouble, most importantly via relocation to safe areas where trouble is unlikely to come to visit. But there may come an unavoidable day that you have to make a stand to defend your own family or your neighbors. Further, if you value your liberty, then be prepared to fight for it, both for yourself and for the sake of your progeny.

**Even if you have a millionaire's budget, you need to learn how to do things for yourself.**

Night-vision equipment is a key force multiplier that may prove to be crucial in defending lives and property in the event of a major disaster.

## Post-Collapse "Foraging" Is Morally Bankrupt

I am concerned that some pundits on the Internet have recommended what they call "foraging" through buildings, in the aftermath of a disaster. In that context, foraging is just a polite term for looting. Importantly, here I am not talking about true foraging for wild edibles. Urban "foraging" would be conscionable only in near extinction-level die-offs, where many properties (buildings with intact contents) are left truly abandoned and *without rightful heirs*. However, don't plan on that because the chances of such an event are very small.

I align myself with the geographical determinist way of thinking, in both history and predicting future outcomes. This is the belief that the environment around a society helps shape its development. (Although some new transformational technologies, such as large-scale desalination plants, inexpensive photovoltaics, and perhaps even seasteading may make my determinist stance less firm.) In general, though, geography and climate have historically shaped human settlement patterns and, in many ways, they will shape future events. The core risk in a grid-down collapse will be directly proportional to population density. Think of it this way: during a full-scale societal collapse, the actuarial risk of having a high-velocity lead pellet pass through your chest cavity or brain on any given day increases with the population density of your locale. There will simply be more starving people with guns surrounding you in cities than there will be in the "hinterboonies." While geographic isolation is not a panacea, it certainly beats the odds of hunkering down in the Big City and hoping to persevere to the far side of a

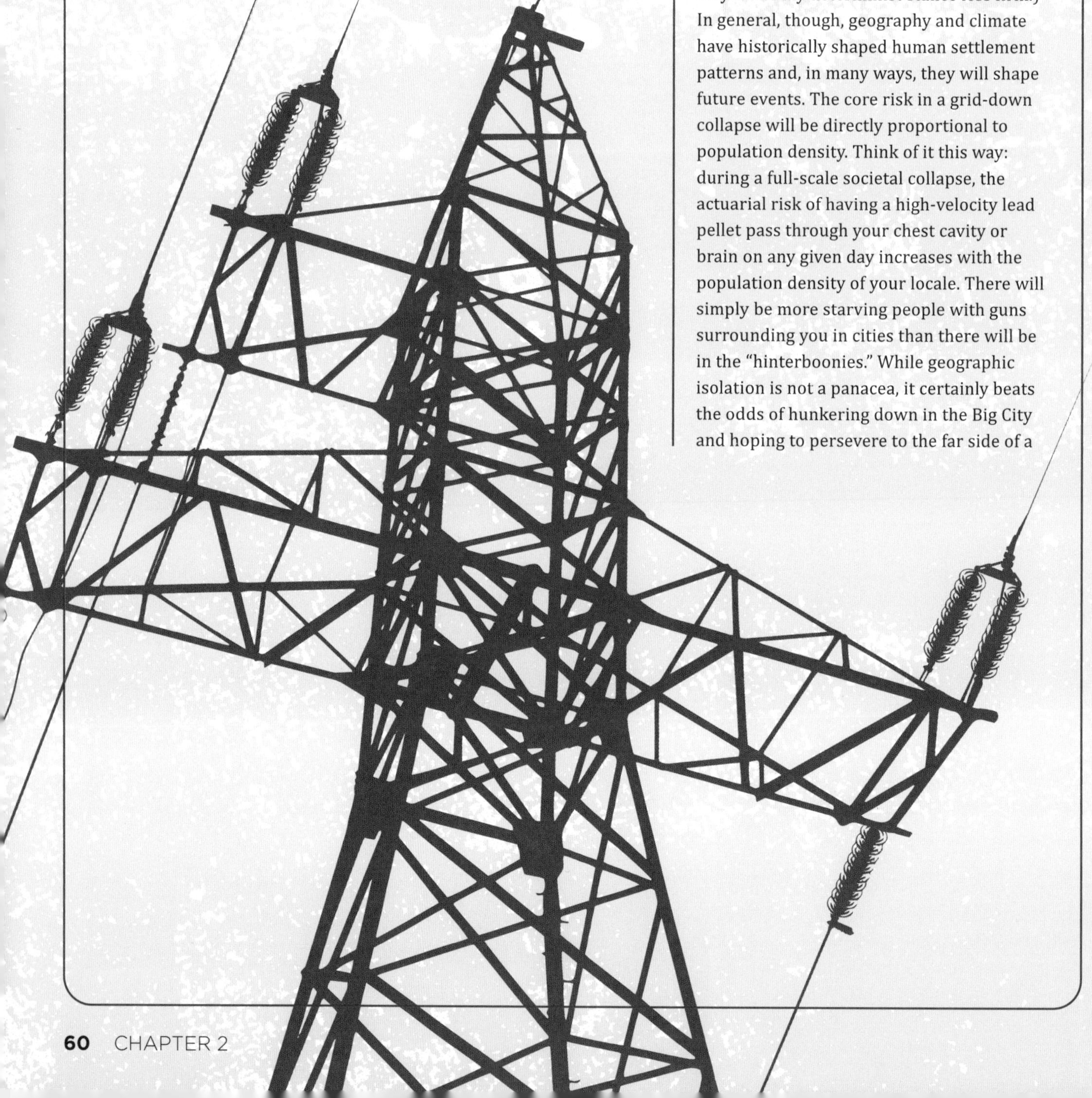

massive population crash, with the intent of "foraging," *post facto*. That would be armchair-commando naiveté, at its worst.

You might feel comfortable with 50 to 200 people per square mile, but I prefer five people per square mile.

In my estimation, after the first winter without grid power and pressurized natural-gas pipelines, virtually everyone north of the 40th parallel worldwide who feels the need to bug out will head *south*, to warmer climes.

In the United States, this means that many of the colder climates such as the inland Northwest and Michigan's Upper Peninsula will not be seeing any substantial in-migration. Exceptions will include Vermont and Maine, as they will likely face temporary in-migration from both New York and from the heavily populated Montreal region.

If the grids go down and stay down, then in any given area I expect population die-off ranging from 15 percent to 90 percent, depending on local population density. In the United States, it is likely that the highest losses will be in urban centers in the Northeast. The lowest losses will be in the inland Northwest and the more lightly populated portions of the Southeast. However, even southern metropolitan centers such as Atlanta, St. Louis, and Dallas/Fort Worth may suffer over 60 percent population losses—and notably not from cold weather. Those will mostly be losses from instantaneous lead poisoning.

After the second winter, we will see an entirely transformed society. It will be a harsh existence, at least for the first decade.

I cannot emphasize enough that the ideal solution is to relocate well in advance of any collapse to a lightly populated farming region that enjoys reliable annual precipitation for growing row crops. (In the western United States, these are called dry land farming regions.) It should be country that is well removed from major population centers. There, you should look for a property with spring water or shallow well water that is geographically isolated from the natural lines of drift that refugees and looters will follow.

The key phrase for your property search is: "on a side road of a side road."

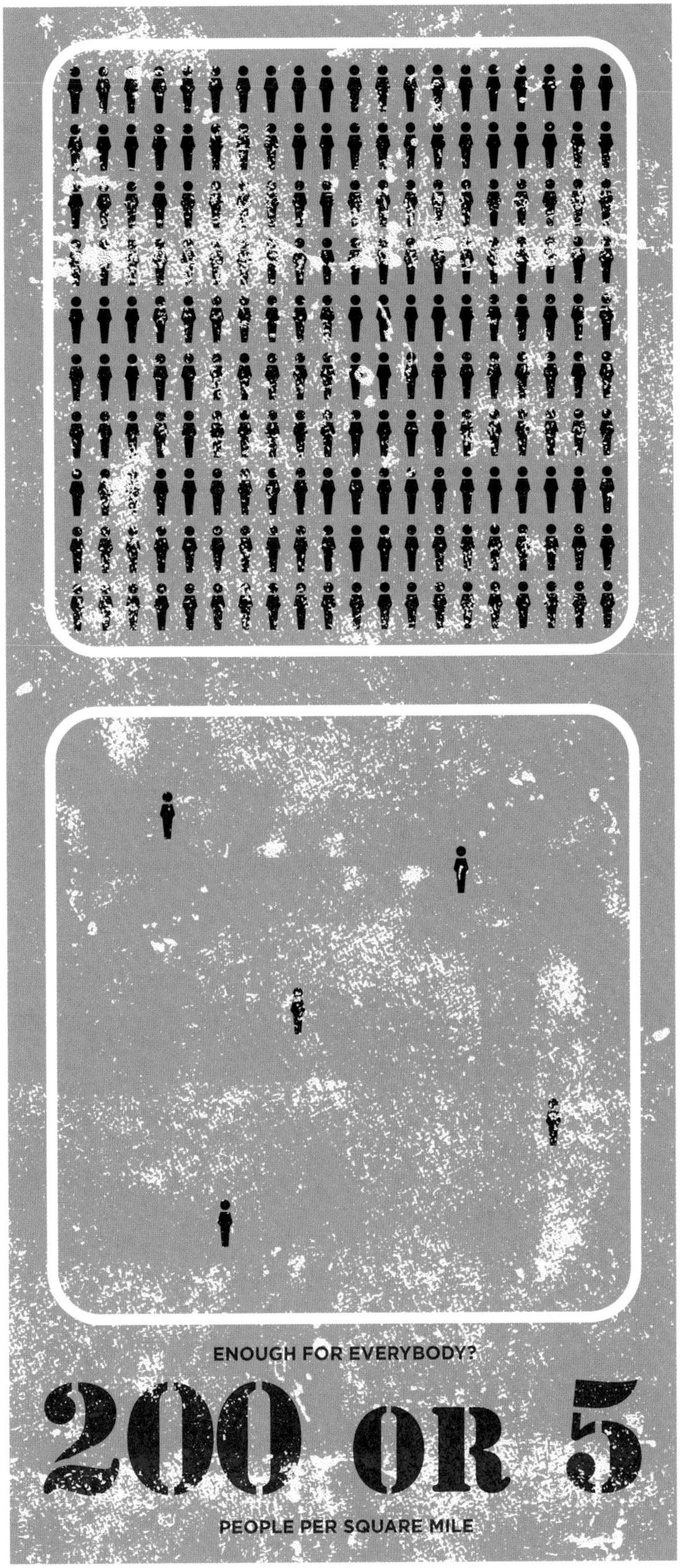

# A STORE OF WEALTH

Most nations stopped issuing silver coinage by the mid-1960s.

One other key aspect of preparedness in the twenty-first century is sheltering part of your wealth in assets that are not dollar-denominated. In my estimation, tangibles always trump intangibles.

I have three primary reasons why I distrust intangibles:

### Nearly all intangible investments are denominated in fiat currencies

Because of this, there is an underlying currency inflation, currency revaluation, or currency repudiation risk. Even when buying stock in the safest, most secure, and impeccably managed company, it still has some risk when the investment is denominated in dollars. Ditto for dollar-denominated bonds, redeemable life insurance policies and annuities, business investments, money market funds, and for certificates of deposit (CDs). Whenever you have any investment that is denominated in a fiat currency, there is the risk of degradation of the currency unit itself. It is only tangibles that have innate, intrinsic, and intuitively obvious value that is not vulnerable to the whims of international currency markets, interest-rate changes, or government insolvency.

### Most intangible investments represent a debt taken on by someone else

When you deposit funds in a financial institution, nearly all of it is loaned to a private party, a company, or a government. So your investment's security is dependent on someone or some entity having the willingness and ability to earn a profit and consistently pay down that debt. In essence, the vast majority of investments are *buying someone else's liability*. But a personally held tangible is something of substance that has true intrinsic value, in and of itself. That rock-solid value is not dependent on the action or inaction of any individual, corporation, or government.

#### Intangibles are outside of one's personal control

Your very best intentions have little or no influence on the bad intentions of others. The news headlines are replete with tales of how people have their investments wiped out: bad corporate management, government ineptitude, corruption, pilfering, swindling, embezzling, "official" confiscation, and wholesale larceny. We also live in the electronic age, so many investments are mere digits in computers. Thus, they are further vulnerable to hacking, malware, ransomware, EMP, solar flares, as well as various other threats to the power grids, phone networks, and computer networks.

In contrast, a tangible that you keep at home in your personal control is subject only to your own failings. Granted, there are vulnerabilities to rust, mold, and theft. But each of those can be mitigated with proper planning, secure storage, and some concealment. And in the modern context, I would add: Concealment of the paper trail of your acquisition of a tangible. I recommend that you pay in cash or in cryptocurrency for most of your investment tangibles. This will minimize the risk of confiscation by thieves with badges.

### The Tangible Difference

In a world of ongoing currency inflation, tangibles make sense. Whether you are buying Colt Python revolvers, slabbed and rare coins, Beta C-MAG drum magazines,

**Once a body of knowledge is between your ears, then you own it.**

bags of junk silver, stripped AR-15 lower receivers, Swiss self-winding wristwatches, or case lots of .45 ACP hollowpoints, there is not very much that can go wrong with buying tangible investments. With proper storage, the downside risk is minimal, and the upside is almost always pleasing. Just be sure to do your research first and *buy low*. This means at or below wholesale. Estate sales, divorce sales, gun shows, and business-liquidation sales are often the best places to achieve this.

As a small aside, in my estimation, there is only one intangible investment that comes close to investing in a tangible, and that is investing in your own education or the education of your children. A well-educated individual betters themselves and hence their prospects for earnings — whether self-employed or employed by others. That is why I'm a proponent of both homeschooling and continuing education well into adulthood. One of my lifelong friends was conferred a PhD by the London School of Economics when he was 54 years old. That is commendable. Once a body of knowledge is between your ears, then you own it. Only senility can take it away. Personal knowledge is invulnerable to market cycles or currency fluctuations. It is also fully portable, and cannot be confiscated.

That, in a nutshell, is my tangibles investing rationale.

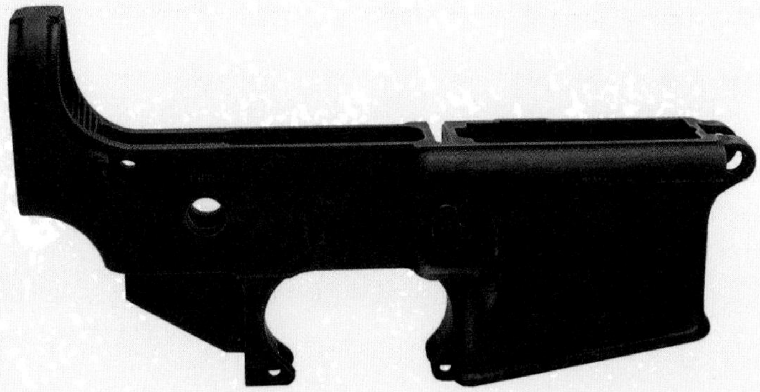

Tangible goods will hold their value in the midst of a currency crisis. Shown are a wristwatch and a stripped lower receiver used to build a complete AR-15 rifle.

**A WHOLE QUARTER WEIGHS 6.25 GRAMS, AND THE SILVER WEIGHS 90 PERCENT OF THIS, OR 5.63 GRAMS.**

## On Silver

Of all of the precious metals, my favorite, by far, is silver. Silver coins are ideal for day-to-day barter. As becomes apparent in my first novel, *Patriots*, gold is too compact a form of tangible wealth to make it practicable for day-to-day barter.

Pre-1965 dimes, quarters and halves from the U.S. Mint are ninety percent silver and have a hardener added, in order to hold up to the rigors of circulation. They are also made in odd fractional weights—for example, a silver quarter weighs 6.25 grams.

For up-to-date details on U.S. silver coin specifications, a good resource is coinflation.com.

When in Rome... The silver coins that you buy as an investment or for barter should be ones that are the most recognizable in the nation where you live. Shown are some older Thai Baht coins.

I recommend printing those specifications for your reference binder. Here in the United States, my preference for barter is for U.S. Mint pre-1965 silver quarters, since they are so widely recognized and trusted. (If you reside in another country, then you would want to invest in whatever silver coin is the most widely recognized.)

I also like dimes for barter. When you are bartering silver coins for goods, for smaller items you won't want to be limited by the inability to "make change." For example, if the item you want costs two silver dimes and all you have is a silver quarter, the new price will be a silver quarter. Quarters are certainly the most recognized, and the bulk of your junk silver should probably consist of quarters. But having both larger and smaller denominations on hand can help assure a fair barter transaction.

All silver American Eagle bullion coins are minted from .999 fine silver. Most commercially made rounds and various silver bars are also .999 fine silver and the majority are made in 1 Troy ounce increments. (Only rarely are they ½ ounce, or smaller.) Note that .999 fine coins, rounds, and bars are *too soft* to use as circulating coinage. They would wear too quickly.

## All That Stuff

Every well-prepared family has mountains of stuff. Storage-space planning presents three major challenges:

- Where to fit it all
- How to keep it safe from deterioration
- Keeping it organized, so that you can quickly find, retrieve, and replenish it

I will attempt to address all three of these issues, from my perspective.

### Mouse- and rat-proof storage

One crucial design feature of storage containers is that they be mouse- and

Storage space is at a premium for most preppers. Use your storage space efficiently!

rat-proof. This is particularly important for clothes and for any items that have even the slightest hint of a food smell. A typical Sterilite translucent bin with a white HDPE lid is *not* rodent-proof, and they are surprisingly fragile when handled roughly. I have myself bought a few of those, to my regret. In contrast, heavy-duty mil-spec transit chests, and Pelican cases (and comparable cases from Plano) will keep out all but the most determined rodents. And most tool boxes, tool cabinets, tool carts, and freestanding steel cabinets with tight-fitting doors are also usually rodent-proof.

Because of their relatively high cost (per cubic foot), it has taken me nearly three decades to gradually accumulate my current assortment of Pelican cases. These range from micro boxes all the way up to some of their big rolling chests. Our other mil-spec transit chests (mostly Mil-Tope and Hardigg brands) were also gathered gradually, but only when bargains were found. Savings can be made: most of these were purchased used, at gun shows or via eBay and Craigslist. When buying used mil-spec containers, inspect them closely for any broken or missing latch hardware, as that is their most common weak point.

## Tote Boxes

We often store some clothing items, canning lids, and magazines in heavy-duty totes with hinged lids. Ours are made by Akro-Mils (in Akron, Ohio), and sold under the trade name KeepBox. These old, reliable KeepBoxes have steel full-length hinge pins, which are much superior to the more recent knock-off totes from other companies that use all-plastic hinges. I've had most of my KeepBoxes since the late 1980s, and, although scratched up, they are all still intact and still fully functional. I have dragged some of these to more than 100 gun shows. Just keep in mind that these totes are *not* waterproof, so they are strictly for indoor use. And *never, ever* step on top of one of these. They will not support your weight and the lids will form a bear trap for a human foot. (Don't ask me how I know that!)

More recently, I've supplemented my KeepBoxes with some similarly sturdy but much more water-resistant Homz brand heavy-duty black plastic totes with removable yellow lids. These stack particularly well, and are fairly vermin-proof. They are classed as water-resistant, but not waterproof. The only improvement would be if they made them in all-flat olive drab.

## Ammo Storage Space Planning

Nearly all of our ammo is stored in USGI milsurp ammo cans that range from the classic .30 caliber size all the way up to the huge 20 mm Vulcan ammo can size. We use the latter mostly for storing shotgun shells and 26.5 mm flares. Our current favorite ammo can is what is commonly called a "tall .50." I've found that this is one of the most versatile sizes for rifle and pistol ammunition. Consequently, most of the ammo shelves in JASBORR ("Jim's Amazing Secret Bunker of Redundant Redundancy") are adjusted to accommodate that height. On the shelves where we have a mix of standard .50s and tall .50s, we fill in the gaps above the shorter cans with .30-caliber cans, lying on their sides. No wasted space.

## Tall but Earthquake Resistant

For the sake of efficient use of your available floor space, you should use tall shelves in your storage room(s). The price of wire rack shelves has dropped appreciably in the past few years. But there is one key safety note: Your shelves should be strapped to walls, for earthquake protection. For additional protection in earthquake-prone areas, you can use long bungee cords to keep bins in place on your shelves. It would be the ultimate irony for a survivalist to be crushed to death by his own stored gear and supplies.

Here is the earthquake strapping method that I recommend: use loops of galvanized pipe hanger tape and large-head 4" TORX power screws that make a solid connection to wall studs. Similarly, you can use pairs of self-tapping power screws directly through the upper backs of wall cabinets, to firmly attach them to studs. (You do own a stud finder, right?)

If you have a fully freestanding set of shelves, then you can make it at least partially earthquake-proof by using 2x2 or 2x4 boards to cross-brace them at the top to other nearby shelves and/or to cleats firmly attached to walls. These cross-bracing boards can be attached to metal shelves with nuts and bolts, heavy-gauge wire, or the newly available stainless-steel zip ties.

The lightest and most heat-invulnerable items should be placed on the uppermost shelves. But note that storage foods—even the lightweight freeze-dried and dehydrated variety—need to be stored "low and cool." Ditto for candles and your canning wax.

## Shoehorning It All

Shoehorning all of your *stuff* into a house can be a challenge. Take a close look at each room, look for any wasted space. Underneath beds is an obvious void. There, I like to use under-bed footlockers for items like extra bed linens, off-season clothes, and towels. And if there is room for a second row of footlockers out of reach, then fill those with more valuable items. I'd expect that Mr. Burglar Inahurry will likely give up on searching under your bed after only finding linens. Like the late comedian George Carlin said of burglars: "They only want the good stuff."

Other useful spaces in a house can include:

- Under or behind desks and tables;
- Behind books on bookshelves;
- The *full* depth of kitchen cabinets;
- Inside hassocks;
- Underneath or even inside couches and upholstered chairs;
- Stacks of canned food boxes *in place of* a coffee table (with a cloth cover);
- Crawlspaces (but beware of moisture and vermin);
- Attic spaces (but beware of heat and vermin);
- Beneath the bottom drawers of dressers;
- Shelves added above clothes rods in closets and armoires;
- Behind clothes in closets;
- Beneath workbenches; and
- Overhead in a garage or shop (you may need to add extra joists and 3/4" plywood decking)

## For Food, Use FIFO

Here at the Rawles Ranch, we use the first-in-first-out (FIFO) storage method for foods and other perishables. It takes just a few extra minutes to mark the purchase month and year on the top of cans. I typically use a medium-point Sharpie pen. Some folks use dedicated FIFO racks for canned foods, but if you use standard shelving, then just remember to stock the newest cans in the back.

We also use FIFO for our assorted animal feedstocks. Storing grain in 80-pound feed sacks is a mistake. Those are just for transport. Much of our grain is stored in standard galvanized trashcans with tight-fitting galvanized lids. Lids can be marked to prevent guessing games about which ones hold chicken feed, and which ones hold corn, oats, or barley. Those barrels are all stored in a secured room that cannot be accessed by the livestock. It would be tragic to have a horse or cow gorge itself on grain and then founder and perish.

One other safety note: with grain stored in barrels, it is important to always *completely* use the contents of each barrel, and brush it out before you refill it. If you only partially empty a barrel and keep adding to it, then eventually you will end up with moldy grain.

Cansolidator racks make it easy to use "first-in, first-out" (FIFO) rotation of canned foods.

**BARRELS WITH LIDS ARE ESSENTIAL FOR THE SURVIVAL OF YOUR VARIOUS PERISHABLE GOODS. ALL OF YOUR PREPARATION WILL BE WORTHLESS IF THEY CANNOT LAST THE DURATION OF YOUR HUNKERING DOWN.**

A handheld electronic Brother label maker has already made my life immeasurably easier.

## Storage Space Planning: Labels

Keeping track of what you have in storage and where you have it is very important. Distinct, easy-to-read high-contrast labels are a key part of that. I just recently (and belatedly) discovered a game-changer in Brother brand electronic label makers. These are a far cry from the Dymo "analog" rotary labeler that I bought back in the 1970s. The Brother machine can print in dozens of fonts, on half a dozen background color tapes, and even print in reverse, for labeling the back side of glass cabinet doors. The Brother labeler itself is available for under $20 and comes supplied with just one short "teaser" label strip. The extra cartridges of blank label tape made by Brother are expensive, but I've found that the generic knockoff brand cartridges work just fine.

Storage takes planning, budgeting, prioritizing, family cooperation, a bit of OPSEC and, of course, *space*. Sometimes, I wish that I had a *Doctor Who* TARDIS closet that could defy geometry and provide unlimited space.

No matter what method you use for organizing: be consistent, be tidy, make prominent labels (except for valuables), and keep lists. The rest of your family will appreciate that, perhaps even after you are dead and buried.

Contadina
Organic
SAUCE
Call 1-800-922-7455 with any comments or questions.
Barilla America, Inc.
Bannockburn, IL 60015
Product of U.S.A.
Cream of
Mushroom
SOUP
PROGRESSO
DISTINCTIVE RECIPES
French Onion
GREAT FOR COOKING
Cream of
CHICKEN
Campbell's
CLASSICS
TOMATO
NOODLE
100% NATURAL
Petite
Diced
Campbell's
CONDENSED SOUP
OLD FASHIONED
TOMATO RICE
Since 1895
WOLF
BRAND
CHILI
Authentic Texas Recipe
NO BEANS
KRAFT
PREMIUM
PASTA SAUCE
Mushroom
Del Monte
Quality
WITH
Fresh Cut.
WHOLE

# A VIABLE OCCUPATION

One of the great quandaries faced by many American preppers is that their desire to move to a lightly populated rural region is usually not consistent with the ability to earn a good living. Let's face it: job opportunities in the hinterboonies are scarce. Unless you are retired, self-employed, you telecommute, or you are in a high-demand profession (such as medicine or dentistry), then it might be difficult to have the same standard of living that you've enjoyed in an urban or suburban community.

## Making a Living in Remote Retreat Regions

Even if you are currently employed somewhere in a "safe and secure" job, keep in mind that there are no absolutely secure jobs. You could have a small town civil service job, at a water treatment plant, for example. But what if the city or county that you work for goes bankrupt? You could be laid off in a heartbeat. Likewise, the phrase "Under New Management" often means firing you and hiring the nephew or an old pal of the new boss. So, hedge your bets.

I recommend that you develop a second stream of income through self-employment. Typically, this can be found in a moonlighting service job, or a home-based Internet mail-order business. To have the opportunity to pursue an online business venture or to telecommute, find a rural community that is served by high-speed Internet. You probably don't need gigabit speed, but try to find a place with at least moderate-speed DSL Internet service available. Better connectivity means more options. Poor connectivity (read: at "dial-up" speed) means fewer options.

I've often encouraged my consulting clients to develop a second income stream. Why is this important? "Living off the land" self-sufficiency is an admirable and commendable goal. But even if you are living truly debt-free, you will still have property

Making a living in a small town can be challenging, especially for new arrivals. It is best to bring an income with you.

taxes to pay. That means that you will need at least a part-time depression-proof revenue stream in the event that you lose your primary job.

I generally do not recommend starting up any sort of brick-and-mortar retail store. The brick-and-mortar business model is dying quite rapidly. This is now the era of e-commerce. Small businesses can no longer compete with major retailers, nor with small overseas mail-order companies in Asia that have amazing wholesale inventory sources and minimal overhead. If you feel that you *must* invest in a business, then keep it small, keep it at home (to minimize your overhead), keep it in a defined niche, and develop a unique product that you manufacture yourself. That will minimize competition, at least in the short term. Lastly, stick to mail-order or e-commerce!

Successful home-based businesses usually center around filling otherwise unfilled needs. Find something that your neighbors buy, or rent, or a service that they hire on a regular basis that currently requires a 30+ mile drive to town, for example. Those are your potential niches.

A successful recession-proof home-based business is likely to be one where the demand for your goods and services is consistent, even in a weak economy. These include services such as chainsaw-chain sharpening, septic-tank pumping, home security/locksmithing, care for the young and the very old, installing home-security webcams, and escapist diversions such as DVD movie sales, to name just a few. (It is noteworthy that the movie industry was one of the few sectors of the U.S. economy that prospered in the 1930s.)

Another market segment that prospered all through the Great Depression of the 1930s was repair businesses. Obviously, in hard economic times, people try to *make do* with what they have rather than throwing things away and replacing them. So repair businesses are a natural. If the business revolves around some small appliances that you could repair and mail back to the customer, then so much the better. That way, you could have a nationwide business rather than just a local one. For instance, these might include DVD player repairs, or laptop computer-screen replacements.

E-commerce businesses that do retail sales of small merchandise that can easily be mailed are ideal for preppers who want a home-based business.

If you are willing to take dirty jobs that most other people shun, then you will nearly always be employed, regardless of the state of the economy.

## It's a Dirty Job, but Someone Has to Do It

If you want to work for someone else, yet still be employed in a recession-proof field, then consider the dirty jobs. These are some of the least likely to suffer a layoff. In Japan, these are called the "Three-K" jobs: *kitsui* ("hard"), *kitanai* ("dirty") and *kiken* ("dangerous"). If you are willing to take on any of the Three-K jobs, do cheerful and hard work, and have exemplary attendance, then you will likely have a job that will carry you all the way through a deep recession or even an economic depression. If times get truly bad and you get laid off, then be willing to "think outside the box" and consider taking a Three-K job. Some of these are low-level city and county payroll jobs. By low level, I mean things like sanitation worker, animal-control officer, sewer technician, solid-waste-transfer station worker, highway-maintenance worker, and so forth.

Think about it: A steady job beats no job. Don't let your family starve or end up homeless. There is no shame in accepting good old-fashioned hard work. If you take a job that brings in only one-half of your existing income, then consider that you'll actually come out ahead of any of your contemporaries who are laid off more than half of each year. Furthermore, you will have uninterrupted benefits, such as health insurance, that they will also lack. Again, a menial, low-paying job is better than no job.

One other important point is that you need to be willing to work several part-time jobs. This redundancy could prove crucial if one of your ventures fails. (And the unfortunate odds are that at least one of them will fail.)

## Be Proactive

I have observed that the folks who find good-paying employment in a rural area are generally those who are proactive. If you sit around and read the "Help Wanted" ads, then you will probably be disappointed. Your best bets are to either bring an income with you (via telecommuting) or to launch your own businesses. If possible, get those businesses established and profitable *before* you make your move.

## SOME STABLE EMPLOYMENT POSSIBILITIES

**1: Mining and manufacturing** processes that, because of shipping expenses, cannot practicably be moved offshore.

**2: Service industry** jobs that are essential and non-discretionary. Let me differentiate so that you will know what to avoid: "Discretionary" would be jobs like a Pilates instructor, hairdresser, massage therapist, and manicurist; non-discretionary jobs would include mortician, sanitation worker and emergency room doctor.

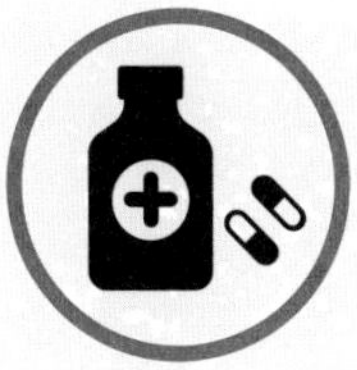

**3: Retail sales (face-to-face or mail-order) of crucial items** such as soap, vegetable garden seeds, vitamins, spices, batteries, etc. The value of concentrating on items like these is that there will still be orders/customers, even in a deep economic depression.

**4: Retail sales (face-to-face or mail order) of "comfort" items** such as DVDs, video games, escapist books, and MP3 players. (To explain that last item: In really remote areas where there is no cell phone service available, few people own smartphones. Where there is no cell coverage, no audio or video streaming is available. Therefore, dedicated MP3 players are still popular.) In the midst of an economic depression, people will crave escape.

**5: Repair work,** including repairing small appliances, laptop PCs, chainsaws, boat engines, guns, vacuum cleaners, and so forth.

**6: Sales of a patentable small product** that you can manufacture at home—or at a workshop in a small town—and sell nationwide through the Internet. A patent is important, to give you several years of production without competition—especially from China or other foreign countries.

# A LEVEL HEAD

Being prepared for the new reality of TEOTWAWKI will require what my father often called "a level head." Getting to this point necessitates understanding ourselves and an awareness of how our mind processes events. This is the key to staying sane while under immense pressure. As my frequent correspondent J.S.F. pointed out to me, keeping a level head involves a number of things. These include:

1. Looking objectively at ourselves as we take into account our perceptional process will help keep us in check and move us toward a greater objective reality. We all have ideals and values, so our perception of how or why things happen will always differ a little from the objective reality. But that shouldn't deter us from trying to strive for a realistic paradigm. Honest self-assessment is needed.

2. Stay positive, but not *too* positive. Don't put on rose-colored glasses! Staying positive is a key to maintaining sanity. A positive person will always outperform a negative one. Remember: A positive person will have a "How can we do it?" attitude versus a negative person having a "We can't possibly do it!" attitude. The goal in survival and life is be as creative as possible. If you have a defeatist attitude, then I submit that you will not last long in extremis.

3. We must know the difference between the subjective reality that our perceptions create, and the objective reality of the world around us, and our circumstances. Stepping outside the subjective reality box once in a while to exercise objectivity and honesty will help us immensely.

4. Keep your emotions in check. Life is full of hardships, pressure, and stress. Whether or not the Big Event or TEOTWAWKI actually does come in our lifetime, it is always best to have the ability to control one's emotions. Emotions cloud our judgment. And in the case of TEOTWAWKI, an uncontrolled emotional cascade could be fatal!

5. Develop honest and healthy coping methods. The use of these throughout one's life can only be beneficial. Whether you are a "go it alone" type or have a significant other for conversation, even the simple act of taking a walk when you get upset can be beneficial on many levels. There are lots of coping methods. Just make sure that you choose healthy ones. Obviously, drinking is *not* a healthy way to cope. There is actually a biological process in the brain that balances your emotions as you use both sides of your brain (i.e., walking, running, or punching—get a punching bag if you are the latter type.) My personal favorite activity is splitting firewood. Not only is it a cathartic release of stress and anger, but it is also productive time. At the end of it you have not only dealt with stress, but you are building muscle, burning fat, building up calluses, and practicing your heel-toe balance. Not to mention the pile of useful firewood at the end of the workout!

In localized survival situations, most people tend to unite. Even for the few that don't pitch in, the others help them out. In larger-scale situations, people generally tend to separate. You have the people who expect to be taken care of or that can't take care of

**COPING METHODS ARE KEY. MY PERSONAL FAVORITE IS CHOPPING WOOD. FIND YOUR OWN BEFORE SOCIETY COLLAPSES.**

themselves, and the other group of people who realize the extent of the disaster and are barely able to take care of themselves and their families. If the situation is dire and lasts long enough, then there will be confrontations between the two groups. In such situations, it will be important to find others of like mind, not only for physical needs, but also for emotional needs. Try to find others who aren't only prepared like you, but those who have the same morals, religious beliefs, political ideals and values that you have.

## People Will React Differently

As my friend "Tona" pointed out to me in a letter, big events have an impact on minds and bodies. Once the initial phase of a disaster has passed, doctors begin to see many more patients showing up with MUPS (medically unexplained physical symptoms). When human beings experience a traumatic event, it releases a cascade of stress hormones and other chemicals in our bodies. Sometimes, the body reacts as though the threat is ongoing and the condition can become chronic. When the body is out of balance, we often begin to experience stomachaches, headaches, fatigue, dizziness, trouble sleeping, pain, and changes in appetite. The distress experienced by someone who has those symptoms is *real*. The *pain* is real. It's a real response to a real physiological change in the body. However, it is not related to a disease, infection, or injury. Rather, it is the body's response to chronic stress.

## Something Like Triage

As you interact with others in your community during a disaster, take the time to objectively evaluate how they are coping, both as individuals and as families. Are they on top of the situation, or overwhelmed? Are they emotionally coping, or emotionally broken? Are they making progress in remediating the disaster's effects on their property, or are they just "treading water"? Do they have a plan, or are they befuddled? Are they part of the solution for your community, or part of the problem? Are they sheep, or sheepdogs—or are they wolves?

Then, for those who are in the "sheep" category, ask yourself: In what ways can I help them? Charitably? Through trading or bartering, to our mutual benefit? By investing some time? Or are they completely beyond help (read: very likely to soon perish), and should I instead concentrate on helping others who will have a better chance of survival and a return to improvement/normalcy?

In pressurized situations like this, we also commonly experience cognitive or thinking changes such as difficulty in making decisions, difficulty with remembering things, trouble concentrating, and recurring thoughts about what has happened, and what we've witnessed. Moreover, our behaviors and emotions can change due to the stress we've undergone, making us more likely to be irritable or aggressive, cry more often, withdraw from our loved ones, feel guilty or depressed, feel panic, engage in more risky behaviors, or "self-medicate" with drugs or alcohol.

We may experience a change in our relationship with God, becoming angry over what has happened, losing interest in prayer or avoiding worship settings and rituals, which formerly were very important to our spiritual lives. Occasionally, the opposite may also happen, where there may be a renewal of faith following a terrible loss.

## Young Folks

Children and teens are most vulnerable to all of the aforementioned as well. In addition, children may regress in their development, acting much younger than their age. They may begin to wet the bed or play like a younger child, and have trouble being able to separate from their parents or loved ones. Nightmares are common among those who

It will be crucial to keep a level head in the midst of disaster. The better prepared you are physically, the better you'll fare emotionally. It will be those who have no stored supplies who are the most likely to suffer emotional breakdowns, resort to suicide, or descend into lawlessness.

survive disasters. In young children, you may see repetitive and obsessive play, which reenacts the event(s) they have experienced. This is the way a young child attempts to make sense of the event and regain some sense of control.

Interestingly, the elderly can often do better under such stress than others, possibly due to their life experiences, which have provided some "stress inoculation." Seniors can provide wisdom from their perspectives as well as information from their life experiences. On the other hand, seniors who have some dementia may become very agitated and confused due to being away from familiar settings and routines.

Individuals with preexisting mental health issues, such as anxiety, depression, or psychosis may, in the short term, temporarily get better. It was reported that following the September 11, 2001, terrorist attacks, many patients in psychiatric wards temporarily "cleared" their psychoses and that rates of suicide declined. However, without the access to appropriate medication, patients with significant psychological disorders will need care and support. Individuals with mental disabilities such as developmental delays or head injuries may experience confusion, fear, and disorientation.

Following a major disaster, many people will have lost loved ones, but may be unable to access the services and rituals that would typically help them through the grieving process. For example, mortuary services and funerals may not be possible in the event of mass casualties, civil breakdown, or pandemic diseases. Community support may be limited because so many have experienced deaths in their own families and are unable to reach out and help others. For many, this may lead to complicated bereavement and depression.

From my perspective as a Christian, I do not look at the prospect of a disaster and potential personal loss with trepidation. Rather, I come from the perspective of Blessed Assurance. My first wife passed away more than ten years ago. Although I went through an intense period of grieving, I did so with prayer and the inner calm of a sincere trust in God. Less than a year later, I happily remarried, to a young widow. Our Lord is good, always! I trust in both his providence and his protection.

I'll have more on my perspective as a Christian in chapter 11.

An elderly Syrian man walks past a destroyed building in the town of Azaz on the outskirts of Aleppo, Syria.

CHAPTER 3

# WATER

**Floods and the Water Supply**

**Water Treatment**

**The Myth of Household Storage**

Aerial view of a flood in Thailand. Ironically, it is in the midst of floods when fresh drinking water is at its most scarce.

# FLOODS AND THE WATER SUPPLY

It is certain that civic water supplies will be disrupted in any disaster that takes down the power grids. Very few civic water supplies are gravity fed from end-to-end. If there is an electric pump moving water anywhere in a civic system, then it is vulnerable to any interruption of grid power. More than 90 percent of American homes rely on piped civic water systems. Just a few homes have their own wells or springs.

## Water Everywhere, but Not a Drop to Drink

Most ironically, it is at times of floods that safe drinking water is most scarce. This is because floodwaters often foul the piped civic water supplies. All too often, rising floodwaters comingle raw sewage with civic water sources. The end result can be a public health nightmare.

If your house is supplied by your own well, then you will need to plan ahead.

Do you have an off-grid power system?

Do you have a reliable generator?

If so, can it handle the high current-load of a well pump?

And does that power system provide the correct voltage to match your well pump? (Here in the United States, most home generators only provide 120 VAC power, but most well pumps require 240 VAC power!)

In a long-term crisis, a generator for your well won't suffice. At some point you will run out of fuel. At that time, you can revert to a pitcher-style hand pump if the static level of your well water is less than one atmosphere (33 feet) deep. Deeper wells require the use of a sucker-rod actuated pump. With those, the pump cylinder is in the bottom of the well, rather than at the surface.

Floods in more economically developed countries cause fewer deaths, but can often result in billions of dollars of damage to urban areas.

**Some Notable Modern Floods:**

**1931** Yangtze–Huai River floods, in China. (Caused between 1 million and 4 million deaths.)

**1937** Ohio River flood, in the U.S. (Caused 385 human deaths and $2 billion in damage—in 1937 dollars.)

**1993** Mississippi River flood in the U.S. (Caused fifty human deaths and $15 billion in damage.)

**2013** Uttarakhand, northern India floods. (Caused 5,748 deaths in floods and landslides.)

**2014** Southeast Europe floods, mainly in Serbia and Bosnia and Herzegovina. (Caused 86 deaths and €3.5 billion in damage.)

**2015** Winter floods in northern England. (Caused £1.6 billion in damage.)

**2018** East Africa floods. (Caused 500 deaths and a multi-country humanitarian crisis.)

**2019** Nebraska flood in the U.S. (Caused $2 billion in damage—primarily from crop losses and cattle deaths.)

For many preppers, the idea of water damage is very low on the list of priorities. However, rising waters frequently claim lives and property, and rescue services are quickly overwhlemed during widespread floooding.

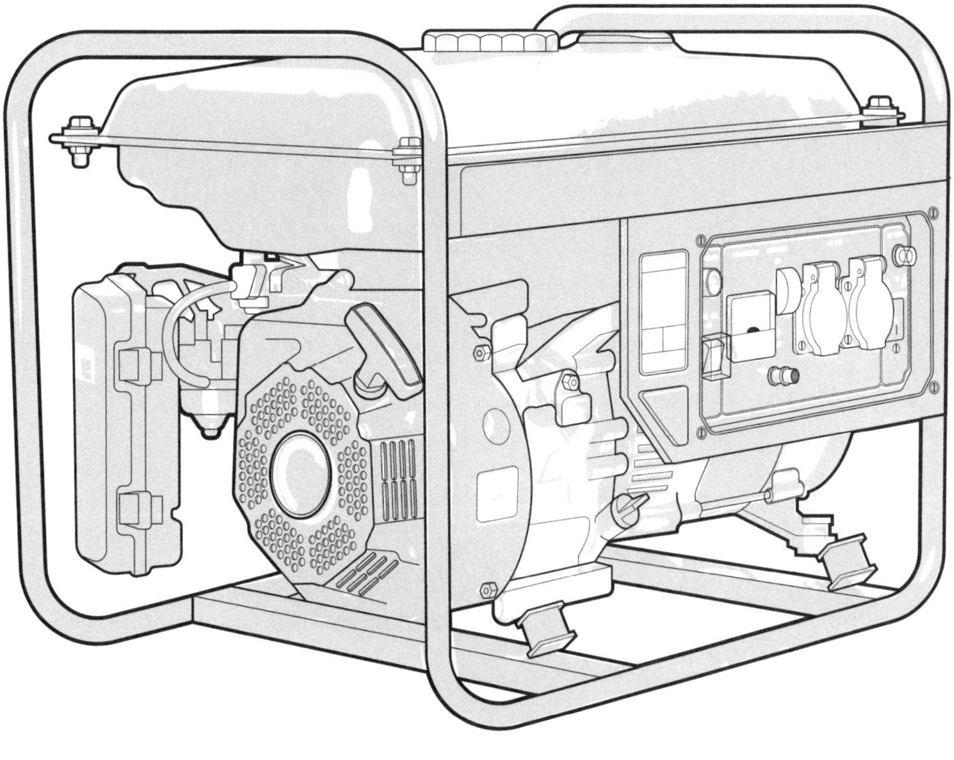

## 240 VAC

Generators are essential in grid-down situations. It is important to maintain a dry outside space for them, as indoor use inevitably leads to carbon monoxide deaths. Keep in mind that most well pumps require 240 VAC, so look for a generator with both 120 VAC and 240 VAC windings.

## Floods in England: A Case Study

In August 2007, I received a letter from England that gave an excellent description of the turmoil that even a relatively brief flood in a highly developed country can cause. I include it as a warning, and hopefully as a real-life experience to be learned from.

Sir:

You might have seen the news reports about the flooding in Central England last week. We're in amongst it, but fortunately (and thanks to forward planning) high enough to have remained dry.

The primary cause of the floods was a prolonged period of exceptionally heavy rain, up to 131mm (c.5-1/2 inches) in one day. This followed hot on the heels of a very wet summer which left the ground sodden and unable to absorb the downpour, which caused flash-flooding as it ran off.

Areas not normally flood-prone have been inundated. Rivers broke their banks and filled their flood-plains.

Now this part of the country is used to flooding, although not in the summer months, as it has two of the UK's most unstable rivers, the Severn and the Avon, passing through it. This episode, however, has been notable for the sheer amounts and force of the water and depths of flooding.

The mayhem and disruption caused has been bad enough, but it has been compounded by the behaviour of some, which can only be described as moronic. Conversely, the bravery of many, both in the response services and the public, has been humbling to see.

The floods caused chaos with the transport links, with railway lines and roads under several feet of water, even the M5 and M50 motorways (our equivalent to freeways) were closed after they disappeared under anything up to a foot of floodwater. This caused huge tailbacks with several thousand people stranded for up to twenty hours in their vehicles. One woman went into labour whilst in the jam on the M5 and the emergency services were unable to reach her either by ambulance or helicopter because of the conditions. Fortunately a truck-driver stuck near to her car realised the situation and used his vehicle to force a way through the water and the traffic to tow the woman's car to the ambulance. He then apparently had to tow the ambulance, as it too had become overwhelmed by the water. They managed to get the woman to hospital in time for the child to be born in the dry.

Towns and villages have been cut off for several days with residents needing rescue by boat or helicopter as the waters rose so quickly. As is always the case, some residents opt to stay with their property and many of these had to be rescued later as levels continued to rise.

The situation has been made worse by the failure of mains services; the electricity and water plants were flooded, even though they were sited above normal flood levels. A water treatment plant was overwhelmed and engineers are having to wait till flood levels drop sufficiently for

**TOTAL DEATHS**

# 13

**2007 UK FLOODS:**
**ESTIMATED PROPERTY DAMAGE: £6 BILLION ($8 BILLION).**
**MAY–JULY RAINFALL: 414.1 MM, THE MOST SINCE RECORDS BEGAN.**

them to get in and assess the damage. It is estimated that mains water will be off for at least two weeks. This has resulted in the water company having to import bottled water into the area for drinking purposes and, when the floodwaters dropped sufficiently, the placing of water bowsers to enable people to obtain clean water for sanitation. Sadly, although not surprisingly, there have been cases of people vandalising the bowsers, by breaking open the taps and even by polluting the contents. There is one confirmed case of someone urinating into a life saving tank. Looting has become a problem in areas that have been evacuated, forcing police to be diverted from rescue to deal with the crimes. There was an attempt to steal a length of temporary flood barrier, supposedly for its high scrap value. It is perhaps a pity that the thieves were thwarted in their attempt as on the other side of the barrier was several feet of floodwater.

Shops outside the affected zone have seen their entire supplies of water, milk and bread bought out by "enterprising" individuals who later tried to sell them at highly inflated prices to the stranded people. Fortunately the police dealt with this unsavoury bunch and the practice has all but ceased. It is now just a week since the worst downpour, although the unseasonal rains continue to add to the misery. It took considerably less than a week, however, for the infrastructure to break down. With no water or electricity, empty shops and no means of re-supply, many people were in dire straits within a couple of days. The elderly, infirm and those with young families were, and in many cases still are, in deep trouble.

For families who could remain in their homes, or who have since returned to areas which are still without power and mains water, basic sanitation is an increasing problem. Toilet flushing has to be rationed, clothes washing is virtually impossible and personal hygiene requires a level of thought and discipline that few are used to. One woman in her forties was seen on the television stating that she thought it appalling that the authorities had not been round to each home to "tell us what to do". Personal responsibility and the thought that maybe the "authorities" had other things on their mind at the time did not seem to enter her thinking. As the swollen rivers send the excess waters downstream the floods, power outages and disruption travel along with them.

There has been some respite from the rains which has allowed the levels upstream to drop, and flooding to recede, but at the time of writing (Friday, 27th July) more heavy rains are forecast for Saturday night and key personnel have been placed on stand by within the response services. Further flooding is predicted, as the ground is still sodden and unable to absorb any more water.

Michael in England

# WATER TREATMENT

Any water gathered from open sources should be considered unsafe to drink unless it has first been treated by any of these three methods:

- Heated in a pan to nearly the boiling point, or
- Treated with a chlorine solution for thirty minutes (*see illustration below*), or
- Filtered with a good-quality (1 micron) microbial filter

Note that when using the heating method, water does not have to reach "a full boil." As long as the water temperature briefly reaches 200°F (93.3°C), it will kill or render sterile all known pathogens.

I do not recommend using liquid chlorine bleach because it gradually degrades over time, losing strength. Thus, you have no way of accurately estimating the remaining strength of any particular batch of laundry bleach. It may have been in the wholesale and retail supply chain for more than a year before you bought it. Instead, I recommend that you store and use granular calcium hypochlorite powder. This is available from various online merchants.

Any water that has been treated by the heating or chlorine method can be made more palatable by aeration with an egg beater, or by repeatedly pouring the water from one container to another.

To provide consistently safe water for drinking and cooking—without burning precious fuel (for near-boil heating) and

**IMPORTANT NOTE**
Water that is contaminated with toxic chemicals (such as fuel, pesticides, or herbicides) will not be made safe to drink by heating, chlorination, or home filtration. If you suspect that your water might be contaminated, then instead use bottled drinking water or only water from a known uncontaminated source.

**DIRECTIONS TO MAKE AND USE A BATCH OF CHLORINE SOLUTION:**

**1** Dissolve one-quarter of an ounce (1 full teaspoon) of high-concentration (78 percent) granular calcium hypochlorite powder for every two gallons (7.57 liters) of water. Mix thoroughly.

**2** Carefully measure and add one part of this chlorine solution to 100 parts prefiltered water to be treated.

**3** Let the "1-to-100" treated water mixture stand for at least thirty minutes before using it for drinking or cooking.

without the sharp taste of chlorine—the crucial item that you will need is a water filter. These are made in two types: compact filters—designed for backpackers—and kitchen countertop filters.

The former is typified by the Katadyn Combi Filter (pictured far right and in use below), and the gold standard for the latter is the British Berkefeld "Big Berkey" filter (illustrated on right). This is a large stainless-steel filter unit that can be equipped with either white ceramic filters or black-carbon activated filters. Given their relative size and weight, each type of filter has their own purpose. If you can afford to, buy one of each.

When treating cloudy water from open sources, it is important to prefilter it. Using a pre-filter will greatly extend the life of your filter's cartridge(s). A pre-filter can be constructed by simply stacking together four to eight thicknesses of cotton shirt material. Pour the water though this slowly, and then run that prefiltered water through your main filter. Note that when filtering water, it is important to avoid having any unfiltered water contaminate the filtered water, so beware of spills that could reach your filtered water reservoir.

The Big Berkey countertop water-filter system comes in a variety of sizes, from 1.5 to 6 gallons. They are excellent for everyday use in normal situations, and potentially a lifesaver in a grid-down scenario.

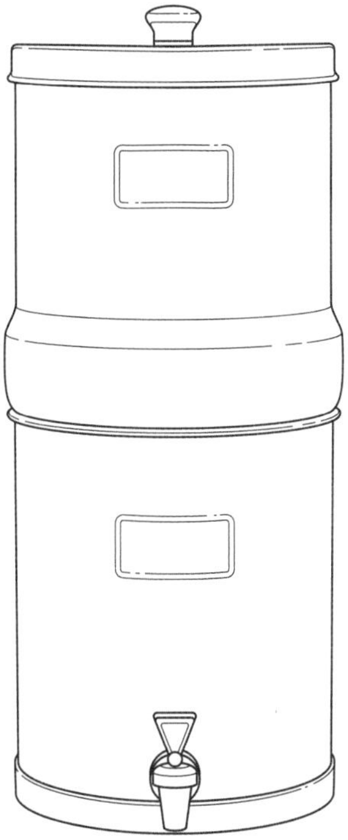

This Katadyn Combi Filter (in use below) is 30 cm high and lightweight, perfect for a small group requiring clean water on a multi-day journey. It can be used on very cloudy or muddy water, and has a 13,000-gallon capacity per filter.

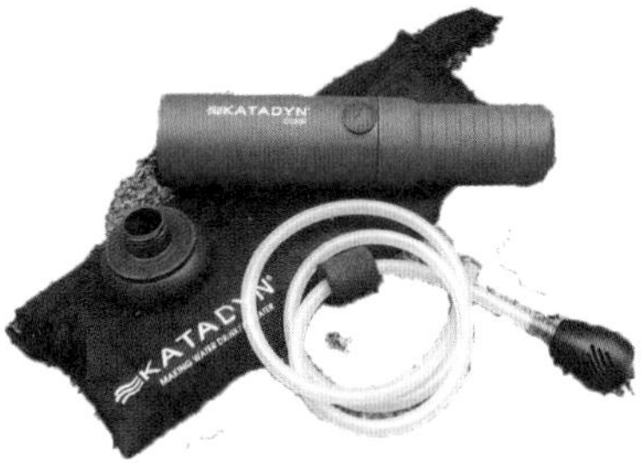

# THE MYTH OF HOUSEHOLD STORAGE

Many disaster-preparedness publications often make reference to "stored water, for emergencies." In the context of a crisis lasting more than a few months, that advice is patently naive. You simply won't have the requisite space to store water indoors for your family's needs for a year, or even for just a few months. The space required would be enormous, and the weight (at 8.34 pounds per U.S. gallon, or 1 kilogram per liter) would overstress the floors of most typical houses or apartments.

Even without water needed for toilet-flushing and showering, most people use three to eight gallons of water per day for drinking, cooking, and dish-washing. Assuming an absolute minimum of just *one* U.S. gallon of water per person, per day, a family of four would require 1,460 U.S. gallons for one year. That would equate to 12,176 pounds (5,523 kilograms). Picture that: ***six tons*** of water! If your floors could take the strain, depending on the containers chosen that would likely take up all of the available spare floor space in your house, leaving no room for other stored food or supplies.

More realistically, you should store just 20 to 30 gallons of water per family member, sufficient to provide for a short-term crisis. Thereafter, unless you have your own shallow well and a hand pump (a rarity these days), plan on gathering and treating rainwater or other surface water for your long-term needs.

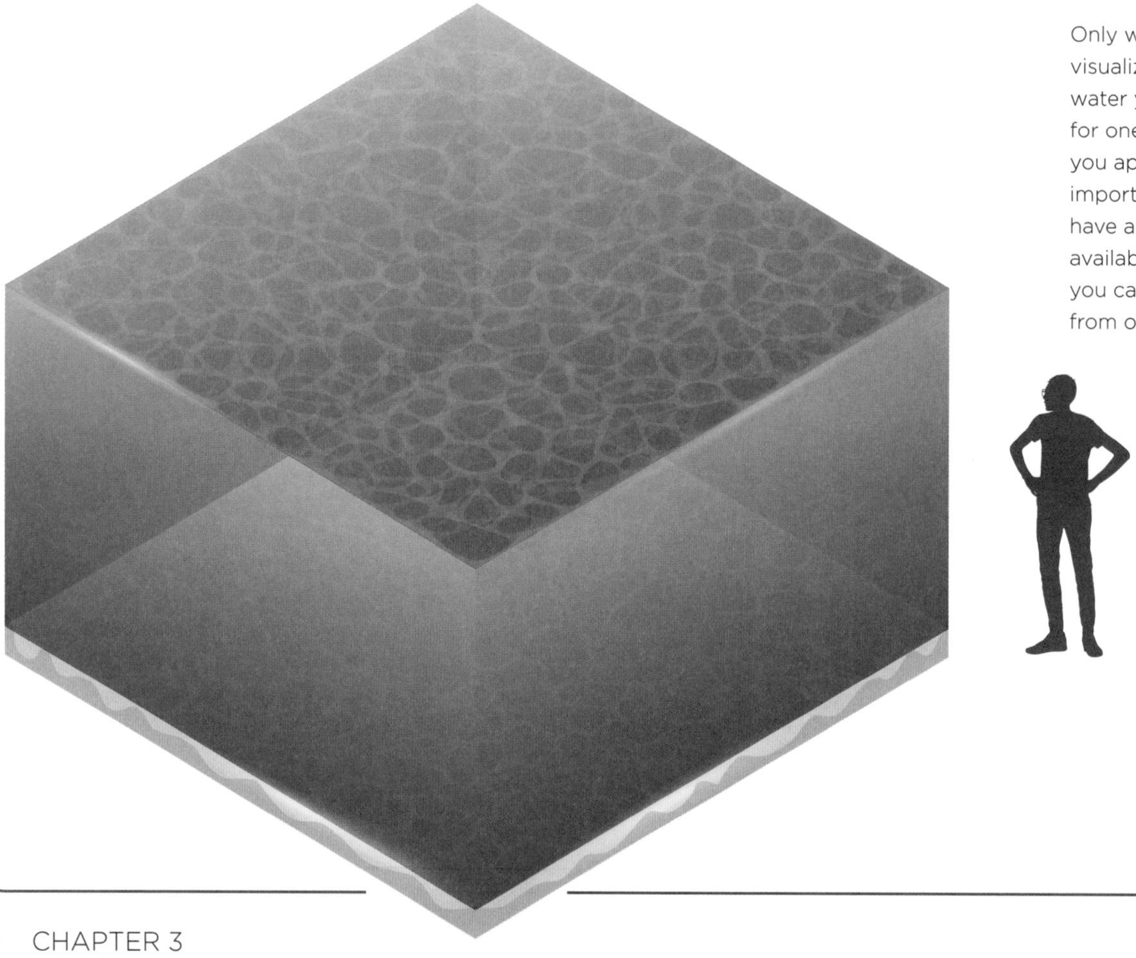

Only when you visualize how much water you will need for one year can you appreciate how important it is to have a water filter available—so that you can treat water from open sources.

## Water Sources and Transport

Most floods only last for a month or two, but a grid-down situation may persist many months, or even years. In this case, how will you gather rainwater, or water from ponds, streams, or brooks?

If your house has rain gutters, then it is important to install downspout diverters and rain barrels. Once a solid rain has washed your roof clean, you can flip the diverter and fill a rain barrel with relatively clean rainwater.

If you live in a region with unreliable rains, or if you don't have access to downspout rooftop water, then you will need to plan to transport water from other open sources such as lakes, ponds, rivers, streams, or brooks.

In a short-term crisis, it would be feasible for you to transport 5-gallon (20-liter) plastic water cans full of collected water in your car or SUV. But in a long-term crisis, during which fuel would surely become unavailable, you would need a "plan B" to transport water by hand. As previously noted, water is quite heavy, so carrying it by hand for more than just a short distance is not realistic. A better solution would be to use a two-wheeled wheelbarrow or garden cart. Most of these are rated to carry up to 400 pounds (181 kilograms). The effort required to push a cart laden with 250 pounds (113 kilograms) of water on level ground or up a gradual incline for half a mile is well within the capabilities of most physically fit adults.

A downspout diverter: it is important to be able to capture rainwater from your roof.

**AIM TO STORE FOUR TO SIX 5-GALLON WATER JUGS PER FAMILY MEMBER WHEN PREPPING FOR A FLOOD.**

# CHAPTER 4
# HEATING

Heating Options

Minimizing Heating

Fuel Storage Alternatives and Safety

# HEATING OPTIONS

Keeping yourself alive in a grid-down crisis will also depend on having an independent source of heat—at least for those of us who live north or south of 30 degrees latitude, depending on which hemisphere you live in. Much of the population of the United States resides in these cooler climes.

Passive solar heating is a good option for anyone living south of 40 degrees latitude. And while its duration is limited in a disaster, propane heating is a far better option than electric heat—full dependence on grid power. I've already described the vulnerability of grid (mains) power. Sadly, because of the huge current drain, electric heating is not an option for a home with an off-grid photovoltaic power system.

## The Rawles Ranch

We heat our house with a masonry wood stove. Because of the thermal mass of its masonry construction, the stove holds heat and, therefore, provides a much more consistent heating effect. At least, that is the case for at least three-quarters of our house. As our stove's wood box is large, there is the unfortunate risk of overheating the living room, especially in the fall and spring when the afternoons warm up. In those seasons, we have to be careful to keep the stove's air vent nearly closed almost all of the time. However, we are careful to let the stove burn "full rip" for a short time each morning, to prevent an accumulation of creosote in the chimney. This is of course no substitute for proper chimney cleaning, which is a lengthy annual chore, accomplished each spring. I usually do this after the roof is clear of snow and dry for the first time in the spring. A brief daily hot burn keeps a stove safe in more snowy climes where you can't safely get up on a roof for five or six months of the year.

Our house is just one story, which greatly simplifies the spread of warmth for wood heat. Two-story houses tend to be too

Masonry stoves have several advantages. Most importantly, their thermal mass holds and slowly disperses heat.

hot upstairs and too cold downstairs. We typically stoke the stove three times a day—around 5:30 a.m, at midday, and just before we retire for the night.

Personally, I prefer to burn Red Fir and Western Larch woods. The latter is commonly but erroneously called "Tamarack," locally. Last year we burned an odd assortment of wood, because we had just manually cleared two wooded acres of our property in order to make room to expand our fruit and nut tree orchard. We have about a dozen varieties of native trees on the ranch, including one sizable stand of Western Larch. However, most of the trees that I cleared were a mix of various types of fir and a bit of pine. Even though the wood was well-seasoned, this "Duke's Mixture" made for more erratic heating and more creosote buildup than we experience in a typical year. In contrast, Red Fir and Western Larch both consistently burn hot and clean. To heat our house, which is well insulated and around 3,000 square feet, we burn between five and eight cords each winter, depending on the weather and how much we travel each year.

Depending on the wood supply available where you are—preferably taken from your own property, but supplied from elsewhere if necessary—you will most likely have to experiment with different woods to find the cleanest and most consistent.

All in all, we enjoy heating our house with wood. One great advantage is that it is nice being able to keep the house at 75 to 80 degrees Fahrenheit and not feel guilty about it. To do the same with electricity or propane would be prohibitively expensive for a house of our size.

I typically have 80 percent of our annual wood supply split and stacked before winter each year. The remainder is kept under tarps and is split gradually, to provide some winter exercise on sunny days. Clear but unseasonably cold days make perfect weather for wood splitting. When a piece of wood is frozen at 10 degrees Fahrenheit, it doesn't just split; it fairly well *explodes*, when the splitting maul hits it. What fun!

For kindling, I typically burn cedar. I specially cut these rounds just 8 inches in length, to make for easy splitting. I split them either with a short-handled mine axe or with a shingle froe.

Lay in a large supply of firewood!

# MINIMIZING HEATING

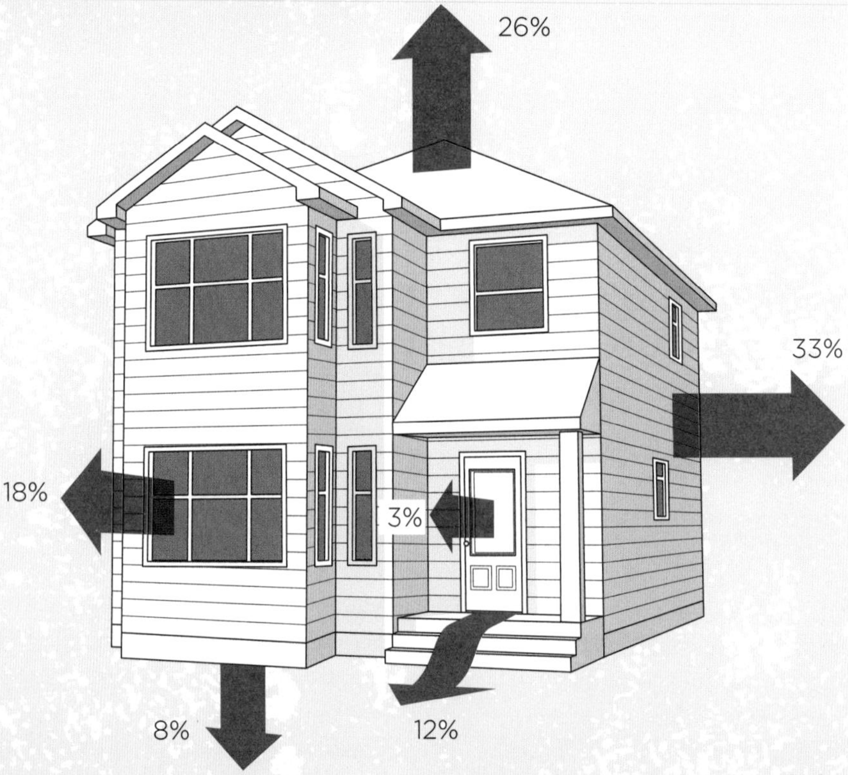


The estimated heat loss from an average U.S. family home from the roof, walls, doors, drafts, floors, and windows.

The simplest way to minimize your heating needs is through insulation. Start by insulating your house with upgraded double- or triple-pane windows, fresh door seals, and an extra layer of attic insulation. This is the simplest and most effective way of retaining whatever heat you generate inside your house. However, you can also insulate yourself. Let me explain several methods:

## Layered Clothing

The first and most obvious way to reduce home heating requirements is to wear layered clothing indoors as the season requires. Simply by wearing long underwear, a sweater (or a sweater vest), and a felt cap, you can easily extend the seasons in which you can go without heating your house.

## Sleeping Bags

Sleeping comfortably in an unheated house at night will require more than just standard bed linens, especially if you live outside of the 30-degree (north and south) latitudes. You should make it a high priority to buy a winter-weight sleeping bag for each member of your family.

Sleeping bags have changed a lot since I used them as a teenager. Back then, most sleeping bags available in the United States were made there, and filled with goose feathers and/or goose down. These days, synthetic insulation has become the norm, and sadly most locally available sleeping bags are made in China. However, there do remain a few truly great American brands. One of the best is a company called Wiggy's. I've used their bags almost exclusively since the early 1990s. They are very well made, comfortable, and durable.

Sleeping in a sleeping bag atop your bed and then draping it with a down comforter (a duvet) can greatly extend the seasons in which you can go without heating your house. It is also important and extremely sensible to wear a sleeping cap in the winter. The human scalp is very vascular, making it a prime avenue for the escape of body heat.

A French couple in a Breton *lit-clos* box bed, with father below, circa 1900.

#### THE 30-DEGREE (NORTH AND SOUTH) LATITUDES

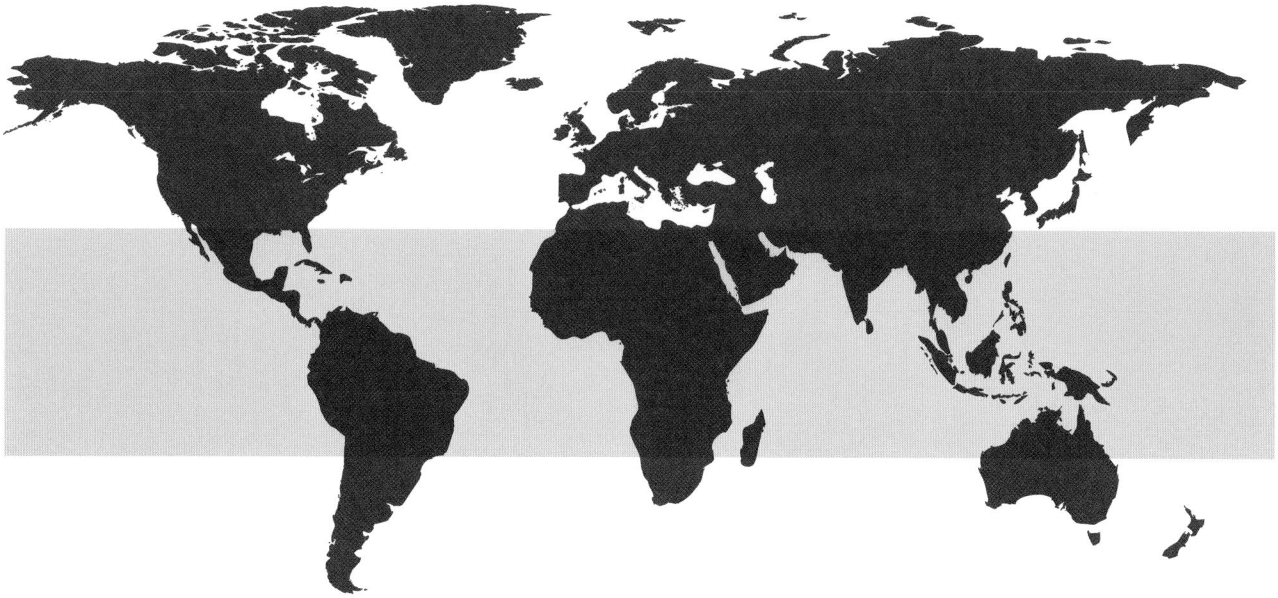

If you opt for sleeping in a sleeping bag for extended periods, then it is important to use a sleeping bag liner of sheet-weight material. Cotton works fine, but a flannel liner feels warmer and more comfortable for most people. Using a bag liner will minimize the number of times that you need to wash a sleeping bag, thus greatly extending your sleeping bag's useful life.

## Box Beds

One usually overlooked aspect of insulating yourself is through the use of a medieval-style box bed—also known as a cabinet bed. In Francophone countries, this is called a *lit-clos*. Now largely forgotten, these beds create a tiny "house within a house" that is heated with just your own body heat. In ancient days, people would also carry in buckets of heated stones, for radiant heat. The use of a box bed can greatly extend the number of seasons you can go without heating your entire house.

Box beds—typically with sliding doors—are still custom-built by carpenters, but can be expensive. If you are handy with carpentry tools, you can construct your own. Just keep in mind that they need *some* ventilation, to avoid asphyxiation!

# FUEL STORAGE ALTERNATIVES AND SAFETY

For many living in first world countries, a lack of grid power will mean an immediate loss of house heating. Most households now rely upon either AC-grid power heaters or upon natural gas heaters that use electrically powered fans to push heated air through ductwork. Very few families now use wood stoves for heating.

In an emergency and with proper venting, if you are one of the many without a wood stove, then you can safely use a kerosene (liquid paraffin) or propane heater in your home. Many wick-type kerosene heaters also have a cook top, making them serve double duty. These are sold under brand names in the United States such as Alpaca, Lamptti, and Lembeauty. Most kerosene heaters weigh 15 to 25 pounds, and refilling a kerosene heater should be done outdoors, in case of fuel spills.

Another alternative is a freestanding propane space heater. These are usually fueled by 20-pound (typically 18 inches tall, and 12 inches in diameter) tanks. These tanks weigh around 19 pounds when empty, and 39 pounds when full, meaning that they

The Manhattan skyline in darkness as the result of a blackout, in 2003.

**IMPORTANT NOTE**
Because of its combustion process, burning propane with a compact heater will release some moisture into the air. If your home has poor ventilation, then over a period of weeks or months you may begin to have a condensation problem that can lead to the growth of mold. So once again, proper ventilation is important.

are light enough that they can be transported in a passenger car's trunk, for refilling. In the United States, these are commonly called "barbecue tanks." Two brands of portable propane heaters that are offered in many countries around the world are sold under the brand names Little Buddy and Mr. Heater. Keep in mind that some of those model variants are designed to be fueled only by small 1-pound (½-kilogram) propane cylinders. Those are *not* cost-effective! The models that you should be looking for are the ones that have fuel line fittings compatible with external 20-pound tanks.

Regardless of the type of heater you choose, you must buy a carbon monoxide (CO) detector alarm. These should be installed at or below knee level, since CO is heavier than air, and settles. A CO detector is inexpensive life assurance!

The versatile Mr. Heater propane heater is especially popular with recreational vehicle owners.

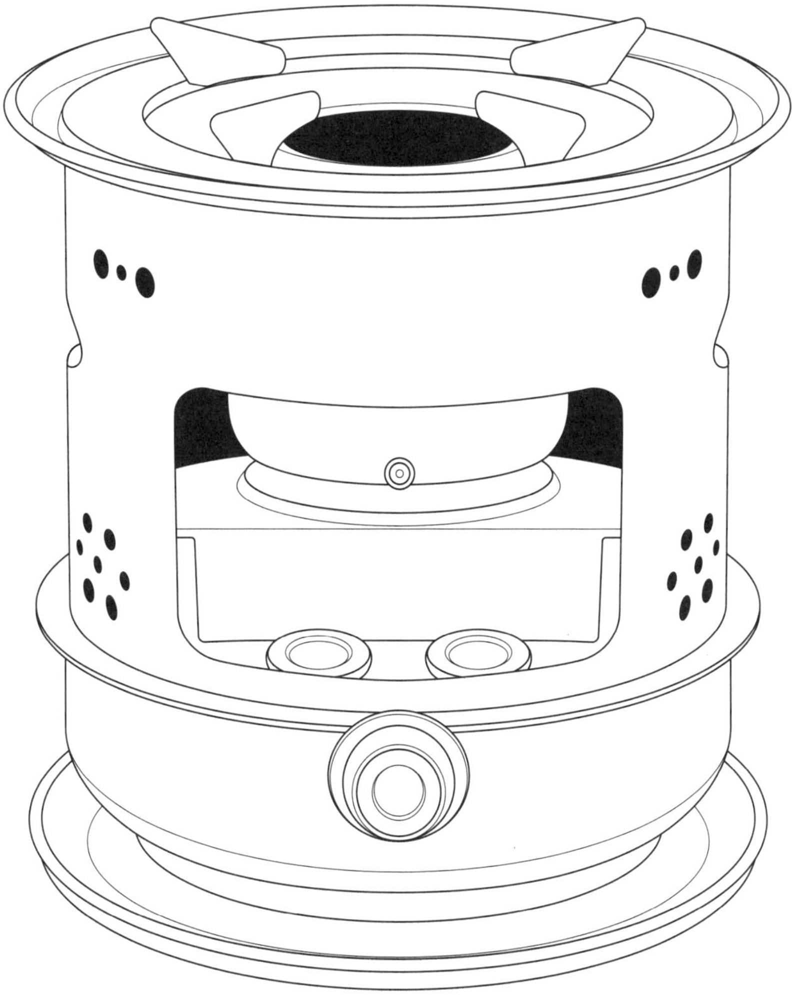

A kerosene cooker, such as the Alpaca, allows you to cook without grid power or piped natural gas or propane.

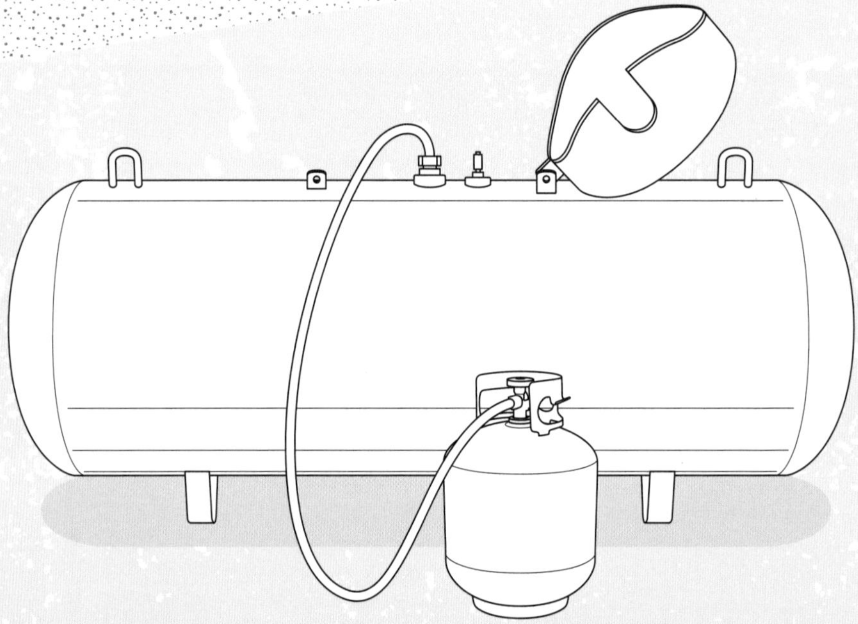

For propane storage, buy the largest tank that you can afford and that is allowable under your local fire code. A wet leg connection is then important for transferring to a smaller tank when necessary.

## Fuel Storage Safety

For fire safety, any kerosene cans (or jugs) and propane tanks should obviously not be stored indoors. However, this poses a dilemma for preppers: how to store extra fuel outdoors, but avoid having it stolen in the midst of a disaster. As discussed, times of disaster are naturally times of copious larceny.

One good solution is to buy a small plastic garden shed with a door that has a padlock hasp. Get in the habit of always keeping it locked up. These garden sheds have become ubiquitous in the suburbs and even in the yards of urban freestanding houses. Typically, they are used for storing lawn mowers and assorted gardening tools, but if you are surreptitious you can put numerous propane and/or kerosene containers in your shed without it being noticed by your neighbors. For this, the hours of darkness are your friends.

In English-speaking countires, many homes in rural areas have large aboveground propane tanks. In many other countries, butane is more normal. Propane tanks are usually refueled at regular intervals by a commercial delivery tank truck. To be ready for emergencies, I recommend that you buy

**IMPORTANT NOTE**
Be sure to first consult your local laws to determine fuel container type and volume restrictions. For optimal safety, a garden shed used for fuel storage should be positioned in your yard as far away as possible from your house or your neighbors' houses.

(or lease) the largest tank that you can afford and that meets local zoning restrictions. Inside the limits of many U.S. cities, the limit is a 500-gallon tank. But if you live outside of city limits, you might be able to install a mammoth 2,000-gallon propane tank. A 2,000-gallon tank can provide a couple of years' worth of heating and cooking fuel, if you use it conservatively.

## DIY Propane Fuel Transfer

What is not commonly known is that residential propane tanks can be used to fill 20-pound tanks, if the larger tank is equipped with an extra valve and a short high-pressure line commonly called a "wet leg." This is tubing connected to your tank that has a portable propane tank fitting at the far end.

There needs to be a temperature differential between the two tanks—with the smaller tank cooler. This can be accomplished by, for example, trickling cold water from a garden hose over the 20-pound tank while it is filling. The transfer process can take up to one hour. To measure the progress, place the small tank on a properly zeroed bathroom scale. Watch the scale at frequent intervals and stop the filling process once the weight of the small tank reaches 36 pounds. *DO NOT* overfill the tank! (For safety, a propane tank should never be filled more than 80 percent, to allow room for expansion on hot days.)

Similarly, 1-pound propane cylinders are easily refillable from 20-pound tanks if you know this trick. Get a brass cylinder-filling adapter. (They are available inexpensively from Harbor Freight and various Internet merchants.) You need a full 20-pound cylinder as the "donor" tank. Place it in a warm place or in the sun for a couple of hours, while chilling the empty 1-pound cylinders in your freezer. Join the cylinders using the filling adapter and make the transfer. The filling procedure is that you invert both of the joined cylinders and open cylinder valve. Refills take about one minute each.

Either of these propane fuel transfer methods could come in handy for your family in a disaster. You will probably also have neighbors that you will want to help charitably with the smaller cylinders. Buy the necessary fittings now, so that you will have that option, in extremis.

**I CANNOT STRESS ENOUGH THAT YOU SHOULD NOT OVERFILL THE TANK. IT IS FAR SAFER TO LEAVE IT 80 PERCENT FULL.**

EXTRA VALUE 10 PACK
Great Value
Quick Oats
Campbell's
25% BIGGER
Chicken Noodle
SOUP
Nutrition Facts
Great Value
Vegetable Beef
DICED TOMATOES
18 VALUE PACK
Great Value
Taco
Original Syrup
B-17G Flying Fortress
Scott
SWEET TEA
PURE LEAF
BREWED TEA
BASIC

# CHAPTER 5
# EATING

- Food Storage
- Grid-Down Cooking
- Special Considerations in Societal Collapse
- Seed Gathering and Storage

"After much research and real-world testing, I'm now posting the Woodpile Report Comprehensive Guide to Survival Food:

**Best Survival Food** – Food you have.
**Worst Survival Food** – Food you don't have."

Ol' Remus, in his YerOl' Woodpile Report blog

# FOOD STORAGE

**Food storage is one of the key differentiators between preppers and the general populace.**

Officials from disaster-preparedness agencies like FEMA recommend having a three-day supply. That is pitifully unrealistic. I'd consider a four-month supply a bare minimum, a one-year supply more realistic, and a three-year (or more) supply ideal.

One food storage option is to buy commercially packaged long-term storage foods in #10-size cans or 2-gallon pails, but those are expensive and often high in salt, sugar and MSG. (This varies by brand. Do some research before placing an order.) These are also generally foods that will probably not match your palate and accustomed menu.

In contrast, budget food storage usually involves home-packing the staple foods that you mostly already use in your day-to-day cooking, typically in 5-gallon or 7-gallon food-grade HDPE storage buckets. Inside of those, you should use Mylar bucket liner bags and oxygen-absorbing packets to kill any insects, larvae, or insect eggs. For those buckets that you'll access the most often, I recommend getting Gamma Seal lids. These lids have an inset threaded "spinner" cap, and they provide much quicker access than repeatedly using a bucket-lid wrench.

The foods most commonly stored in buckets include: wheat (or flour), rice, legumes, oats, pasta, salt, sugar, and honey. You will also need a source of fats and oils. Our family accomplished that through storing plastic bottles of olive oil in our freezer. If left out at room temperature, a bottle of olive oil only has at most a two-year shelf life before going rancid. But if kept frozen, it can be stored for up to six years with no discernable change in taste or consistency after thawing.

Whole wheat has a shelf life measured in decades, whereas ground-wheat flour only stores well for two or three years. If you store whole wheat, you will of course also need to invest in a good-quality hand-cranked grain grinder. At the Rawles Ranch, we use a grinder from the Country Living brand. But there are also several other brands available.

We often use an AC-powered dehydrator for drying fruit, vegetables, chicken, herbs, bell peppers, onions, beef jerky, venison jerky, and *biltong*. Dehydrating most of these is probably familiar to you, but it is biltong that might take a little explanation.

Huguenot and Dutch South African settlers created biltong. The recipe that we use is very simple: four pounds of beef strips, rinsed under tap water and then koshered for thirty minutes in salt water. Next, put the strips on a scrubbed dish drainer with an incline, at the side of your kitchen sink. Sprinkle them with rock salt on both sides, and leave it to sit for ninety minutes, allowing the juices to drain into the sink. Scrape off the salt with a knife, and put the beef strips

A five-gallon bucket with a Gamma Seal "spinner" lid for easy access.

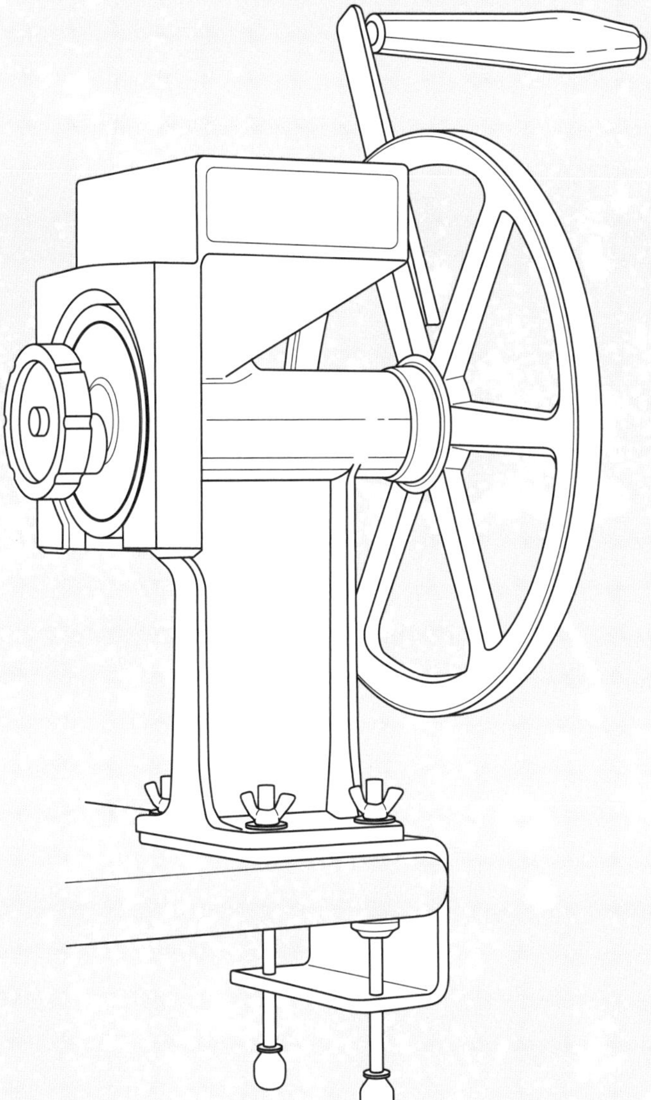

**IMPORTANT NOTE**

Since proper *biltong* is hung in strips to dry, rather than dried flat on trays, I do a little temporary conversion to our Excalibur-brand dehydrator: I remove all of the trays except the uppermost one. Through the broad mesh of that uppermost tray, I hang steel S-hooks that were leftovers from a batch of bungee cords. They have proved to be perfect for hanging *biltong* strips.

Owning a hand-cranked grain grinder will allow you to store whole-grain wheat rather than flour. The storage life of wheat is up to ten times longer than that of flour.

A food dehydrator will save both money and food storage space.

in apple cider vinegar, two at a time, for 2–4 minutes. Finally, heavily sprinkle both sides with coarsely ground black pepper and coarsely ground coriander. Put hooks in the meat and hang them in the dehydrator to dry for 12 hours at 155°F.

One of my blog readers who uses the pen name "John Adams" had this advice on dehydrating vegetables:

## JOHN ADAMS'S ADVICE

**GREEN BEANS** are dried in the southeastern United States. The end product is called Leather Breeches. You can do a web search for recipes. Traditionally, you use a sewing needle and sew a string through the green bean and then hang them to dry. We blanch the beans prior to drying in our dehydrator. After the beans were dried, we wrapped a handful of them in a paper towel and shrink-wrapped the package. The paper towel protects the plastic bag from the pointed ends of the beans.

To cook, simply soak them in water overnight and cook as if you were cooking fresh green beans. We made ours with pork hock, some shelled dried horticultural beans and potatoes. We cooked them for 12 hours in a crock-pot. Be sure to freeze the beans for three days before putting them in storage because those pesky moths will hatch in them if they are around your area.

**POTATOES.** We recently came into some free potatoes, some will store in the root cellar but the biggest part needed to be worked on right away. We scrubbed them, sliced them and placed them in a salt brine for a few minutes. (This helps keep them from turning brown.) Then they were placed in the dehydrator for 24 hours. The dehydration ratio for potatoes is 5:1. Thus, for every 5 lb. of fresh potatoes, you will get 1 lb. of dried. The next batch we'll run through the food processor and make hash browns, and then we'll dry them like the slices. Vacuum-packed, these, like the dried green beans, will keep for several years.

**TOMATOES,** we sun-dried when there was sun available and then finished the tomato pieces off in the dehydrator. We cut the tomatoes into roughly ¼" wedges and gave them a light coating of salt before setting them out. Use caution as they make a lot of juice. At first, we filled a dehydrator without first air-drying them in the sun, and drowned the dehydrator in tomato juice. After the wedges are dry but slightly rubbery, tightly pack a jar and cover with olive oil. The olive oil keeps the oxygen off the tomatoes, we ate some from last summer last night—six months later—and they were great.

# GRID-DOWN COOKING

While I've already addressed wood stoves for heating in the previous chapter, I should also say a bit about wood-stove cookery. If the power grids go down, and propane deliveries cease, then folks will have to revert to cooking with wood or charcoal heat. Modern residential fireplaces are mostly ornamental and almost wholly unsuitable for cooking. And even wood-fired space-heating stoves with flat tops are not much better. To be a safe and productive cook in a long-term societal collapse, you will need a proper wood-fired cook stove.

In the United States, my personal recommendation for a wood-fired cook stove is sold under the brand name Kitchen Queen. These are manufactured in an Amish community near Hopkinsville, Kentucky, and distributed by the Stove Works in Knoxville, Tennessee. Alternatively, there were dozens of other brands of wood-fired cook stoves made up until the 1940s and many of these can still be found, and can often be restored, with new firebrick and door seals. However, be careful to check for cracks, burned-out grates, and any threatening rust. (Minor rust can be handled by wire-brushing or sandblasting, followed by the application of specialized high-temperature stove paint.)

Unfortunately, because the heat generated by firewood has several variables, it is difficult to generate steady heat at a desired temperature for the cooktop and oven compartment. This is more of an art than a science, and there is a steep learning curve. You will probably overcook, undercook, and downright burn a few dishes before you master the care and feeding of a wood stove! Do not expect to learn how to manage your stove's firebox until after several weeks or even months of practice. And if you ever change stoves, change your chimney or damper configuration, or change the type of firewood that you use, then you will probably have another small learning curve.

**In a long-term societal collapse, you will need a proper wood-fired cook stove.**

If adding one of these doesn't work with the layout of your kitchen, then consider installing one on your back porch instead, or perhaps even in your workshop, if it is close to your house. If you are a renter with access to a deck or patio, then at least get a charcoal-fired barbecue. As they say, "Something is better than nothing." For a barbecue, you will also want to lay in a large supply of charcoal briquettes—best stored in galvanized steel trash cans to protect them from moisture.

One other alternative for grid-down cooking is a Japanese slow-cooker. Imagine the combination of design elements of a crock-pot and an insulated ice chest. In this case, the insulation holds heat in, instead of cold. With the efficient Japanese slow-cooker design, you quickly bring soups, stews or casserole dishes up to high heat. Then you ladle them into a steel or ceramic cooking cylinder, which is enclosed in a heavily insulated sleeve, with an insulated lid that clamps down. The internal heat of the food is used to slowly complete the cooking process, over several hours. Surprisingly, a full cooker with contents at boiling temperature will still be at serving temperature after seven or eight hours have elapsed. The same effect can be achieved with a standard cast-iron Dutch oven with a tight-fitting lid used in conjunction with a heavily insulated cooking bag. These bags are sold under the trade name Wonderbag.

Automatic rice cookers on display in a store. More traditional non-electric products are available as well and function more simply, like a Thermos bottle.

# SPECIAL CONSIDERATIONS IN SOCIETAL COLLAPSE

Life in the midst of a societal collapse will be radically different than what we experience today. The threat of violent crime will be almost constant. Theft, kidnapping, rape and murder will skyrocket. Constant vigilance will be required. Even items that are "locked up or nailed down" will be at considerable risk of theft. When most people are out of work and preoccupied with hunger, any compunctions about law and order will surely slip away. This will be most starkly seen in big cities. But even small towns will see an upswing in property crime. If you live in or adjoin a populated area, then you may literally have to set up a night watch over your garden to prevent people from stealing your crops.

And if times ever get *really* hard, then just the smell of food cooking may attract desperate looters. In the cities or suburbs, you may have to start cooking without spices, and with your windows shut. History has shown that desperate times lead people to desperate measures.

Food and supplies are looted as society collapses towards the end of World War II in Hanover, Germany, circa June 1945.

# SEED GATHERING AND STORAGE

It has been asserted by several authors that the garden space required to feed a family of four could be as little as a quarter-acre plot. However, the pessimist in me says to at least triple that. And my Christian conscience dictates that I double that again, to be able to provide some food for charity. Therefore, if you are the head a family of four, to allow requisite room for a house, a shop *and* a garden plot, you will need at least four acres. A larger family would, of course, necessitate a correspondingly larger parcel of land.

## Non-Hybrid Gardening

Famines could be caused by disruption to supply chains, but they could just as easily occur thanks to disruption of hybrid seed production. In recent decades, the lure of high yields has forced the vast majority of the world's farmers into the ongoing use of hybrid seeds, because cross-bred seeds can have more favorable traits. Unfortunately, this has led to the majority of farmers using the same hybrid seed to produce the same crop, which is called monoculture farming. This is like an enormous, inviting, invisible trap that has taken in nearly all of the commercial farmers on the planet.

I will discuss hybrids further later on, but one major hazard of hybrids is that the exact same seed type is planted on a large scale. This means that a disease that could wipe out just one type of plant could kill all of those plants: all are identical, and all would have the same lack of resistance. You can think of hybrid seeds as identical twins. The beauty of non-hybrid seeds is that they offer genetic variety, you can think of them as cousins. They are from the same family, but each has unique attributes. Among a field of non-hybrid plants would be *some* with resistance to most diseases. Thus, when disease strikes, you would only lose part of your crop. Moreover, if you saved the seeds from the plants that had the most resistance, then you would have more disease-resistant plants the next year.

Therefore, saving non-hybrid seeds year after year is of vital importance. In this section, I will depend on the hard-earned wisdom of my wife, "Avalanche Lily," and also of blog reader "P.R." At first glance, saving seeds might seem obvious and easy, but there are a lot of questions (see opposite box).

There are many books and references that can be found on seed saving. The problem is that the answers to these—and other—questions tend to be scattered in numerous sources, often with conflicting information. What's more, many of them are overwhelming, with family names and cross-pollination data. It is true that saving seeds can be a challenge, especially if you have large crop operations or you have many varieties of each type of crop, but for the home gardener or small community operation, seed saving doesn't have to be difficult.

## Where to Start

The seed you start with is perhaps the most important aspect of it all.

With so many choices of seeds out there between grocery stores, catalogs and the Internet, it's difficult to figure out where to begin. It's even more difficult to be motivated to learn to save seeds, because there is such an abundance of them available for purchase, or so it now seems. From one view, it may seem silly to waste time and energy on seed saving when it's so easy to stock up on an item that takes so little space, and with so many places offering a variety of survival seeds for a small budget.

But, truth be told, this is a huge mistake. First, not all crops will grow in your area. This may seem like common sense, but it needs to be said. If you live in an area with a short growing season, then you won't be making tomato sauce every summer, and if you live in a hot climate, then you won't be growing many dark leafy greens. Second, the viability of seeds degrades with time, even if kept in the best of conditions. Seeds, like all stocked food, should be rotated as time goes by.

### SAVING SEEDS

- How do you save the seeds?
- What do they look like, for different plants?
- What conditions do you need for plants to produce seed?
- When is the best time to harvest them?
- How many do you get?
- Can you eat the same plants that you get seed from, or do you have to keep food crops separate from seed crops?

**4 BILLION**

**THE ESTIMATED NUMBER OF AMERICAN CHESTNUT TREES KILLED IN THE EARLY 1900S, WHEN THE TREE WAS VIRTUALLY WIPED OFF THE CONTINENT BY A SINGLE STRAIN OF FUNGUS.**

It is possible to grow a wide variety of vegetables in even the smallest of home gardens.

The growing season and temperature variables are not the only things to consider in making your seed selection. Your elevation will matter as well, along with the amount of precipitation and type of soil. Rather than tying yourself in knots attempting to mitigate these issues, it is much easier to grow crops that are suited for your local conditions.

Your first decision will be to decide what crops you want to grow. Let's say you want to grow the following:

- Tomatoes
- Carrots
- Spinach
- Broccoli
- Cabbage
- Cucumbers
- Salad mix
- Potatoes
- Sweet potatoes
- A nice melon to satisfy that sweet craving

Let's start with the tomatoes. There are so many varieties out there, you can get lost in pages upon pages of choices. It can be daunting and cost a lot of money. So, here's what you want to do: find a few varieties that are known to be favorable for your climate, your elevation and your soil. Look for disease resistance and look for non-hybrid, heirloom varieties. Also, make sure the variety you choose does not require a second variety to pollinate. Most basic garden foods do not, but it's still good to check. You should pick several varieties to allow you to experiment to see what you can successfully grow in your soil and climate.

However, there is an important point to note about this: experiment with growing *only one* seed variety at a time. Pick one, just one, and *only* one. Plant and grow that one seed variety to start. Follow the same

**THE APPROXIMATE NUMBER OF KNOWN VARIETIES OF HEIRLOOM TOMATOES WORLDWIDE.**

**IMPORTANT NOTE**

If you try to save a potato or a related family that you purchased in a store, there's a good chance it won't sprout. This is because the distributors commonly spray them with a chemical to suppress the hormones that occur naturally in the root, which normally would cause the root to sprout. Depending on what chemical was used, you may be able to soak the tuber root in water for an hour prior to planting, but this is not a guaranteed method. It's really best that you start off with something that is a sure thing with known qualities.

Store-bought produce is a gamble. Potatoes you get from a CSA will probably sprout before you have a chance to use them. This would be a better option.

I also usually do not recommend starting with transplants. Generally, these plants have started off with ideal conditions that include a heating mat, moisture control, and whatever disease-preventive spraying that took place. Unless you know exactly how that plant was treated from seed, and you can replicate these conditions for its offspring, then do not buy it for seed saving.

selection process for your other fruits and vegetable choices, selecting only one variety of each to try growing, initially.

Next, you must decide where to get your seeds. Some of the varieties might not be available locally, so you may have to settle for a variety that you *can* find locally. The good news is that the chances are good that if it's grown locally, then it already has most of the features you are looking for.

My first recommendation is to find a Community Supported Agriculture (CSA) farm or co-op in your area. These are mostly available in the United States and Canada, but there are a variety of similar organizations set up around the world. Contact them and find out if they sell seeds from their locally grown food. If not, then find out who they buy from. The reason I recommend a CSA is that it's local, which means the food is grown in your locale, your climate, your elevation, and your soil. This means that this type of food will actually grow in your area, and these seeds are worth saving.

My second recommendation is to find local farmers in your area, and see if they offer seeds. You may have to call or drive around a lot to get what you're looking for, as many farmers specialize in monoculture farming. Therefore, you may have to go to several farmers to accumulate the seeds you want to start with.

Lastly, I recommend Internet research, but *be careful*. Call and ask questions. Find out where the seeds are grown and find out if they are hybrids or heirlooms.

## Hybrids

A hybrid is a mix of two different parent plants, and its offspring will not be the same. Hybrids are great for disease resistance and temperature tolerance, but they are not good choices for saving seeds, because the seeds likely will not carry the same properties as the parent, and will not produce the fruit or vegetable you started with. Worse, some hybrids won't produce seeds at all. When thinking of a hybrid, think of a horse mating with a donkey. You get a mule, which is a sterile animal that is a hybrid of its parents.

## Where the Seeds Are and How to Save Them

We are so used to buying products that are processed, that it's difficult for the inexperienced to know how a cabbage or a carrot will develop seed. Some produce is obvious. A tomato is filled with seeds when you cut into it, and potatoes sprout. Those seem easy, but what does a cabbage or a carrot do? Some crops need two years, and some crops need the right temperatures to "bolt" (go to seed).

One key aspect of seed saving is that the seeds that you save cost almost nothing.

**24 HRS**

**RECENT RESEARCH HAS SHOWN THAT 24 HOURS IS IDEAL FOR SOAKING TOMATO SEEDS, AND ALLOWING THE SEEDS TO SOAK LONGER REDUCES VIABILITY.**

A tomato is fairly easy. You plant the seed, your plant grows, it develops tomatoes, they mature and turn red, and you eat them. Tomatoes are one of the fruits that you can enjoy eating and still save seed. You don't need much; a few tomatoes will suffice. The tricky part is getting the seeds to store for a long period of time.

Tomatoes are also a special case study,

because they're one of the few plants where you will elicit the help of fungus to help you with your seed. The issue is that tomato seeds are naturally covered in a gelatinous concoction that keeps the seeds from germinating inside the tomato.

When gardening, there are many cases such as this, when it is helpful to ask yourself a very important question: what would nature do? At one point during life on Earth, plants reproduced without the help of humans, and nature helped these plants along the way. So when thinking about how plants might spread their seeds in nature, ask yourself: if you were a tomato, what strategy would you use to spread your seeds so that you reproduce? First, you have to get the seeds out of the tomato, and then you have to break down the gelatinous concoction so that they can sprout. Next, you have to disperse the seeds. So how would you do that?

Nature—or tomatoes—developed an amazing process. Imagine an animal ate the bright red (ripe) tomato. The tomato would then be digested in the stomach of the animal as it moved to another location. The seeds are protected and do not break down during digestion, due to their protective coating, and eventually the animal defecates in another location. A natural fungus that occurs naturally with the seeds then helps break down the gelatinous concoction, just in time for the seeds to be firmly planted in the perfect roll of soil. Thus, the next generation of tomato would grow!

The problem is that it's highly impractical to depend on wild animals to digest your tomato seeds to meet your needs. The solution is that you place the gelatinous seeds in a container, add some water, cover partially, and let them stand for 24 hours. The fungus that comes naturally with the seeds will then break down the gelatinous layer. Then all you have to do is rinse, dry on a towel or paper plate, and store. No wild animals are needed. The important part is that you do not store the seeds until they are *fully dry* after rinsing them. I usually allow mine to dry for a couple of weeks on a flour-sack towel.

## Collecting Carrots

Carrots are a very different story. If you eat the carrot, you can't get the seed. This is okay, though, as you don't need to set aside many unharvested carrots to get enough seed; one carrot can produce quite a bit of seed. The trick here is time.

Carrots need two growing seasons to produce seed. In the first season, they will produce the root vegetable that you would normally eat. However, if you leave it in the ground, then, during the second season, the carrot will develop flowers, and, eventually, seed. Again, you have to look at nature and what strategy nature—or the carrot—has employed. When you look at the flowers of the carrot, you will quickly realize that whatever seeds develop will be very susceptible to the wind, because they are very fine. This is where you have to beat nature and collect the dry carrot seeds before the wind scatters them. You may have to check your seeds quite often to see if they are ready to harvest.

Watch the weather to make sure you don't miss your opportunity to a windy day, and collect between rainy days, so that they are already dried on the plant. If the seeds don't fall off in your hands easily, they need more time to mature. If you pick too early, the seeds won't germinate. It can be a bit tricky to learn when the time is right, and you may have to collect the seeds more than once from the same plant to get the most viable seeds.

TOMATO

PEPPER

CABBAGE

CARROT

Collecting carrot seeds can be tricky.

## Spinach Seeds

Spinach requires that you learn yet another strategy of nature. Spinach is a cool-weather crop, and oftentimes, unless you get a variety that is slow to bolt, spinach will go to seed if the temperature gets too hot. With some varieties, this can occur as low as 80°F. With most spinach, you can harvest the leaves up until it bolts. This is nice, because you get the best of both worlds—that is, you get to eat the spinach *and* you get to save the seed. Just don't eat the leaves once they bolt—they won't taste good, and the plant will still need to undergo photosynthesis through its leaves in order for the seeds to mature. I suppose if you have nothing else to eat, and you don't need the seed, then go ahead and eat it but, again, note that the flavor becomes very different once spinach goes to seed.

Spinach is unique because it requires two plants in order to pollinate—a male and a female. It also requires wind to pollinate. This means that when planning on saving seeds, you need to save double the plants as you would for any other plant that doesn't require both a male and female. The wind pollinates the spinach, and the seeds develop on the female once pollinated. The trick here is time, yet again. The seeds usually turn dark brown when ready, but they need to be dry. Because of the length of time to mature, some gardeners collect the spinach stalks, tie them in a bunch, and hang them upside down in a paper bag in a garage or other dry place. Then, several weeks later, they shake the stalks and watch the seeds fall to the bottom of the paper bag. This method can also be used for collecting seeds from other plants. Exercise your judgment for when this method is appropriate.

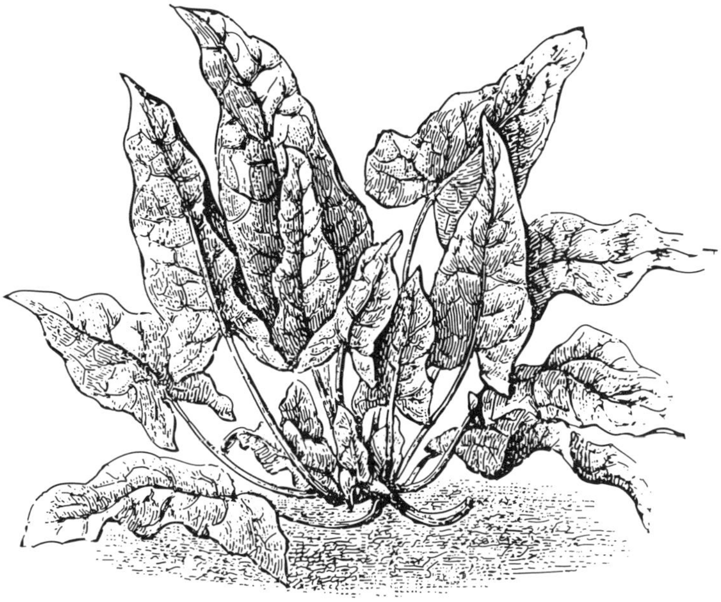

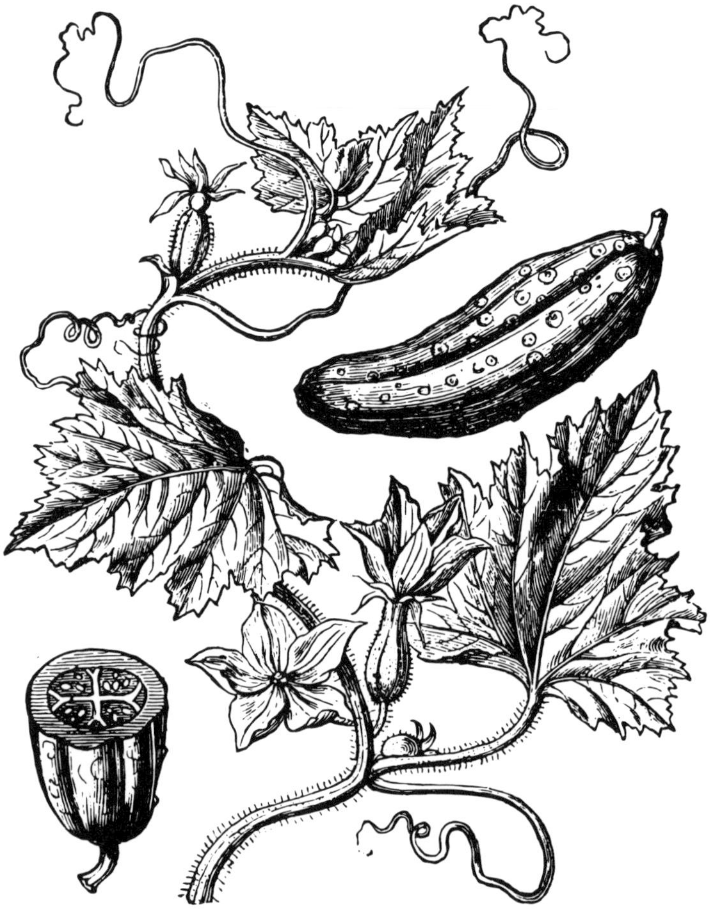

## Broccoli and Cabbage

Broccoli and cabbage are two plants that you do not get to enjoy eating and also save the seed. You have to choose one or the other—food or seed. I list these together because they are in fact in the same family—Brassica.

With broccoli, the very part that we eat (the "florets" or "crowns"), if left uncut long enough, will eventually turn into flowers.

Small insects, such as mason bees or certain flies, would then pollinate these flowers. Once pollinated, they turn into pods, mature, and then dry. Inside each pod, you will have a few dark brown seeds ready for planting.

With cabbage, if the "head" (the part we eat) is left without cutting, it eventually splits open and grows flowers from the opening. The flowers are pollinated, then turn into pods, then mature, dry and, again, inside each pod you will have seeds ready for planting.

It is a more difficult question to answer what strategy nature uses to physically spread cabbage or broccoli seed. Any plant that produces flowers naturally entices bees and other flying insects to pollinate it, which is all well and good, but once the pods are dry, what animal would want to eat it? The pod will continue drying out until it splits, and the seeds will simply fall out onto the soil and grow anew. Thus, no animal is required to spread the seed. All you have to do is collect the dry pods when they crack easily in your fingers. It is best to remove the seeds from the pods before storage.

## Cucumbers and Potatoes

Cucumbers are another crop that you cannot both eat and save the seed. The seeds in the cucumbers that people eat are nowhere near ready for planting. Cucumbers must over-ripen, when the seeds will finally develop fully inside the fruit. In the wild, or nature, or whatever you want to call it, a cucumber would mature, become heavy, then start to dry after it falls off the vine. The seeds inside would continue to mature until the cucumber rotted, and then the seeds would be able to take life again, using the mixture of rotting cucumber and soil for nutrients.

To save the cucumber seeds, you want to let your cucumber overmature, but *not* rot. Cut it open, remove and wash the seeds, and then let them dry. One way to tell viability is to see if the seeds float or drown during washing. Think about it this way: if it's an empty shell, it's likely to float; if it's full of life, it's likely to sink. Dry the sinkers for a few weeks, and store away.

Everyone likes a good salad with tomatoes

and cucumber, and generally, salad lettuces and greens are fairly easy to grow. You pick them, and they grow right back. It's a great crop to have around, and the best part is that you can cut and cut, and still get seed. Once salad greens (most varieties) bolt, they become bitter and most gardeners stop harvesting. However, if you let them go, flowers spring up from the center stalks, the mason bees pollinate, and seeds develop over time. They produce lots of seeds, but you have to beat nature by collecting them before the wind sets them free. Don't pick too early though: just like carrots, you have to wait until they dry and fall off easily.

Potatoes can have seeds, but the viability of these seeds is usually not great. It's really better to give up a few servings of mashed potatoes, and save some tubers for planting rather than trying to save potato seed. Again, if you consider the strategy of how potatoes will reproduce in nature, the potato has to do nothing but stay in the ground.

Eventually, the eyes of the potatoes will grow sprouts, and those sprouts, chitting, will then grow new potatoes. The flowering period is usually an indicator of when to harvest the potatoes—six weeks after flowering is ideal (the same also applies for sweet potatoes).

## Plant Families

The best way to determine if different plants are related is by looking at two things—growth patterns and flowers. If two plants follow the same growth patterns and their flowers develop and look about the same, then they might be related. It's best to choose only one of the plants to go to seed at the same time. If you allow two plants—let's say broccoli and cabbage—to flower at the same time, then the bees just might cross-pollinate. In this case, the seeds you get would produce duds, with neither the broccoli nor the cabbage producing viable seeds. This is why I recommend you start with one variety of each plant, so you reduce your chances of cross-pollination and, thus, seed failure.

## When You're Not Sure

Always ask yourself: what would nature do? Sometimes just sitting back and studying how a plant grows, at what point it develops flowers, or how it looks, can tell you a lot about that plant and the seed it produces. You can ask yourself questions about the plant, like how fragile the seeds are, how they would be spread, and so on. These questions can help you to figure out what it will take to save the seeds from that plant.

I haven't covered cross-pollination too much because I think it can be overhyped for the simple gardener. Cross-pollination only occurs if you have two plants of a related family flowering at the same time. First, if you only grow one variety at a time, as suggested above, you don't have to worry about cross-pollination because a carrot obviously won't cross with a tomato. Second, if you are set on growing two different varieties in the same family, you can prevent cross-pollination simply by planting them at different times, or choosing varieties that take different lengths of time to mature. For example, if you have two tomato varieties, and one matures at fifty-six days, while the other matures at eighty days, and you pay attention to make sure they have not flowered at the same time, then they will not cross.

A final way to prevent cross-pollination is simply to physically isolate the plants. This could be done by separating each with insect netting (for those that require insect pollination), or by separating in greenhouses or cold frames (wind-pollinated).

If you are someone who only grows one type of tomato, one type of cucumber, and one type of dark leafy green, then you don't have to worry about cross-pollination. This is why I suggest you start out experimenting with one variety at a time.

However, this doesn't necessarily mean that you cannot think at all about cross-pollination; you still have to use your head. As mentioned earlier, plants in the same family *can* cross-pollinate. For example, broccoli and cabbage are related, and to make matters more complicated, so is kale—all are Brassicas. If you were to compare seeds and flowers from all three, you would not be able to tell them apart. So, if you plan to grow and save seeds from two or three plants from the same family, you will need to keep them sufficiently segregated, or schedule the planting so that they flower—and seed—at different times.

**Always ask yourself: What would nature do?**

If you want seeds, and you see flowers on different plants that are alike or very similar in appearance, then decide which crop you want to save for seeds, and eat all the others. Stick to the rule of one variety per family blooming at a time, and you won't have to worry about saved seeds growing into sterile duds or not germinating at all.

### When Nature Is Confusing

There are plants that break all the rules, and even though they might develop seed, they won't germinate from seed, because they have found a better way to reproduce. Blackberries, strawberries, and other common berries are of this nature. Rather than going to seed and dying, the root system throws out shoots and upon hitting soil, these

shoots will develop roots, giving you a new berry plant. Those who swear off thorny blackberries and prune them to the bottom often realize only a short time later that the plant has found a way to beat them.

The upside to this is that we can use this method to our advantage. Let's use fruit trees as an example. A fruit tree can take years to grow from seed before it is old enough to produce fruit. So people have discovered a shortcut—rooting. In short, select a branch, cut it off the tree, place it in water (and ideally also a plant growth hormone), and that branch will develop roots. The advantage here is that you take a five-year-old tree branch, root it, and you have a second five-year-old tree. This also works with certain other long-maturity plants.

Plant-hormone growth stimulants are not always required. In some cases, you can simply place the branch in water and see if roots develop. However, the plant hormones do help increase the success rate. You can try just sticking the branch in water, but sometimes diseases will win the race with the development of roots, and the twig will die before it has a chance to grow. With the aid of rooting hormones, however it usually wins the race. A small container of plant-hormone powder will go a long way, store for a long time, and take up less space than a bunch of trees for which you might not yet be ready.

Another trick that nature might play on you is that your seeds might not germinate. You did everything right, you collected them at the right time, dried them properly and stored them correctly, and yet, the seeds just won't grow. Again, you have to ask yourself: why would nature do this?

There are many plants, especially fruit trees, which require that their seeds be kept cool for a certain period of time before germinating. Basically, the "right" conditions are required for the seeds to germinate. Though not a fruit tree, I'll use the oak tree as an example. If you collect oak acorns and plant them, the chances are they won't grow until the second year. Some seeds require a certain amount of cold or "freeze hours" before they will break dormancy and sprout.

Some berry plants and fruit trees will also not produce fruit if they do not get enough "freeze hours." This is nature's way of making sure the seeds don't germinate before the conditions are right. The seeds stay dormant until conditions are favorable, such as after winter. Ideally, then, make sure you get a variety that is appropriate for your climate. However, where that is not possible, you can try to trick the seeds. Just place the seeds in moist soil in a plastic bag, and place it in your refrigerator for ninety days. This is called cold stratification; you are effectively mimicking winter. After ninety days, seed dormancy should be broken.

**Where there's a will, there's a way. And, if nature can do it, rest assured, so can you.**

## HOW TO PROPAGATE A CUTTING

Cut through the branch at the point where the current year's growth begins. This will appear differently from plant to plant, but one trick is to bend the branch back on itself. The point where it begins to break is the perfect spot.

Make a straight cut ¼ inch above the nearest bud. Many people advocate for an angled cut, but the chance of getting bacterial or fungal disease in your cutting is slightly higher with an angled cut.

Remove a thin layer of the bark wood from the base of the cutting using a sharp knife or secateurs. This will wound the cutting, which makes it more likely to root. Take care not to crush the delicate end of the cutting.

Dip the base of the cutting into hormone rooting powder. This will help to stimulate root growth from the cutting. Ensure that the cutting is kept in a cool, moist environment until ready to plant. Do not let it dry out.

Plant the cutting in a pot and water the soil regularly. Check frequently to make sure the soil is slightly damp, but avoid overwatering it. You can place the pot in the cold frame of a greenhouse if you have access to one, as this can help to speed up the root formation.

Transplant the cutting into your chosen permanent ground location during the next fall season. The larger the cutting grows before it is transplanted, the greater its chance of success.

## On Storing Your Seeds

It is best to store your dried seeds in a cool, dry place. Refrigerating your seeds will increase the length of time they remain viable. Many references will recommend that you freeze your seeds for the longest shelf life. However, it is important to remove as much moisture as possible *before* placing them in the freezer, as water crystals in larger seeds—such as peas and corn—will cause them to crack and leave the seeds unviable.

The first step to removing moisture is to allow your seeds to dry at room temperature. I recommend a minimum of a couple of weeks. You can place the seeds on dry flour-sack towels or you can use other bedding, such as paper towels or paper plates. Next, place the seeds in paper coin envelopes or another paper storage container. I find that storing seeds in paper helps to absorb any extra moisture and allows the seeds to breathe.

Once the seeds are dry and in a paper envelope, prepare a glass jar, such as a home-canning (preserving) jar. Place oxygen-absorbing desiccants into the bottom of the jar. These desiccants are included in packaging for a variety of products and can be saved and reused. You can collect the desiccant packets, and then dry them in the oven just prior to use. Be careful not to burn or melt the desiccants with too high a temperature, though—I keep the temperature below 180°F. Once the desiccants are in the bottom of the jar, place the seed envelopes, put the lid on, and leave it be for about a week. Finally, open the jar and quickly transfer the seed envelopes to the freezer.

## Food Storage Quantities

You can develop large, productive vegetable gardens, but they will probably not be enough to provide nutritional adequacy for your family, year after year. There are simply too many variables and imponderables. What if you have a sudden influx of relatives who will depend on you for food? What if there is a disruption in your water system? What if there is simply a poor or short growing season? What if your gardens are stripped clean by marauders?

Anyone with a preparedness mindset can see that it is wise to store food, in quantity, with most of it hidden. But what qualifies as "in quantity"? The LDS (Mormon) church has a recommended food-storage program that hasn't changed much in more than a decade. For one adult for one year, they assert that you will need the amounts of food as shown on the opposite page.

While those will provide complete proteins, and an adequate nutritional baseline, there will likely be some vitamin and mineral shortfalls. So, for more complete nutrition, I would add to that list:

- A good-quality double-encapsulated multivitamin and mineral tablet (365 tablets per person, per year). However, it is my opinion that most of these tablets are inadequate in both vitamin C and magnesium, so I also recommend adding: a) 365 vitamin C tablets (500 mg per tablet); and b) 365 magnesium tablets (250 mg per tablet).
- A sprouting kit with an assortment of sprouting seeds.

The preceding numbers would of course have to be multiplied by your number of family members and by the number of years that you want to be supplied. I recommend a two- to four-year supply, if you can afford it, and if you have adequate storage space.

To close this chapter, I should mention that there really is no such thing as a family having "too much" storage food. Any excess quantities will be useful for barter and charity.

**OF WHOLE GRAINS.**

This should be a mixture of wheat—part of this can be pasta—rice, corn and oats.

**OF FATS.**

This can be a mixture of oils, such as canola oil, but it can also include high-fat foods like peanut butter.

**OF DRY BEANS.**

These can last up to seven years before becoming as hard as a rock.

**OF SALT.**

Half iodized and half plain salt.

**OF SUGAR.**

These can be a mixture of honey, sugar, molasses, sorghum, maple syrup, and various jams and jellies.

**A WIDE VARIETY OF GARDEN SEEDS.**

**OF DRY MILK.**

Ideally buy the nonfat variety.

CHAPTER 6

# SELF-DEFENSE

# LEGALITIES AND LOCALITIES

Just as when buying guns, it is best to buy ammunition with cash at a gun show so that you do not leave a paper trail. (First consult your local laws.)

## Self-defense Basics for Urbanites

To fend off intruders, you will need to be well armed. Preferably you should also be teamed up with at least a half dozen other armed and trained adult neighbors.

Look into local legalities on large-volume pepper-spray dispensers. These are marketed primarily as bear repellent, with brand names such as Guard Alaska, Bear Guard, and 17% Streetwise. If they are legal in your jurisdiction, then buy several of the big one-pound dispensers, first making sure that they are at least a 12 percent oleoresin capsicum (OC) formulation.

If you can get a firearms permit—which is a bit complicated in localities like New York City, and in various countries around the world, but not an insurmountable task—then I recommend that you get a Remington, Winchester, or Mossberg 12-gauge pump-action shotgun with a mounted SureFire flashlight. Note that #4 buckshot (not to be confused with the much smaller #4 birdshot) is the best load for defense in an urban environment where overpenetration (into neighboring apartments, for example) is an issue.

If getting a firearms permit proves too daunting, there are several nice exemptions in the laws of many large cities. For example, New York City exempts muzzleloaders and pre-1894 manufactured antique guns that are chambered for cartridges that are no longer commercially made. It is not difficult to find a Winchester Model 1876 or a Model 1886 rifle that is in a serial-number range that distinguishes it as pre-1894 production (see Savage99.com for exact dates of manufacture on twelve different rifle models). You will be limited to chamberings like .40-65 and .45-90. You can have a supply of ammunition

**500**

**MINIMUM NUMBER OF ROUNDS PER FIREARM.**

## STRAIGHTFORWARD ADVICE ON SELF-DEFENSE:

1. Arm yourself well, with the most capable weapons that you can afford and that are allowable under your local laws.

2. Get plenty of training, with the best instructors that you can afford. A firearm, bow, or an edged weapon is not a magical talisman that instantly transforms you into an armed, confident, and competent combatant. Without training, the tools will be nearly useless, and can lead to a false sense of security.

3. Buy plenty of extra ammunition, magazines, and cleaning equipment. I'd say that 500 rounds per firearm is the bare minimum. Some good round numbers to consider (these could vary, depending on your locale, your level of firearms training, and whether or not you plan to hunt):
   - 3,000 rounds per rimfire rifle or pistol;
   - 2,000 rounds per battle rifle;
   - 2,000 rounds per centerfire pistol;
   - 400 rounds per hunting rifle;
   - 750 rounds per shotgun (or *more*, if you don't yet own a battle rifle)

4. If you can afford to, buy extra guns and ammunition. These will be useful barter, if nothing else. And if you fall victim to burglars, these extra guns—kept very well hidden—may become vitally important.

custom loaded. A Winchester Model 1873 or an early Model 1892 chambered in .38-40 might also be an option, but I would recommend one of the more potent calibers available in the large-frame (Model 1876 or 1886) rifles. Regardless, be sure to select rifles with excellent bores and in nice mechanical condition.

For an antique handgun (legal to own without paperwork in most major cities, but check local laws around the world), I would recommend the S&W double-action top-break revolver chambered in .44 S&W Russian. None of the major manufacturers produce .44 S&W Russian ammunition. However, look for semi-custom extra-mild loads. These are so-called cowboy loads, made especially for the Cowboy Action Shooting enthusiasts. Mild loads in .44 S&W Russian are now available from Black Hills Ammunition. The S&W double-action top break revolvers are very fast to load, and you can even use modern speed loaders designed for .44 Special or .44 Magnum cartridges with the stumpy .44 S&W Russian loads, since it has the same cartridge "head" dimension and spacing.

### Those Who Would Disarm Us

Of course, all the training and preparation in the world will count for nothing if you are denied the ability to arm yourself properly. Unfortunately, around the world,

In the United States, guns manufactured before 1899 are exempt from federal background checks. They can be purchased across state lines without creating a paper trail. (First consult your local laws.)

governments of all stripes are making it harder for well-intentioned citizens to defend themselves. Self-defense is a key tenet of preparedness. To have the personal right to self-defense denied coalesces power in the hands of government. And by extension, this removes the veto power of the citizenry over any eventual ill intent by their government.

Amidst the rancorous debate over gun control in the United States, I am incredibly thankful for the Second Amendment, the Tenth Amendment, and the rest of the Bill of Rights. Unfortunately, such explicit reservations of fundamental rights are something conspicuously absent in the government of most other nations. God bless America!

However, as I'm writing this, civilian disarmament is back in the news. Even though the murder rate in the United States is declining—and at a 33-year low—the media's much-heralded "threat of gun violence" has politicians in a frenzied state, much like in 1968 and 1994. For anybody in the prepping community, it is important to pay attention to this. Such laws and decrees should be called out for what they really are: systematic civilian disarmament. In Western nations, most such legislation usually starts small but progresses quickly, leaping from simple registration to wholesale confiscation. First one category of weapons is banned, and then another. Gradually, these draconian laws can ramp up to the point where most citizens can't even possess air rifles and crossbows.

I would like to take a short period of time to examine this from an historical perspective, because we can learn much from systematic disarmaments that have gone before, and why they are so dangerous for those who choose to be prepared.

## Civilian Disarmament Around the World

Many people mistakenly believe that systematic civilian disarmament was an invention of the twentieth century. However, here in America, gun restrictions actually got a very early start. The first General Assembly of Virginia met in Jamestown in 1619. There,

**Self-defense is a key tenet of preparedness.**

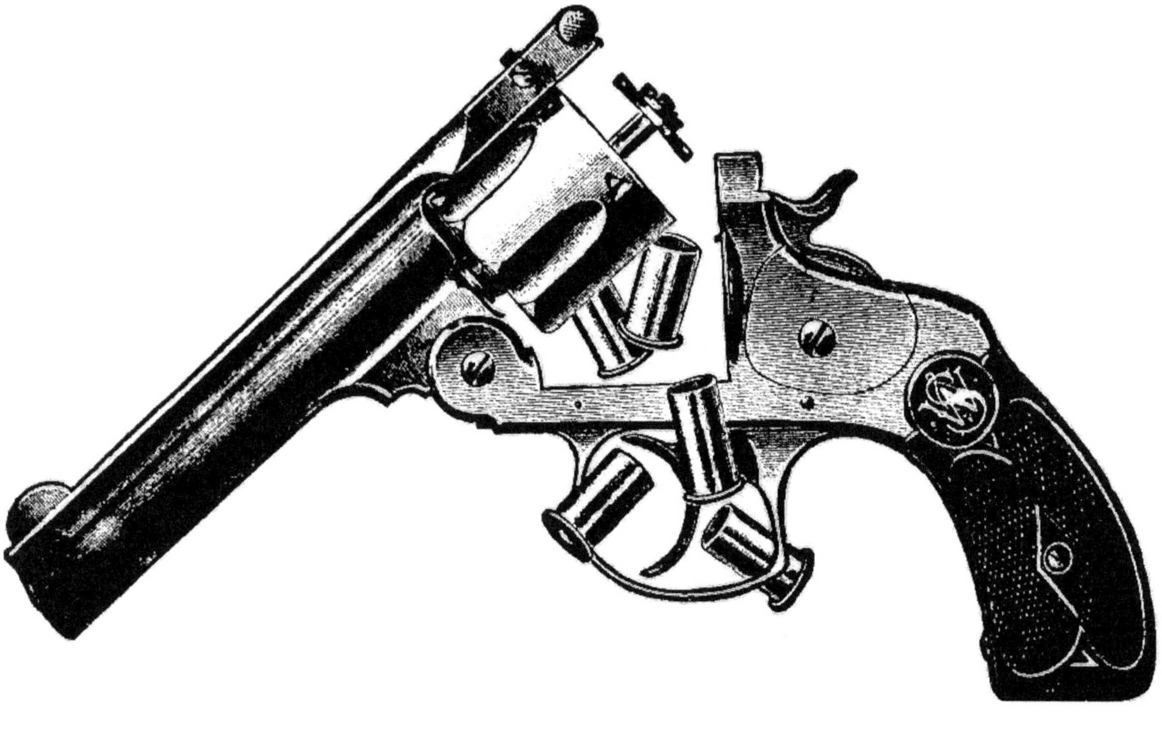

Pre-1899 antique top-break revolvers are affordable, federally exempt, and can be reloaded very quickly.

the settlers enacted more than thirty laws to govern the fledgling colony. One of these laws was a monopoly of force provision that included this wording:

> **"[...t]hat no man do sell or give any Indians any piece, shot, or powder, or any other arms offensive or defensive, upon pain of being held a traitor to the colony and of being hanged as soon as the fact is proved[...]"**

Yes, they introduced the death penalty for selling a firearm or gunpowder to a Native American!

While state laws began expanding in some areas from the 1860s onwards, there were no federal gun laws until 1934. Then, in the midst of the Great Depression, with Franklin Delano Roosevelt in the White House, the National Firearms Act of 1934 (NFA-34) was enacted. This law put a $200 tax on machine guns, silencers, short-barreled rifles, and short-barreled shotguns.

The machine-gun law was expanded in 1986, when an outright freeze on the production or importation of any new machine guns transferable to civilians was enacted. After the NFA-34 tax morphed into a quasi-ban, the prices of transferable machine guns rose astronomically. Just a two-ounce AR-15 registered drop-in auto sear now sells for as much as $34,000!

Elsewhere in the Americas has been a similar story. Cuba established systematic civilian disarmament soon after Fidel Castro took power on July 26, 1959. By restricting almost all gun ownership to the military, police, and a few loyal communist paramilitary cadres, any organized resistance to the Castro regime was virtually impossible. Guatemala disarmed its citizens in 1964, and from 1964 to 1981, roughly 100,000 disarmed Mayan Indians were rounded up and killed.

Mexico amended its constitution in 1917 in response to a revolution led by Pancho Villa. Since then, they have been successful in

**IN THE U.S. THERE WERE NO FEDERAL GUN LAWS UNTIL**

# 1934

A mass gun seizure in Australia in 1997.

The Armenian genocide was specifically targeted and ruthlessly systematic.

**1.5 MILLION**

**PEOPLE KILLED IN THE ARMENIAN GENOCIDE.**

stopping several revolutions. Gun laws were a key part of their strategy. But now, in the twenty-first century, there has been an unintended consequence: Mexico's drug cartels run rampant. They just ignore the country's gun registration, caliber restriction, and firearm-category restriction laws. The police are outnumbered. And because of civilian disarmament laws, the general citizenry is vastly outgunned by the drug gangs. They are at their mercy.

Over the centuries, disarmament has reached all corners of the globe. For example, during the sixteenth century in feudal Japan, civilians were free to carry swords either for defense or decoration. This ended during Oda Nobunaga's ascent to power. He was a Japanese lord who attempted to unify all of Japan under his rule, and to this end he ordered a sword hunt (*katanagari*) in the late sixteenth century.

Katanagaris occurred several times in Japanese history, when the new ruler would consolidate his position by calling for one. They were simply to ensure that no other person could rise up and take the leadership of the country for themselves by force. During these times, the state military would search homes all over the country—focusing especially on those people who were enemies of the new regime, of course—to confiscate all of the weapons that they could find.

In Europe, there have been various disarmament programs in place since at least the twelfth century, when the Holy Roman Emperor Frederick Barbarossa the First issued the Peace Ordinance of 1152. This law forbade peasants from carrying swords and lances. Only nobles were allowed to be armed in peacetime.

However, it wasn't until mass production of arms in the 1800s introduced the standard practice of stamping serial numbers that efforts truly became systemic. That opened up the opportunity for governments to register not just owners but particular guns to particular owners.

## The Twentieth Century: The Century of Genocide

What is now called commonsense gun control was adopted by many nations around the world in the twentieth century, with disastrous results for human life and liberty.

One such example was when the Ottoman Turkish government began systematic civilian disarmament in the 1890s. These laws were not equally enforced—Armenians were specifically singled out. The Armenian Genocide (1915–1922) saw some 1.5 million disarmed Armenians—mostly Christians—killed. They died at the hands of the Turkish army, police, and civil administrators.

Similarly, in 1918, just a year after the Russian Revolution, the Soviet Union also established systematic civilian disarmament. In December of that year, the Council of People's Commissars issued a decree on the surrender of weapons. While normal citizens were disarmed, members of the Communist Party were allowed to own a single weapon. Illegal gun possession was severely punished by up to five years in prison. In 1935, the same penalty was imposed for possession of knives.

From 1929 to 1953, around 20 million disarmed dissidents in the Soviet Union were systematically starved, exiled to Siberian gulags, or exterminated. Some of these pogroms were on a grand scale, such as the aforementioned *Holodomor*.

Nazi Germany also established systematic civilian disarmament in 1938. But as early as 1935, Jews were named in particular as prohibited from "acquiring, possessing and

German soldiers rounding up civilian women and children during World War II. Approximately 11 million disarmed people were systematically murdered.

carrying firearms and ammunition," as well as "truncheons or stabbing weapons." From 1939 to 1945, no fewer than 6 million Jews and more than 4 million others were segregated, rounded up, and systematically worked and/or starved to death or outright exterminated by gassing or gunfire.

During World War II, Nazi Germany invaded and occupied parts or all of eighteen countries. In the majority of those countries, the Nazis immediately seized gun-registration records held by local police. Using those records, they confiscated nearly all guns in private hands. This systematic civilian disarmament made occupying these nations much easier, and any organized resistance much more difficult.

Yugoslavia, too, began systematic civilian disarmament immediately after the end of World War II. In the Kosovo War that erupted with the inevitable breakup of Yugoslavia, there were widespread kidnappings, summary executions, and civilian massacres. Programs of "ethnic cleansing"—primarily through forced property dispossession and relocation—caused untold misery in the late 1990s. In the Kosovo War, it was primarily ethnic Albanians who were systematically killed. The worst of these were in the Dubrava Prison massacre, the Meja massacre, and the Orahovac massacre. These massacres underscored the sad truth: Disarmed people can be victimized en masse.

## The Endgame

As you can see, over the centuries governments have continually imposed more and more laws restricting the ownership of weapons. Many other cases—just as shocking—have occurred in Asia and Africa over the years, but the point has already been made. Sooner or later, centralized governments almost always gravitate toward a monopoly of force. As history has shown, even in nominally "democratic" countries, gun-prohibition laws have led to suffering and death on a monumental scale. It is up to us to resist if we want to ensure that we can defend ourselves in the event of any threat, whether this is societal breakdown, a dictatorial state, or a natural disaster.

# TIERED DEFENSE

I envision one possible future for America that is bleak. If the economy deteriorates and the power grids collapse, then it could trigger that dreaded "worst-case" situation. Such a socioeconomic collapse could precipitate a large population die-off in metropolitan regions—less in rural areas—and an extended period of lawlessness. There will be many refugees from cities, and some of them will turn to looting in order to survive. The new paradigm for American farmers and ranchers might resemble the security situation faced by farmers during the Rhodesian Bush War of the 1970s.

As such, it is worth closely examining how the various steps they took to defend themselves. I recommend taking the time to study recent low-level insurgencies in general, and the Rhodesian Bush War in particular. History doesn't repeat, but it often rhymes.

## The Rhodesian Bush War: A Case Study

Starting in the late 1960s, communist guerrillas had been slipping into the country to wreak havoc and terror on the civilian populace. While most of their victims were black people, the communist terrorists (or "terrs" as they were called in Rhodesian slang) began attacking isolated farms owned

No-tech security: Rhodesian Ridgeback dog and guinea fowl.

Rhodesian troops patrolling, armed with FN-FAL rifles, in 1975.

by the white Rhodesians. Early on in the war, they were literally able to catch the farmers sleeping. The steps these farmers took to defend themselves are as relevant today as they were half a century ago.

Since phone lines could be cut, a radio network was established called the Agric-Alert system. With it, there would be a chance to call for help if a farm came under attack.

Rhodesian farmers had to be constantly armed and vigilant. To carry only a pistol was considered foolhardy. Intrusion-detection systems in those days were rudimentary. They were limited to tripwire-activated systems and a few photocell-activated bells or buzzers. These days you can invest in more sophisticated infrared sensor systems.

There was substantial reliance on dogs to give a warning if strangers approached a farmhouse. The Rhodesian Ridgeback breed proved to be well-suited to this task. A few farmers also raised guinea fowl, specifically for their "watchdog" nature.

"Protective works" became the norm at Rhodesian farms. Grilles to stop hand grenades were fitted outside of house windows. Floodlights were set up that could be used to daze attackers. Elaborate perimeter fences topped with barbed wire became de rigueur. Often, these were constructed in depth, with two fences (or more) around a house, sometimes with tanglefoot wire in between. Traditional cowbells were sought after, for attaching to tripwires. At least one fence would be constructed of chain-link material, to pre-detonate rocket-propelled grenades.

Farmers resorted to constructing lethal electrified fences. Most of these were left on all night and were full-current 220 volts AC! They also set up remotely fired shotguns and command-detonated directional mines. These were essentially ersatz Claymore mines and they were positioned to cover the most likely crossing points for fences, and at other choke points that could be seen from a farmhouse. Assuming that terrs might climb up fence posts, some remotely fired shotguns were buried and fired upward, parallel to fence posts.

**1975 POPULATION OF WHITE RHODESIANS: 296,000.**
**1985 POPULATION OF WHITE RHODESIANS AFTER A DECADE OF ATTACKS: 100,000**

Infrared and light-amplification night-vision equipment was very scarce and expensive in the 1970s, so it was out of reach for all but a handful of Rhodesian farmers. And light-amplification gear (such as Starlight scopes) was—and still is—export restricted by Western nations, as "military armaments," under the ITAR treaties.

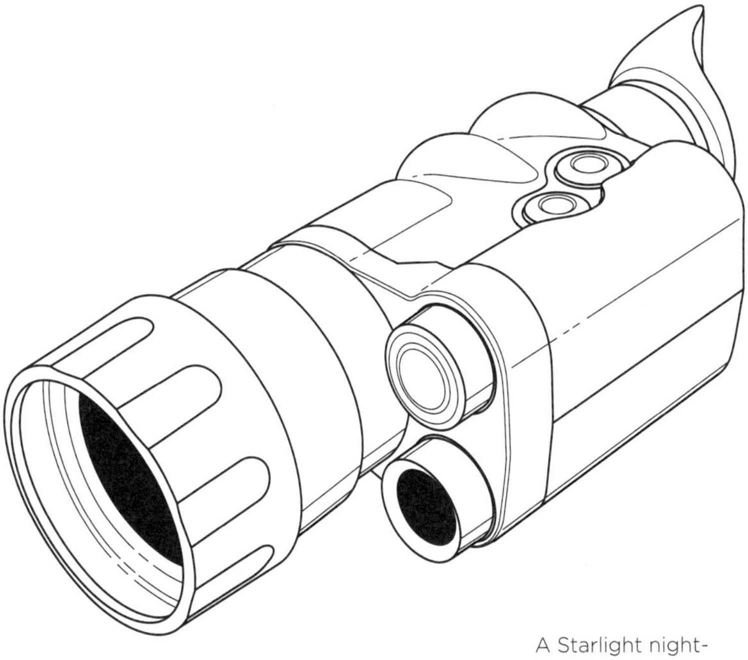

A Starlight night-vision scope.

## The Watchful Daily Grind

Life on Rhodesian farms was largely routine, but farmers did their best to not fall into predictable patterns or lapse into inattentiveness. Each morning, farmers carefully examined their dirt roads, looking for signs that landmines had been planted. They kept in close contact with their resident farmworkers, neighbors, and people living at nearby native *kraals* (villages) to check on reports of any suspicious activities or any sightings of roaming terrorists. By the standards of Rhodesian farmers, anyone living within five miles was a "neighbor."

All through the daily tasks of tending crops and caring for livestock, every adult and the older children went everywhere armed. Many farm tractors were fitted with gun racks, to keep a rifle close at hand, at all times. A surprising number of the guns owned by the farmers were fully automatic. The selective-fire Belgian FN-FAL battle rifle was widely used, and almost reverently cherished. Some HKG3 rifles (by way of Mozambique) were used in smaller numbers. Many folks, especially women, carried Uzi submachine guns, or the Commando LDP (in later years the Sanna 77 variant) submachine guns. The latter were locally produced in Rhodesia and South Africa. Some farmers were also able to legally acquire hand grenades and rifle grenades.

At dusk, unless under the urgency of harvest season, farms "buttoned up" for the night by SOP, and no one ventured outside of the farmhouse's perimeter fence unless there were exceptional circumstances. Dairy farmers felt particularly apprehensive, since at least one of their twice-daily milking sessions would be during hours of darkness, at least in winter months. Therefore, some security precautions were also set up outside of the outer doors of milking parlors.

A young Rhodesian farmer armed with an FN-FAL rifle inspects his barbed-wire fence. He is accompanied by his Rhodesian Ridgeback dog.

# RHODESIAN BUSH WAR STATISTICS

**WAR COSTS:**

**FROM 1972 ONWARD, ROUGHLY $1 MILLION PER DAY.**

**INSURGENTS:**

**Zimbabwe African National Liberation Army (ZANLA)** was the military wing of the Maoist Zimbabwe African National Union (ZANU). It was led by Robert Mugabe and operated from Mozambique. It had 13,500 personnel in 1979. ZANLA also operated training camps in Ethiopia, Libya, Mozambique, and Tanzania.

**Zimbabwe People's Revolutionary Army (ZIPRA)** was the armed wing of the Marxist-Leninist Zimbabwe African People's Union (ZAPU). It was led by Joshua Nkomo and operated from Zambia. It had 20,000 personnel in 1979.

**RHODESIAN SECURITY FORCES (AS OF 1979):**

**ACTIVE:**

**10,800**

**RESERVE:**

**40,000**

**BRITISH SOUTH AFRICAN POLICE:**

**11,000**

regulars (about 60% black) and 34,000 reservists

By 1978, all white males up to the age of 60 were subject to periodic call-up into the army. Those up to age 35 often spent alternating periods of six weeks in the army and at home. Many overseas volunteers came from Britain, South Africa, Canada, Australia, New Zealand, Portugal, and the United States. Black Africans made up 67 percent of the Rhodesian Army.

**CASUALTIES:**

By late 1968, the combat death ratio was 12 security force members for every 160 insurgents killed. By the end of the war, the Rhodesian Army had killed more than 10,000 terrorists inside Rhodesia and 2,000 more in external raids on terrorist camps. It lost only 1,361 service members between December 1972 and December 1979.

About 19,000 black African civilians died in the war, mostly at the hands of the terrorists.

The psychological turning point in the war came with the downing of civilian Air Rhodesia Flight 825 in February 1979. The plane was shot down with a portable Strela-2 (SAM-7b) surface-to-air missile. Of the 52 passengers and 4 crew, 38 died in the crash. The terrorists then approached the wreckage, rounded up the 10 survivors that they could see, and massacred them with gunfire.

**19,000**

**BLACK AFRICAN CIVILIANS DIED IN THE WAR**

# THE DRAW TECHNIQUE

The basic handgun draw has five steps. In this section I will talk through this simple technique, and how to practice it.

I did not gain confidence in my draw until I practiced for an hour or so each evening. It has often been said: "Slow is smooth, and smooth is fast." I practiced this by calling out each step, in turn. I didn't speed up until I felt confident in each phase of the draw.

There are a couple of important points to remember when working on your draw. One is the "Laser Rule." Pretend that the muzzle of your gun is shooting out a high-powered laser. Nobody wants to be sliced with one of these so, naturally, you don't want it pointed at you. Therefore, keep all appendages away from said laser beam at all times. With that in mind, during steps one through four, the support hand should be flat against the body. Keeping the support hand against the stomach will help keep extra appendages away from the muzzle of the gun. Practice and follow through on this step and, during the heat of battle, you will not succumb to any self-inflicted injuries.

When your hands merge, take a moment to examine how you grip the gun. The thumbs should be resting next to each other along the slide rail and not overlapping. This takes stress off the hands and presents a calmer sight picture. The support hand should be wrapped around the strong hand and doing what it is intended to do: support. If you know of anyone who "tea cups" their grip (with the support hand under the gun), after explaining that what they see in the movies is bunk, correct their grip so that they improve their shooting. Be sure to correct anyone else you see who uses the support hand to brace their strong side wrist. This is not an effective technique. Chances are, you will also run across one or two people who think that "lobster clawing" with their support hand is good.

**Pay attention to the details, for they may save your life.**

A CZ-75 series 9mm semi-auto handgun with magazine and 9mm Parabellum cartridges.

## BASIC HANDGUN DRAW HAS FIVE SIMPLE STEPS

### 1. MASTER GRIP

Stand with hands at your side. Master grip is achieved by placing the web of your strong hand firmly against the butt of the pistol grip. This should be as high up as possible to attain the maximum effective grip. Wrap your fingers around the grip, remembering to place the trigger finger in register. This should be extended straight out, outside of the trigger guard.

### 2. LIFT AND CLEAR

After master grip, lift the gun straight up and out of the holster. Don't try and bring it away from the body or move it towards the target just yet. The muzzle should still be down at this point and just clear of the holster. Remember to keep your elbow and arm close to your side. I had chicken wing syndrome when I first did this.

### 3. ROCK N' LOCK

Like the old gunslinger of the West, rotate the gun ninety degrees and point it at the target. Don't forget to think about weapon retention! Like the chicken wing elbow, the gun should stay close to your body in case of a close-quarters battle situation.

### 4. HANDS MERGE

The strong hand should be moving close against the body to the "anchor position" to join the weak hand. Remember how you open a jar of pickles? Keep the gun close against the body to allow for the strongest retention. If you let that gun get away from your body, someone is very likely going to be able to take control of it. Don't let that happen!

### 5. EXTENSION

You should have the weapon in both hands now. Press through the target with your gun and bring your sights onto the target. Don't tomahawk chop, overhand sight, throw the gun out there, or sweep from the floor to the ceiling... Just press the gun smoothly toward the target and align the sights. One smooth and fluid motion will help prevent any pitched shots.

Getting a good grip on a handgun is important for accuracy. Shooting skills are perishable, so they require regular practice.

Lobster clawing is when someone stretches the support hand all around the gun with the thumb firmly planted behind the slide. You will know of those who've learned their lesson by the sizable chunk of flesh missing from their support-hand thumb.

Reholstering your weapon is the exact opposite of the draw. This is pretty simple. Just go through the five steps in reverse. When the muzzle is ready to be placed in the holster, move your thumb up to press against the back of the slide. Keep the thumb against the back of the slide to prevent the gun from coming out of battery. If you are forced to draw again, in the heat of the moment, you may find yourself inventing new expletives when the bang button only clicks.

Pay attention to the details, for they may save your life.

A holstered semi-auto handgun for concealed carry. Pistols that are too bulky tend to get left at home. Remember the first rule of gunfighting: Have a gun with you!

# SURVIVAL GUN SELECTION

There is no single perfect survival gun. Different situations are best handled by using different firearms. There are several requirements that must be considered in selecting guns for use on a farm, ranch, or survival retreat. First and foremost, they must be versatile. A single gun might be pressed into service for shooting crows or starlings at ten yards, rabbits or coyotes at one hundred yards, or rattlesnakes at five feet. While there is no single gun that can handle any task, it is important to select guns with at least some degree of versatility. Further, it is not realistic to believe that you can get by with just one gun, or even just one rifle, one pistol, and one shotgun. Versatility has its limits. Like a carpenter's box of tools, each type of gun has its special place and purpose.

The second major consideration for survival guns is that they must be robust and reliable enough to put up with constant carry and regular use. Good designs not prone to mechanical failures are a plus. When an infrequent repair must be made, a small stock of spare parts that do not require special gunsmithing to install must suffice. When the nearest gunsmith is a two-hour drive away, you have to depend on your own resources.

Since they are carried quite frequently and in all sorts of weather, survival guns need to have durable finishes. Stainless steel is by far the best choice for most situations. Unfortunately, however, not all guns are available in stainless steel. For guns that are only made with a blued finish, there are several alternative finishes available. These include Parkerizing (the military standard gray or black phosphate finish commonly seen on M16 and AR-15 rifles) and various other factory finishes with trade names such as Coltalloy or Armour Alloy. In addition to gun-factory finishes, a wide range of exotic materials such as Teflon and Zylan are now frequently used as after-market gun finishes.

Because trips to town to procure ammunition might be infrequent (or impossible in a severe survival scenario), and reloading will likely be the norm for

**10 GUNS** CHAMBERED IN TEN DIFFERENT CARTRIDGES COMPLICATES LOGISTICS.

SQUIRREL

RABBIT

CROW

RATTLESNAKE

FOX

COYOTE

those seeking self-sufficiency, it is desirable to limit the number of different cartridges that you stock. Having ten different guns chambered in ten different cartridges would only serve to complicate logistics. Further, it is best to select only guns chambered for commonly available cartridges. Small country stores stock ammo like .22 Long Rifle, .308 Winchester, .30-'06, or 12-gauge, but probably not .264 Winchester magnum, .300 Weatherby, or 28-gauge.

## Small Game

There are several categories of firearms that belong in the gun racks of nearly every farm or ranch. The first, and most frequently used, variety are small game/pest shooting guns. These guns are used to hunt small game for the pot (squirrels, rabbits, etc.), to shoot garden pests (crows, starlings, gophers, etc.), and marauding predators (coyotes, foxes, weasels, ferrets, etc.). They also end up being the guns most frequently used to slaughter livestock. Good cartridges for small game/pest shooting include .22 Long Rifle (.22 LR), and .223 Remington. The most common shotshells for this use are .410, 20-gauge, and 12-gauge. The .22 LR will suffice for everything up to the size of rabbits at conservative distances. It is inexpensive to shoot, quiet, and has hardly any felt recoil. The .223 Remington is a good cartridge for shooting perched birds that would be out of range for a .22 rimfire, or for shooting feral dogs, feral cats, or coyotes. Experience has shown that both handguns and long guns are needed for small game/pest shooting. A long gun would, of course, be the ideal choice in most circumstances, due to their inherently higher velocity and longer sighting radius (and hence greater accuracy). However, when mending fences, feeding livestock, hauling wood, riding a tractor, or doing most gardening work, it is usually not practical to carry a long gun. This is where handguns come in.

## Rimfire Handguns

A good quality .22 rimfire pistol may be one of the most useful handguns in your battery. They are used for dispatching those "uncatchable" chickens for the stew pot, for shooting small game/pests, and for inexpensively maintaining marksmanship skills for those more powerful (and more expensive to shoot) handguns. A stainless-steel Ruger Mark II or Smith and Wesson Model 622 are both good options, and available in various barrel lengths. If you prefer a revolver, the stainless-steel Smith and Wesson Model 617 is a good option. It is available in a 4-inch, 6-inch, or 8⅜-inch barrel length. Rifles chambered in .22 LR are often used on farms and ranches.

They are useful for pest shooting, small game hunting, and target practice. Reliable, American-made semi-auto .22s include the Ruger Model 10/.22 (also available in stainless), the Marlin 70-P "Papoose," the Remington Speedmaster Model 552, and the discontinued Remington Nylon 66. If a bolt-action is your preference, either the Kimber Model 82 or the Ruger 77/.22 are good choices. Two good-quality lever action .22s are the Marlin 39TDS and the Winchester 9422. Regardless of which brand of .22 rifle you buy, you should consider mounting it with a telescopic sight. Because of its low energy, proper placement of a .22 rimfire bullet can mean the difference between crippling and cleanly killing small game. Mounting a scope will, in most instances, give you the ability to not just hit an animal's center of mass but rather hit a precise aiming point, such as its head or neck. If you do decide to mount a scope, use a full size (1-inch-diameter) scope, rather than one of the inexpensive ¾-inch-diameter scopes made specifically for air rifles and .22s. Inexpensive scopes generally have a poor field of view, considerable parallax distortion, and are not as ruggedly made as the full-size rifle scopes. For training youngsters, I recommend the diminutive Chipmunk .22 LR single-shot bolt-action, with a 16-inch barrel.

Rifles chambered in .22 LR or .22 Magnum are the top choices for small-game hunting and rural garden pest control.

Multi-caliber handguns—such as the Thompson/Center (T/C) Contender single-shot—offer great versatility. The author's favorite is a stainless-steel T/C Encore.

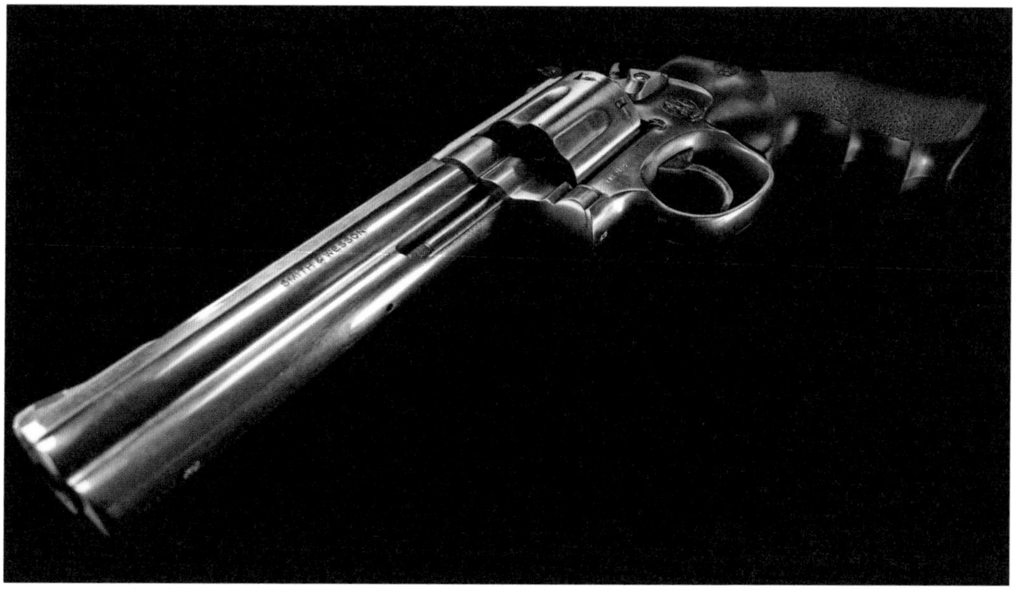

A Smith and Wesson Model 686 .357 magnum revolver. A .357 magnum can also shoot shorter .38 Special cartridges as well as specialized CCI brand .38 birdshot cartridges.

## Centerfire Handguns

If you are seeking a particularly versatile handgun, you might consider the Thompson/Center T/C Contender. This single-shot pistol uses readily changeable barrels in a wide range of chamberings. The Contender is available in both blued and stainless steel. Some of the most useful of the 20-plus chamberings are .22 LR, .223 Remington, and the .45 Colt/.410 shotgun barrel.

The handgun in my battery that I traditionally carried the most was my Smith and Wesson Model 686 .357 magnum revolver. It was black Teflon coated (a short-lived S&W factory variant dubbed "Midnight Black"), with 6-inch barrels and equipped with Pachmayr Signature grips, and red ramp/white outline adjustable sights. The 6-inch barrel length is a compromise between ease of carry and accuracy/velocity. While an $8\frac{3}{8}$-inch barrel would provide better accuracy and velocity, without using a shoulder holster, a gun with this barrel length is not comfortable to carry. This revolver accounted for numerous snakes, rabbits, and even a couple of coyotes thanks to its versatility. These guns also pack a punch, so they allayed any fear of dangerous predators, whether of the two-legged or four-legged variety. In addition to the Smith and Wesson, good-quality stainless-steel double-action

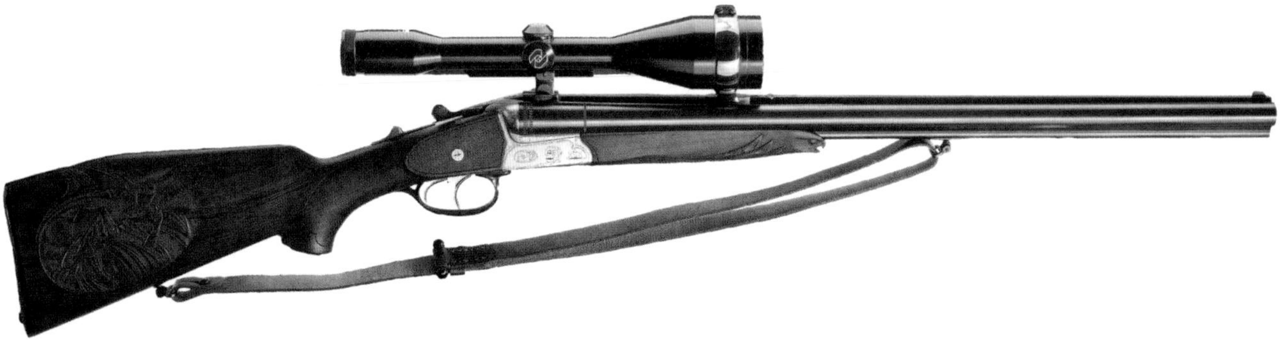

A Krieghoff drilling combination gun with Zeiss scope.

.357 revolvers are made by Colt (the King Cobra and Python) and Ruger (the GP-100).

However, for homesteaders living in brown bear or grizzly bear country, or any other similarly large predator, a more powerful handgun is recommended. A stainless-steel Smith and Wesson Model 629 (6-inch) .44 magnum, or Ruger Redhawk (5½-inch) .44 magnum, or perhaps the Colt Anaconda (6-inch) .44 magnum would be good choices. If you would rather carry an automatic, the LAR Grizzly (.45 Automatic magnum), Wildey (.45 Automatic magnum), Desert Eagle (.44 magnum), or the long discontinued Auto Mag (.44 Auto Mag) would also serve the same purpose, although all of these guns are relatively expensive and heavy to carry.

## Rifles

A lightweight rifle chambered in .223 Remington is particularly useful for shooting both perched birds and predators. Remington, Ruger, and Sako all make good-quality .223 bolt-actions, and selecting one is largely a matter of personal preference. We use our .223s on coyotes, which currently abound in great numbers in the western United States, and are a constant source of trouble in our area. We use three different guns on the uncommon occasions when we have a chance to snipe at coyotes. These guns include a Remington Model 7 bolt-action chambered in .223 Remington, a Colt CAR-15 "M4gery," and a scoped L1A1 semi-auto chambered in .308 Winchester). A .308 bolt-action is used when we spot a coyote at beyond 300 yards. With the Remington Model 7 available, the CAR-15 is largely superfluous. However, it is easy to handle and can get off a quick second shot when shooting at running rabbits or coyotes.

## Combination Guns

The next category of guns is combination or "garden guns." These range from expensive imported rifles and shotguns to inexpensive combination guns made domestically. The European three-barrel combination guns, or "drillings," can easily cost $2,000 or more. Guns typical of this breed are the Colt/Sauer drillings, Krieghoff drillings, and the Valmet over/unders. They typically feature a high-power rifle barrel mounted beneath side-by-side 12-gauge shotgun barrels. Domestically produced two-barrel combination guns, while not as aesthetically pleasing, cost far less than European drillings. These guns offer the ability to fire a single shotgun shell or rifle cartridge with the flick of a switch, and they are by far the best to have at hand when out doing garden work. They provide the versatility to eliminate either a pesky gopher or marauding birds, whether they are perching or in flight. One of the best of the inexpensive combination guns is the Savage Model 24F with a Rynite fiberglass stock.

## Long-range Rifles

Big-game hunting or counter-sniping rifles are the next group of guns to be considered. The selection of a big-game rifle depends on the variety of game to be hunted. In most places, a bolt-action rifle chambered in .308 Winchester or .30-'06 will handle most big game, but regional differences will determine exactly what you need. For example, in the plains and desert states of the United States, you might need a scoped rifle chambered in a flat-shooting cartridge, such as .270 Winchester or .25-'06.

No matter which chambering you select, it is important that you buy a well-made rifle with a robust action. Remington, Ruger, and Winchester, among others, all make guns with these qualities. After you buy the rifle itself, you will probably want to have a more durable finish applied to its metal surfaces. You might also want to mount a telescopic sight, especially if you will be hunting in open country. If you hunt in brushy or densely wooded terrain, you could find a scope is more of a hindrance than a help. It is important to note that scopes are more prone to failure than any other part of a rifle. Therefore, it is wise to select a rifle with good-quality iron sights, whether or not you intend to mount a scope. If and when a scope should fail, you will have the recourse of removing the scope and reverting to iron sights.

In North America, the need for a cartridge more powerful than .30-'06 is normally a consideration only in Alaska or parts of Canada where moose and grizzly bear are found. Several powerful cartridges are currently popular, and these include the .35 Whelen, the .338 Winchester, and the .375 H&H Magnum.

**A CARTRIDGE MORE POWERFUL THAN**

**.30-'06**

**IS NORMALLY A CONSIDERATION ONLY IN ALASKA.**

## Shotguns

Upland game and waterfowl shotguns are important to consider as well. If you will have the opportunity to hunt upland game or waterfowl on your property or somewhere

Though antiquated, a 12-gauge double-barreled shotgun is still quite useful for hunting. They can even be pressed into service for self-defense. Shown is a model with exposed hammers.

The ubiquitous Remington Model 870 12-gauge pump-action shotgun, designed in 1950, has had more than 12 million units produced in its lifetime. They are made in a variety of hunting, police, and military configurations. Shown is an M870 riotgun with an extension magazine.

nearby, you will also want to include one or more good bird-hunting shotguns in your battery. As you will likely be carrying your shotgun more often than the average city dweller, a durable finish is desirable. Remington's "Special Purpose" versions of their Model 870, Model 11-87, and Model 1100 fit this bill nicely. They come from the factory with a non-glare stock finish and a dull gray Parkerized finish on all of their surfaces. Several makers produce (or produced) Parkerized-finish pumps and autos comparable to the Remington Special Purpose series. One such is the Winchester Model 1300 Waterfowler.

Like most other currently produced domestic shotguns, the Remington Special Purpose guns come with screw-in choke tubes as standard equipment. A 26-inch barrel length is best suited to upland game hunting, while a 28-inch or 30-inch barrel is normally recommended for pass shooting at ducks and geese. Because odd gauge shells might be difficult to obtain in rural areas—or regardless of where you live in times of turmoil—it is best to buy either a 12- or 20-gauge shotgun. Also, given the trend towards steel shot, a 3-inch-length chamber is recommended. The longer chamber allows the use of magnum loads, which are needed to give the less dense steel shot the same killing power as traditional lead shot loadings. In addition, screw-in choke tubes are advisable. As steel shot wears out chokes quickly, replaceable choke tubes can greatly increase the usable life of a gun.

**Our Snake Charmer gets taken along on walks where heavier, bulkier long guns would usually be left behind.**

One gun that deserves special mention is the .410 gauge "Snake Charmer II" single-shot shotgun, made by Sport Arms, Mfg. This lightweight gun just barely meets the federal size minimums (18-inch barrel and 28½ inch overall length). It is constructed of stainless steel and has a synthetic stock with a compartment that holds spare shotshells. Because it is compact and lightweight, our Snake Charmer gets taken along on walks where heavier, bulkier long guns would usually be left behind. This gun has been used to kill several rattlesnakes and a good number of quail.

## Retreat Defense

Self-defense guns are the final category to be considered for farms, ranches, and survival retreats. Just as homesteaders in the nineteenth century had to depend on themselves for the protection of their lives and property, many modern homesteaders will find that they must do likewise if society ever collapses. Indeed, post-TEOTWAWKI, we all may be on our own, with no law enforcement to call on. Even in the present day, rural farms and ranches are often a long drive from the nearest sheriff's office, so it makes sense to be prepared. If you expect bad economic times or other sources of

**393 MILLION**

**FIREARMS ARE IN THE HANDS OF U.S. CIVILIANS. THAT IS 46% OF THE WORLDWIDE TOTAL.**

social unrest, you should make a concerted effort to stock up on defensive guns, plenty of ammunition, lots of spare magazines, and a good selection of spare parts, to the extent that your local laws allow you to.

Encounters with poachers, escaped convicts, or other assorted riff-raff might not necessarily take place in the immediate vicinity of your home or vehicle, where you would presumably have access to a telephone or CB radio. If you are walking a fence line at the far end of an 80-acre parcel and run into trouble, the only law enforcement assistance available might be the handgun on your hip. Be prepared. At our farm, we have a variety of guns whose main job is defense, but that are also used for other purposes. For example, our large-frame handguns are primarily self-defense guns, but also usable for hunting and shooting pests.

If you like the ballistics of a .45 ACP but prefer the action of a revolver, you might consider purchasing a Smith and Wesson Model 625 revolver. This is a stainless-steel revolver built on the "N" frame—the same heavy frame used for Smith and Wesson .44 magnums. The Model 625 uses "full moon" spring steel clips to hold six rounds of .45 ACP. Unlike most speed loaders, with the full moon clips, there is no knob to twist or any mechanism that could potentially fail. You just drop the whole works into the cylinder. This makes them just as fast, if not faster, than any speed loader. The Model 625 is offered in 3-inch, 4-inch, and 5-inch barrel lengths—the latter one of which is just about ideal. Because the .45 ACP has the same bore diameter as the .45 Colt cartridge, a spare cylinder and crane assembly can be fabricated for this more potent cartridge. This combination would make a particularly versatile handgun.

Shotguns are also well suited to defensive work. A spare short "riotgun" barrel for a pump or automatic shotgun can make it double as a formidable home defense weapon. For our Remington 870 12-gauge, for example, we have a 20-inch length barrel that is equipped with rifle (slug) sights, and the choke tube that we keep in it is cylinder bore (no choke). It is ideal for shooting rifled slugs or buckshot. With the short barrel and a Choate eight-round extension magazine, the Remington 870 is a particularly handy gun to use at night for shooting feral dogs and cats or other animals that are attracted to our barn full of rabbits and chickens, while also being a reassuring gun to have around for home defense. The short riotgun barrel stays on our Remington most of each year, while the long "bird" barrels are normally mounted only during the quail and pheasant seasons.

The Smith and Wesson Model 625 revolver, chambered in .45 ACP. Using full-moon clips, it is very quick to reload, and can also shoot Remington .45 ACP birdshot cartridges.

# DEFENDING A HOUSE ON ACREAGE

A tiered defense for a home on acreage can be completed without too much expense. And if done right, it will not be immediately apparent to passers-by.

You should start by installing a gate at the end of your lane or access road. A heavy-duty steel gate is the best choice. Keep in mind that "stout" doesn't have to look crude. Adding some filigree or a regional motif can make a sturdy steel gate appear more decorative than defensive. All perimeter gates should be secured by a heavy-duty chain or locking bar mechanism, and a stout, pick-resistant padlock. The best chain to use is the ultra-hardened variety marketed to motorcyclists. These chains often have rubber-coated links. They *can* be laboriously cut with an abrasive cutoff wheel, but they are just about invulnerable to someone using a hacksaw or a pair of bolt cutters.

**A tiered defense for a home on acreage can be completed without too much expense.**

The best locks to use are ones with warded hasps. Often called "disc" or "hockey-puck" locks, these modern designs have limited access keyways, pick-resistant cylinders, and shanks with little or no room for attack with bolt cutters. Most knowledgeable thieves simply give up at the sight of them and direct their attentions elsewhere.

Don't neglect upgrading the *opposite side* of your gate. Imagine installing an expensive lock and chain, but then some miscreant walking up and simply lifting your gate off of its hinge pins. The simplest solution is to reverse the orientation of one of the hinge pins. If one of the hinge pins points upward, and the others point downward, then that will prevent a

A high-security "hockey puck" padlock. These stout locks are difficult to attack with bolt cutters.

## THORNY PRIVACY BUSHES

PYRACANTHA

HAWTHORN

BLACKTHORN

RED BARBERRY

HOLLY

CACTI

simple "lifting" attack. As added insurance, you should also spot-weld the attaching hardware, so that it cannot be defeated by disassembly with a wrench.

You also need to evaluate your shrubbery. Thorny bushes and hedges are best. They can even be set in successive rows if you have enough acreage. But keep in mind that "privacy" bushes will also provide concealment for anyone who is reconnoitering or attacking your home.

The particular arrangement of interior fences, walls, and hedgerows can have advantages. For example, by placing hedgerow plantings at angles, you can *funnel* approaching attackers into places where they can be clearly seen—and in extreme circumstances then engaged with rifle or shotgun fire.

I often get e-mails from readers of my blog asking about installing spikes atop walls. This is a controversial subject. In some jurisdictions, this could mean a civil lawsuit or criminal charges. But in other locales, it is considered customary. For example, in most of Latin America, the norm is to build stout masonry walls, with shards of broken glass on top embedded in the concrete. In South Africa, the contemporary residential standard is to install multiple strands of electrified fence wire with a potentially lethal voltage and current. The only legal requirement is to prominently post warning signs. Obviously, such a fence would be illegal in most Western countries.

Suggested defensive hedges.

Be sure to check state and local laws before installing electric fences. Liability law varies by jurisdiction.

A concrete garden base beneath a range of flowering *Ixora*. A "decorative" barricade such as this will stop nearly all wheeled vehicles.

## A series of vehicular barricades will be important for slowing down the advance of attackers.

**A MODERN BOLLARD CAN STOP A 65,000-POUND TRUCK TRAVELING AT 50 MPH. NON-RETRACTABLE BOLLARDS HAVE COMPARABLE CAPABILITY.**

I'd also like to address vehicular barricades. One significant but seldom-mentioned threat is having home invaders use a vehicle to batter down a house door. But if you build a 20-inch-tall "decorative" masonry planter that is positioned properly, you can virtually eliminate the risk of someone using a vehicle as a battering ram.

On large properties, having a series of vehicular barricades will be important for slowing down the advance of attackers. Simply installing a series of gates or cables across your access lane or road should suffice. The advantage of having movable barriers, of course, is that they can be left open in normal times, but then locked shut if times ever get perilous.

If you live in open country—i.e., a house surrounded by fields—then you will have both advantages and disadvantages. The key advantage is that it will afford you what military planners refer to as "open fields of fire." But a disadvantage will be that attackers can simply bypass your sturdy gate(s) by cutting a wire fence, and driving onto your property and then across your fields. This threat can be reduced by building hedgerows, low walls, terraced earthworks, or perhaps more sturdy fences.

However, keep in mind that obstacles work both ways. The same wall that affords you concealment and some ballistic or antivehicular protection will also provide the same for your opponents. Without supporting "friendlies" in the distance, or indirect fire, or some way to maneuver, then your defensive works also will serve as siege works for those who mean you harm.

# HOUSE HARDENING

The second tier of your defense should be hardening your house itself. In preparing your house for inimical times, I suggest that you use the same mindset as the Rhodesian farmers. Ask yourself: what should I do to make my property's perimeter as strong as possible against a large number of determined and well-armed attackers? How should it be arranged for when there may not be any help coming, perhaps even if we are isolated for days? By preparing for the absolute worst case, then you should be able to fend off lesser threats with relative ease.

It may seem counterintuitive, but it will be in countries where firearms are restricted that you will need to do the most barricading of doors and barring of windows. This is because you will need to rely more upon the local gendarmes to respond. In places like the United States, it usually takes the mere sight of a gun in a homeowner's hands or the sound of just one gunshot to send home invaders running. However, in gun-deprived nations, the bad guys will be more determined to break in, and think less of the threat on the other side of the door to them. And, given the chronically long lag time between a call to police and their arrival, formidable barriers on your home are a must.

Upgrading your house with steel security doors is an obvious first step. Adding "decorative" wrought-iron grills to your windows is an important next step to keep burglars and home invaders out. But to be ready for TEOTWAWKI, you will also need to lay in a supply of dozens of sandbags. These can be filled with sand or gravel, and should be on your list of items to stockpile.

Window bars can range from utilitarian to more decorative, depending on cost.

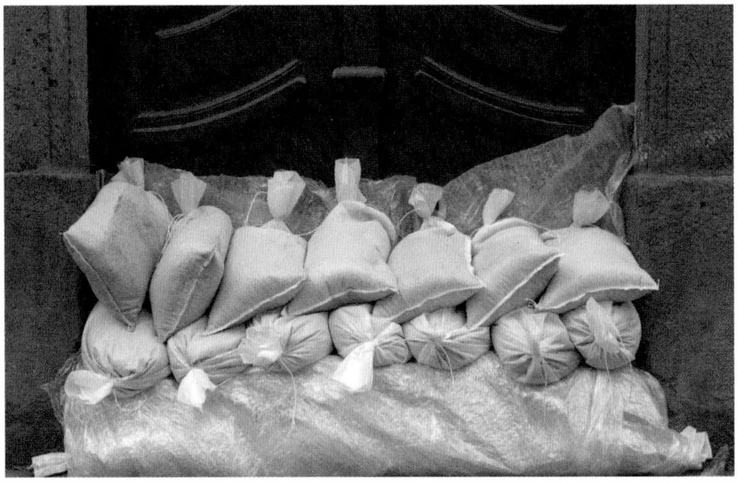

Keeping sandbags on hand will serve you for both ballistic protection *and* for floods.

Once the world goes sideways, you'll need to fill those sandbags and stack them right up to the level of your windowsills, inside of your house. Don't stack them outside, or they will be obvious and attackers will simply aim above them or shoot from odd angles to avoid hitting them. Unless you have a house built on a concrete slab, then you should, of course, check to see if your floors can handle the extra weight.

I generally recommend replacing traditional wooden exterior doors with windowless, hollow steel doors that are hung with at least four heavy-duty hinges. For further protection, most hollow steel doors can be filled with pea gravel, to give them protection against small arms. All exterior doors should also be secured by one—and preferably two—quickly removable interior heavy-duty steel bars.

All exterior doors and even a few interior doors should be equipped with wide-angle view peepholes, but I discourage installing anything larger. The general rule should be: no aperture large enough to allow an intruder to reach a hand through. If you presently have a house with any exterior door that has a window, then you should probably replace it with a steel door. Or, at least upgrade that door with a very sturdy grate or closely spaced steel bars.

## Your Last Bastion

The final tier of your defense should be a hardened vault room or panic room. Ideally, this room will be both beefed up and concealed. For one of my consulting clients, I specified, sourced, and oversaw the construction of a masonry basement gun vault/fallout shelter with an *inward*-opening vault door. Just outside of that vault door was a lightweight paneled wall with a concealed door in the paneling; that was a large hinged wall mirror secured by magnetic catches. To me, this represented the best possible protection: a very secure vault room, with the added advantage of concealment. To attack this room, any home invader would have to first *find* the room. And if they were in a hurry, I'd anticipate that they might entirely overlook it.

Your "last bastion" room should be equipped with independent (battery-powered) emergency lighting, a water tap, a fire extinguisher, and both a spare cell phone and a hard wired (landline) telephone. If you were to take shelter in a panic room in the event of a home invasion, and the invaders persisted in breaking in, then you would certainly be justified in the use of lethal force. I could not imagine any judge or jury—even in a courtroom in a country like the UK, which doesn't have such self-defense laws—ever convicting someone who took the life of an intruder in such a situation.

**$5,847**

**THE AVERAGE COST OF AN ABOVEGROUND SAFE ROOM ACCORDING TO HOME ADVISOR.**

**A PROPER DEFENSIVE DOOR:** A sturdy all-steel door, preferably gravel-filled, with at least four sturdy hinges, a security peephole, and sturdy removable locking bar(s).

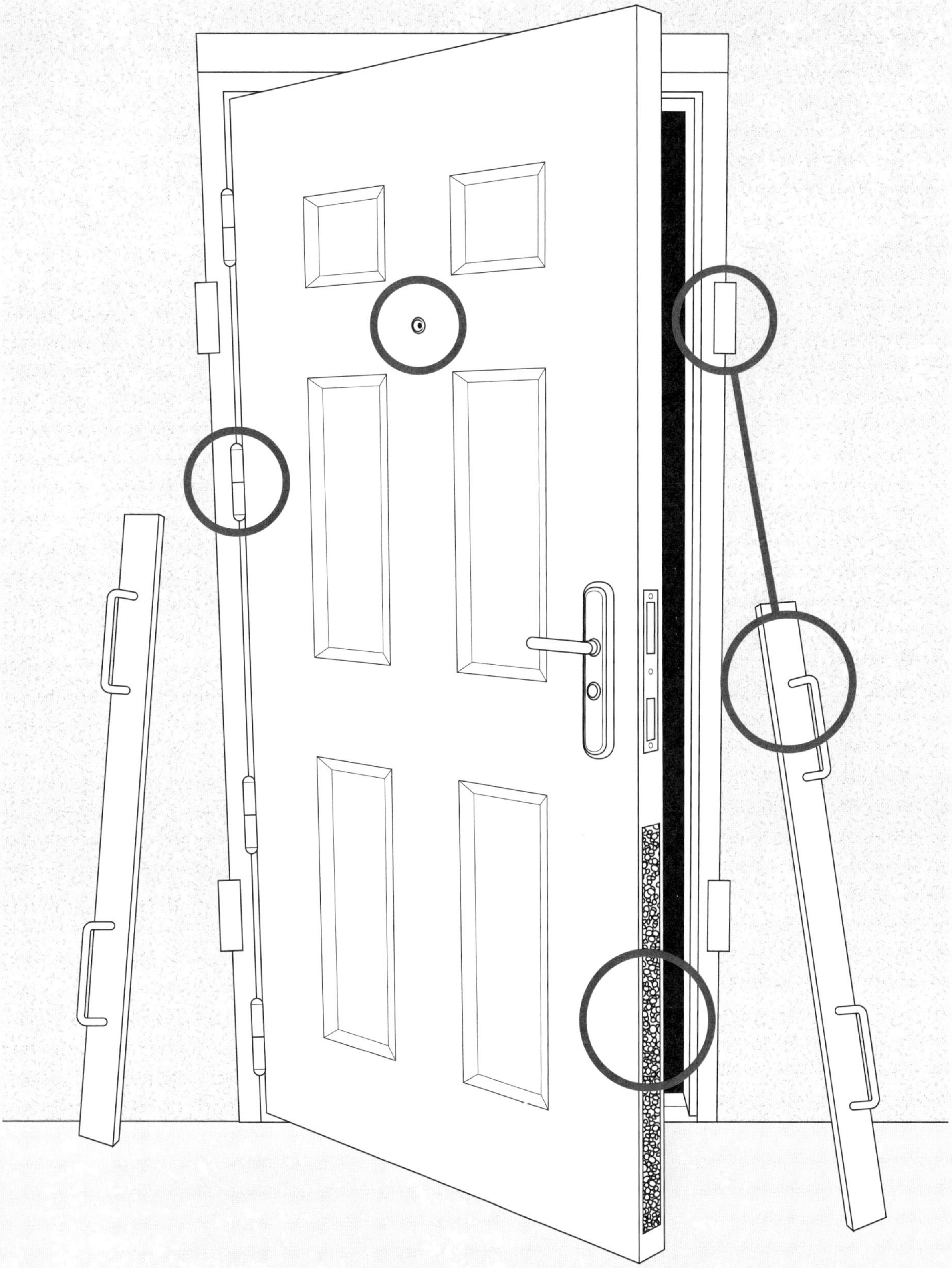

# NIGHT VISION

Most of the commonly used night vision devices (NVDs) amplify existing light from the Moon, stars, or surrounding community artificial lighting. They are crucial tools for self-defense, particularly in "grid-down" situations when streetlights and most security lights will be inoperative. Most NVDs have the advantage of being passive—you aren't emitting visible light—and provide good resolution for safe trail walking and for identifying threats.

Many NVDs can be weapon-mounted in front of a scope or behind a red dot, but this makes it awkward to scan for threats unless you are in a stationary position. The best use of an NVD is mounted on a helmet in front of your nondominant eye. This allows you to scan and move while still having your dominant eye available if you need to use conventional sights in well-lit areas.

When helmet-mounted, the NVD can be coupled with a weapon-mounted IR laser for targeting. This is where lasers provide their most dramatic advantage. You mount the rifle a bit lower than usual (at your chin versus a traditional cheek weld), put the laser on the target, and shoot. The laser must, of course, be sighted in before use and will have an offset from your daylight sight depending on its location. You also need to remember that the targeting laser will be visible to an adversary who is using an NVD.

This same caveat applies to the use of an infared (IR) illuminator with an NVD. The illuminator allows you to see much farther and more clearly through the NVD, but is visible to other NVDs. This is another reason for NVDs—you can detect an attacker using

**A drawback to light-amplification night vision is that it only allows you to see as well as you would without it in twilight.**

A helmet-mounted vision monocular.

Night-vision scope view, as marines from the 1st Battalion, 4th Marines, conduct a night assault on targets at Al Qatrana, Jordan, during exercise Infinite Moonlight in 1998. (Official U.S. Navy photo by PO1 Craig P. Strawser.)

IR devices and it prevents you from being at a huge disadvantage if the attacker has an NVD and you don't.

## Thermal Night Vision

A drawback to light-amplification night vision is that it only allows you to see as well as you would without it in twilight conditions. If a threat hides behind vegetation for concealment and you wouldn't see them in the daylight, then you won't see them with a light-amplification NVD. This is where the less common thermal night vision devices have a huge advantage. Thermal sights detect the heat coming from anything they look at. Yes, they can literally see heat. They can be used for navigating your property as long as there has been enough sunlight to warm the terrain and provide differences in temperature. They are least effective for navigation after a cold, cloudy, foggy day when everything is at nearly the same temperature.

Living things and motor vehicles are dramatically hotter than the surroundings and stand out like a neon sign, regardless of weather. You can literally see through light vegetation if there are any openings. This is also true during daylight hours. While light-amplification NVDs cannot be used during the day, thermal devices can see a heat signature regardless of visible light levels. This allows you to scan your perimeter during the day to see hidden threats.

**GENERATION 1**

**GENERATION 2**

**GENERATION 3**

Each generation of night-vision gear is progressively more capable—and expensive. Three images showing generations 1–3 of night-vision imagery.

Light-amplification night-vision equipment is already ubiquitous. And thermal night vision—though still scarce in civilian hands—is gaining popularity. The prices of both are steadily declining, due to economies of scale. Both are produced in large numbers for military organizations, and some of that production capacity is being used to produce civilian units.

I believe that getting good-quality night-vision equipment will be very important in keeping you ahead of the capabilities of your possible opponents, or at least keeping you equally matched.

Generation-3 night vision is currently used by most of the U.S. military. While there are no substantial changes in the underlying technology from Generation 2, these NVDs have even better resolution and sensitivity. One of the key specs to look for is the line pair (lp) per millimeter count of the NVD's phosphor tube. The higher-quality units will have 64 lp/mm or greater. This rating is generally indicative of the quality of the tube you are getting. The line pair count can only be confirmed if your NVD comes with a serialized data sheet from the manufacturer. Note that lp/mm is only one of three important specifications you will want to check. One good example is the AN/PVS-14.

Some vendors are selling what they are calling "Gen 4" scopes and goggles, but there is not really a Generation 4 classification, according to the U.S. Army. When it was initially introduced, the U.S. Army recognized the Gen-4 technology classification—however, after testing reliability and lifespan of the Gen 4, the army determined that this technology did not meet their strict requirements and thus recanted the Gen-4 definition. So what does this mean for someone looking for the best equipment they can get? In terms of performance, you should buy Gen-3 autogated NVDs.

Pinnacle tube Gen-3 autogated models offer the NVD user spectacular performance, much better tube longevity, increased reliability, and a lower cost. Although some people feel that Gen 4 gives a little better image, it is really a bit of a toss-up, and it often comes down to which unit has the better individual image tube. Only a side-by-side comparison at night can prove that out.

# INTRUSION DETECTION

Another key piece of technology for retreat security is intrusion detection systems (IDS). I cannot overemphasize the need to have a proper IDS for a retreat. Typically, these are electronic systems that produce an alert when a light or infrared beam is disturbed, such as at the activation of a pressure switch, a door or window sensor, or a buried loop that detects the magnetic anomaly of a vehicle passing overhead.

The brand of intrusion detection system that is the most often mentioned in my blog is the Dakota Alert driveway alarm. Beware: there are many other driveway alarms on the market that are made in China. Those are notorious for shoddy construction and vulnerability to moisture. Most of those are not truly weatherproof. By far, the best non-Chinese brand of wireless IR driveway alarm on the market is the Dakota Alert. These are American-made and have long-term reliability.

The wireless Dakota Alert (and some competing brands) use the MURS band frequencies, which I consider a plus. This is because you can get MURS walkie-talkies tuned to the same frequency, so you can have a portable alerting device right on your belt that doubles as a voice "push to talk" walkie-talkie.

## I cannot overemphasize the need to have a proper IDS for a retreat.

Thermal imaging night-vision gear allows you to literally see heat.

Infrared alarms such as the Dakota Alert can be incredibly effective for perimeter security, if properly emplaced on likely avenues of approach. With Dakota Alerts, you can emplace multiple alarm transmitters, each with a distinctive audible alert. That way, you'll know which approach has an intruder—such as "Alert, Zone Two."

The only difficulty that I've encountered with Dakota Alerts is that their BNC antenna connectors and pull-up antennas are slightly leaky. The manufacturer suggests inserting a packet of silica-gel desiccant inside the sensor boxes. But I recommend going a step further by wrapping the BNC connection and each antenna segment joint of the extended antenna with COAX-SEAL (a hand-moldable plastic). This will ensure much better waterproofing of the unit. I also disguised my chromed, collapsible Dakota Alert antennas by covering them with heat-shrink tubing. I then gave each antenna a few blasts of flat brown and flat green spray paint.

A Dakota Alert fake birdhouse. (Shown partially raised.)

The Dakota Alert company also makes a clever fake wooden "birdhouse" enclosure for the sensor boxes. These do camouflage the units well, but I've found that it makes them more vulnerable to cobwebs obscuring the sensor window, resulting in more false alerts. The only way to obviate this is with fairly frequent cleanings.

The other sort of intrusion detection that you will need is a burglar alarm with door and window sensors. I presently prefer the variety that are battery-powered or those that are AC-powered with a battery backup. (If you have a small PV-power system, then most wireless alarms are still operational in the event of an extended power failure. The system can still operate in standalone mode, even if Internet contact with the parent company is lost.) In the United States and Canada, one of the most popular brands of wireless burglar alarms is SimpliSafe. Because they incorporate wireless Web cameras, these sorts of systems also document break-ins by burglars if you are away from your home, thus giving you the chance to bring them to justice.

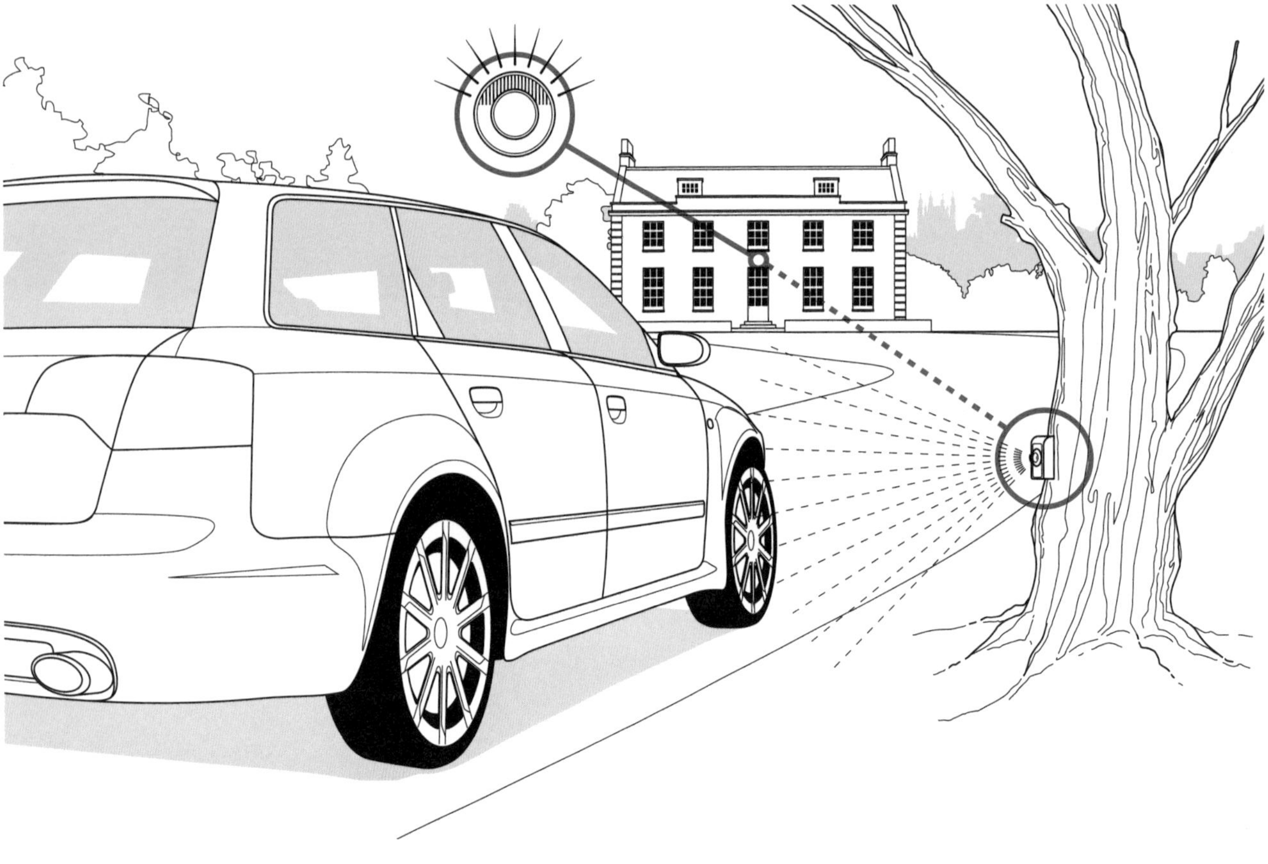

# IMPROVISED WEAPONS

A lit road flare can be quite intimidating to attackers.

I can foresee several potential situations wherein you might have to construct improvised weapons. These could include disaster situations where:

- You are stranded while away from home, or
- Legislation denies new commercial manufacture, or
- You are living in, or traveling through, a weapons-deprived area.

Beyond obvious choices like kitchen knives, nearly any small item of stout construction and some weight can be used as an impact weapon, a penetration weapon, for cover or concealment, or as a distraction if thrown at an attacker. The variety of improvised weapons runs the gamut from do-it-yourself pepper spray to homemade slingshots, baseball bats and other blunt instruments, and road flares. From personal experience, I must mention that the psychological impact of having a lit road flare waved in a perpetrator's face is devastating. I've seen burly grown men shriek like three-year-olds, and even wet themselves when confronted by a lit flare. So I advise that you stock up on road flares—preferably the longer fifteen-minute variety.

Some improvised weapons are not apparent to casual observers when carried on the street. These can include "heavy hands" weights for joggers, lengths of chain, umbrellas with sharpened tips, sword canes, flashlights, hammers, key rings attached to fairly heavy chains, and weighted walking sticks. Even a large ballpoint pen or felt marking pen can be used in lieu of a *tonfa* (a short fighting stick). Laws vary widely, so be sure to research your local, county, state, and national laws before acquiring or carrying weapons of *any* type!

**Improvised weapons run the gamut from do-it-yourself pepper spray to homemade slingshots, baseball bats and other blunt instruments, and road flares.**

The variety of potential improvised weapons is limited only by your imagination and the vagaries of paranoid politicians.

For pedestrians and rail commuters, walking sticks and umbrellas (depending on the season) don't even get a second glance—especially for those of us in the graying generation. Also note that for bicyclists, a frame-mounted tire pump can be effective as in impromptu baton, especially if it is a variety that can have its sliding handle lock in the closed position.

Part of carrying an improvised weapon in modern times is being able to justify doing so. In some jurisdictions, carrying a cane might require a note from a doctor directing you to do so. You should be well-rehearsed in your explanations of carrying such objects. For instance, carrying a cane or umbrella with a sharp tip is justifiable if your local streets get icy in winter. The difference between explainable normal behavior and a punishable offense could very well come down to your glib articulation of *why* you need such an item close by. Practice exactly what you will say if confronted by police or a nosy neighbor.

**Part of carrying an improvised weapon in modern times is being able to justify doing so.**

Travel by bicycle, motorcycle, or automobile will give you carte blanche to carry a wide range of potential defensive tools—such as a hammer, a wrench, a tire iron, a bundle of road flares, a "tire checker" baton, or a large multi-cell flashlight such as a MagLite—that would seem suspect if you were just on foot. Items that seem perfectly normal for a motorist to carry are significantly harder to explain for a pedestrian. Likewise, carrying a length of chain with a stout padlock snapped on the end is easy to explain for someone on a bike or motorcycle, or for someone pushing a baby stroller. Not so for someone who is just out on a walk.

Here in the United States, anyone that works at a retail store can often justify carrying a box-cutter knife. If carried in a well-worn utilitarian leather belt pouch, then they just look like a "tool of the trade." But make sure that you also have a business card that identifies you as a "retail sales associate" or something similar. Of course in the UK and in other highly restrictive countries, that would probably *not* be seen as sufficient justification.

Lastly, I should mention that using a knife or improvised weapon actually requires *more* training and better physical conditioning than using a firearm. So I recommend enrolling at a qualified martial-arts school. The best martial art? For pure hand-to-hand self-defense, I'd recommend jiu-jitsu. But for the use of knives and improvised weapons, I'd recommend finding a Filipino martial arts dojo. They are renowned for teaching their students how to end street fights quickly and decisively, with whatever weapon is on hand.

## A Transcendent Right

In summary, I see self-defense as an inherent and God-given right. This right predates *all* governments and transcends all statutes. To deny someone the right to defend themselves, their family, and their property is the worst sort of nanny state tyranny. If our only recourse if attacked is to summon help from police, then we will be at the mercy of street criminals. In many Western nations, the citizenry has been reduced to just the phrase: "Stop or I will shout 'stop' *again*!"

Again, I am thankful that I am an American. Here in the land of the free, we have the advantages of both the Second Amendment (the universal gun permit) and castle doctrine laws, in most states. (The latter reinforces the long-standing legal precept that "a man's home is his castle.") I urge my readers to resist all legislative attempts at civilian disarmament. Both the safety of our loved ones and the preservation of our other liberties depend on the continuity of our right to keep and bear arms.

The martial arts are perishable skills, requiring regular practice.

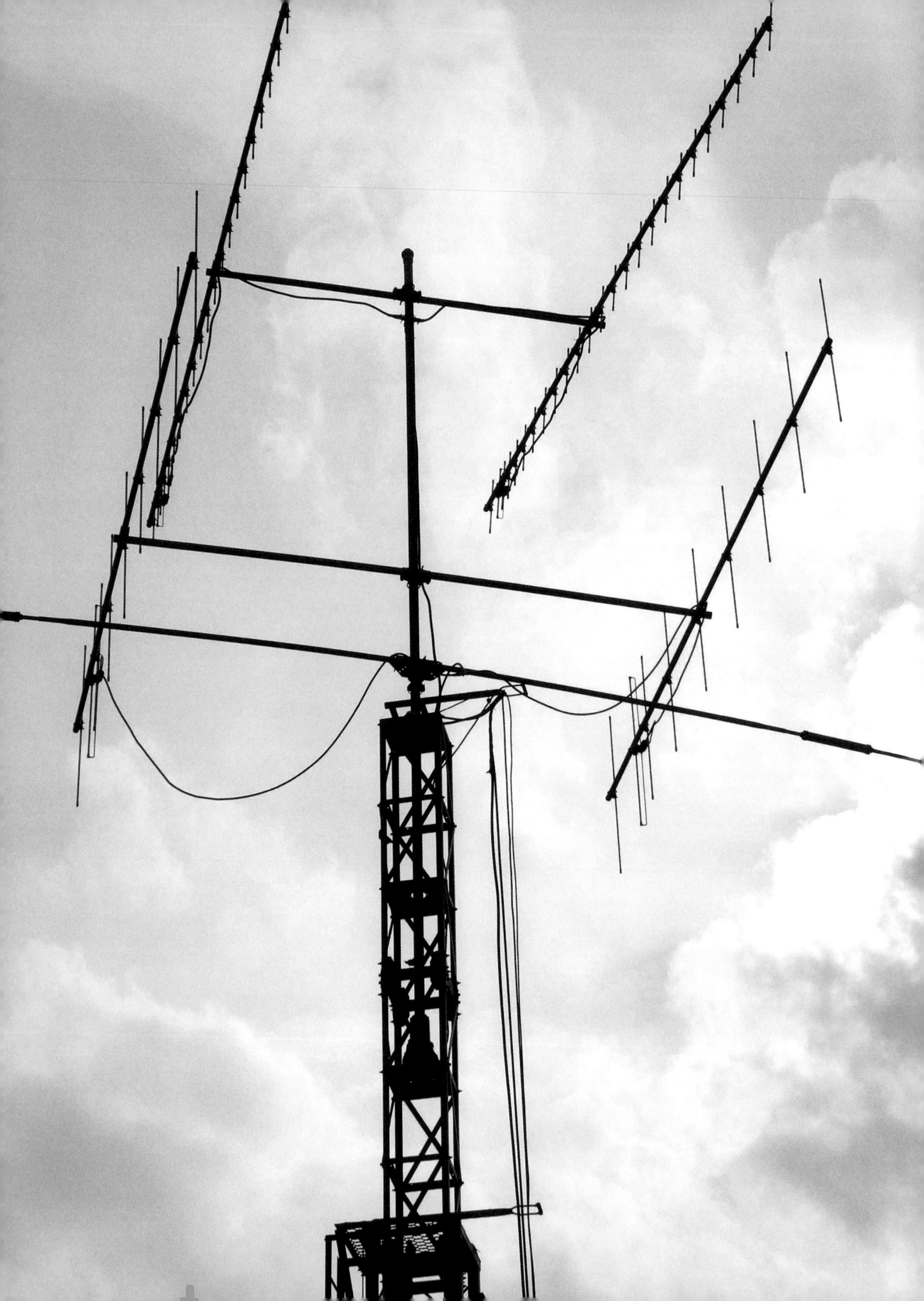

CHAPTER 7

# COMMUNICATIONS

**Hardwire or Wireless**

**Unconventional and Covert Comms Options**

"Quote me as saying I was misquoted."

Groucho Marx

# HARDWIRE OR WIRELESS

An AN/TA-312 field telephone, powered by a pair of type D alkaline batteries.

A multiband Baofeng UV-5R handie-talkie. Sadly, these can no longer be imported into the United Sates.

## Hardwire

Although handheld radios have become inexpensive and ubiquitous, I'm still a big believer in old-fashioned military field telephones. These can be connected in a "hot loop" or point-to-point with your neighbors. In the United States, I recommend the army-surplus TA-312 field phones that are available from Fair Radio Sales. The same company also often sells reels of WD-1 field-telephone wire.

## Wireless

For wireless communications, my current preference is for the multiband Baofeng UV-5R. Please note that many of the bands require an FCC ham license for you to legally operate in the United States, but there are no restrictions on the CB, MURS, and FRS bands. Check your local regulations for restrictions around the world.

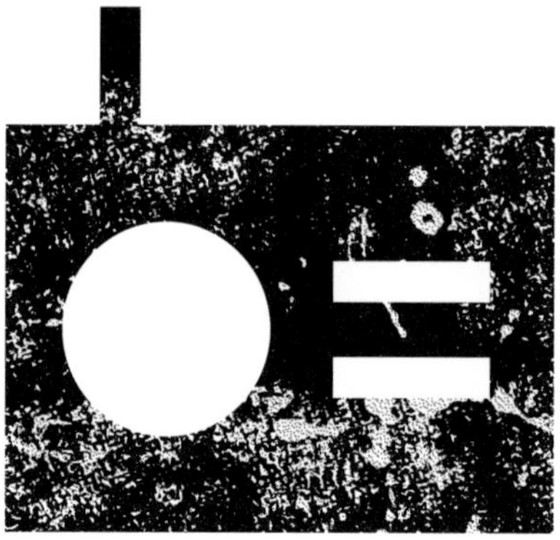

**MORE THAN**

**3,000,000**

**ESTIMATED NUMBER OF HAM RADIO OPERATORS WORLDWIDE.**

# UNCONVENTIONAL AND COVERT COMMS OPTIONS

Couriers transporting messages physically between the sender and the receiver have the best way to handle covert communications. There are, however, a few high-tech options. These include home-brew laser communications and spread-spectrum transceivers. With the latter, it is difficult for anyone to tell that you are operating, much less for them to intercept your transmissions. The Motorola DLR digital two-way radio is a fairly rugged consumer-grade radio that uses spread-spectrum frequency hopping, but at $418 per pair, they are literally ten times as expensive as purchasing Baofeng UV-5R handhelds. Unless you expect to be up against sophisticated opponents who are using multiband scanners, then you are probably better off buying ten to twelve of the Baofengs. That will give you plenty of spares for the long term. After all, it is inevitable that in the course of hard field use, radios will get dunked or knocked around. A $21 spare is certainly more affordable than a $209 spare!

## Move, Shoot, and Communicate

As an army officer, I learned that, in order to be effective, an army must have three key abilities: to move, to shoot, and to communicate. Take away any one, and you are ineffective. But if you get all three right, you can absolutely devastate an opponent—even one that has vastly superior numbers.

Part of my work life in most weeks involves consulting phone calls. The majority of my clients are in the United States and Canada. Not surprisingly, many of them have questions for me about privacy. These questions are generally along three lines: (1) buying guns privately; (2) buying land privately; and (3) how to avoid paper trails on storage-food purchases. One of the key privacy concepts that I often mention is what I call "going analog." But first, I'll mention "going dark"—that is, completely dropping off the grid.

## Going Dark

The "going dark" concept implies someone cutting off all normal contact. This is often coincident with relocating in an attempt to disappear without a trace. This extreme privacy is only required for someone in distress. That would be, for instance, someone who is the target of a manhunt, a witness of a criminal case who is at risk, someone evading an abusive ex-spouse, or someone who is fleeing creditors.

Details on fully going dark are included in several popular books. I would recommend *How to Disappear: Erase Your Digital Footprint, Leave False Trails, and Vanish Without a Trace* by Frank M. Ahearn and Eileen C. Horan.

Realistically though, for most of us, simply lowering our profile is sufficient for whatever needs we might have. What follows are a few of my suggestions for achieving this.

It is eminently sensible to learn how to use your chosen amateur radio setup now, before it becomes the only mode of communication to your friendly neighbors.

**ENCRYPTION**

E-mails, texts, and phone calls can be intercepted, but various apps like Whatsapp and Telegram provide end-to-end encryption. This is currently the only secure way to communicate digitally.

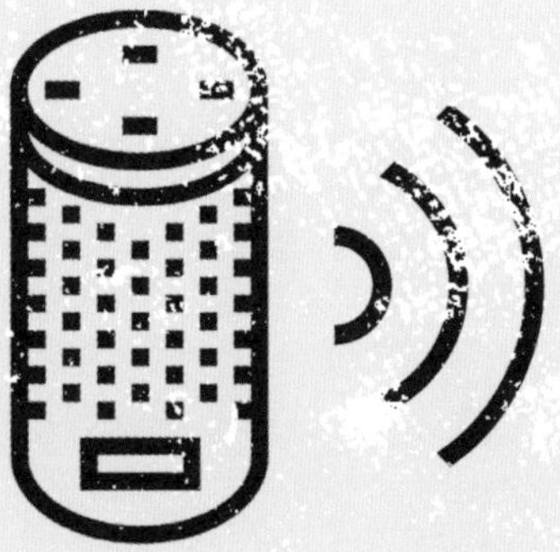

**100%**

**THE PERCENTAGE OF TIME THAT DEVICES LIKE ALEXA OR GOOGLE HOME ARE LISTENING TO YOU.**

An AN/TA-1 field telephone. This variety is sound-powered and therefore requires no batteries.

## Going Analog

The term "going analog" refers to limiting or eliminating all digital communications, for fear of tracking or monitoring. Most of privacy is just common sense: keep your paper trail to a minimum; don't offer your name in transactions if you don't have to; and remember: cash is king, and cash is *private*.

One of my blog readers, "Charles K.," offered some great advice on privacy, none of which is too difficult to implement:

- Don't answer the phone unless you know who is calling. If I don't recognize the number or caller ID, I don't answer. If it's important, they will leave a message. It's amazing how few important calls I get.
- If possible, don't own a computer with a built-in camera or microphone. Mine is 12 years old. It's old, it's a little slow, but it works! It's the next one I get that's going to be a big problem.
- Use credit and debit cards as little as possible. In my case, I only use my debit card at my bank-branch ATM, and credit cards only on large purchases. Otherwise, I only use cash.

A 1970s-vintage IBM correcting Selectric II typewriter. For COMSEC, "old school" mailed letters have their advantages. A typeball is shown below. These can be replaced to destroy the typewriter's "fingerprint."

- I limit my online purchases to Amazon and on rare occasions Wal-Mart.
- Disable Bluetooth and WiFi in your car. Then disable Bluetooth and WiFi on your phone. I don't like that there is a built-in microphone in the car, but without Bluetooth and WiFi, it should not be a problem. I don't want to talk to my car, I don't want my car talking to me, and I certainly don't want it *listening* to my conversations.
- I usually do not answer my front door, depending on who is there. The optical peephole is a wonderful invention.
- Finally, know who you are talking to. Some people couldn't keep a secret if their lives depended on it, and it might.

## Using Old-School Typewriters

We need to assume that *all* e-mail is now monitored and archived. This even includes encrypted e-mail. Instead of e-mails, consider

### SECURITY NOTE

Keep in mind that the film ribbon cartridges for Selectric typewriters retain the exact sequence of letters typed, and that can be recovered, forensically. You can burn the used ribbon cartridges, but that makes a stinky mess. One trick that I learned in my ASA unit was to simply run a Selectric ribbon through a crosscut paper shredder. It will spool out of the cartridge as the shredder runs, and it gobbles up the film ribbon nicely.

If typewriter fingerprint anonymity is not a concern to you, then you might also consider buying a traditional manual typewriter. These are great for off-grid living. Just be sure that it is in very good working order and that spare ribbons are still available before you buy.

**A key tactic in lowering your profile is minimizing your paper trail.**

sending old-fashioned handwritten—or, better yet, typewritten—letters in envelopes. In the United States, it is legal to put the addressee's mailing address in both the "To" and "From" blocks on the envelope, so do so.

For the greatest privacy—especially for letters to newspaper editors or elected representatives—use an electric typewriter. My favorite model is the now-obsolete Correcting IBM Selectric II. I prefer these because they have quick-change 88-character "typeballs" in 30+ different 10-point and 12-point fonts. It is notable that it is the type-head that creates a typewriter's unique "fingerprint." By changing the typeball, you change this fingerprint. Discarding a typeball and substituting another makes a type fingerprint disappear.

Selectric typewriters, typeballs, and correcting ribbons are now available at very reasonable prices on eBay or through your local Craigslist or similar local website. (IBM controlled ¾ of the typewriter market in the 1970s and early 1980s, meaning that there are huge numbers of perfectly serviceable machines out there!) I recently saw a set of 16 assorted typeballs sell on eBay for just over $20, postage paid. Technically, IBM Selectric typewriters are considered digital/analog, but their typewritten output is analog, and that is our goal.

## In Trusts We Trust

To convey land deeds privately, it is best to use a family trust. By using a trust, the names of the owners/occupants do not show up on the deed or tax rolls. Only the trust name is visible. So, obviously, you should pick a fairly generic trust name that does not include your surname or location. A good example of a generic name would be "The Plains Trust."

## Switching to Cash

A key tactic in lowering your profile is minimizing your paper trail. Every time that you use a credit or debit card, you are creating a fairly permanent record of your purchase. The obvious solution is using good ol' *cash*. If possible, you should make the purchases of any controversial books or gear face to face with cash, and don't leave your name.

Many of the smaller storage-food vendors are willing to accommodate cash customers, as long as the purchase is less than $10,000 worth of food. You simply call them and arrange an in-person payment and pick-up. Even companies that advertise that they have no storefront are usually willing to meet customers face to face for a "cash on the barrelhead" transaction. You just need to phone them to confirm they have that particular stock on hand, and schedule a date and time for the purchase.

**31%**

**OF ALL TRANSACTIONS IN THE U.S., AS OF AUGUST 2018, WERE IN CASH.**

25
WARNING
NEIGHBORHOOD
WATCH
PROTECTED AREA

CHAPTER 8

# YOUR NEIGHBORS

**A Neighborhood Watch on Steroids**

**Charity**

**Barter**

**OPSEC**

"The police can't stop an intruder, mugger or stalker from hurting you. They can pursue him only after he has hurt or killed you. Protecting yourself from harm is your responsibility, and you are far less likely to be hurt in a neighborhood of gun-owners than in one of disarmed citizens—even if you don't own a gun yourself."

Harry Browne

# A NEIGHBORHOOD WATCH ON STEROIDS

In lawless times, you will need more than just a traditional neighborhood watch.

When the end arrives, the police will probably be overwhelmed, and unlikely to respond—and that is assuming that the communications network still allows them to receive emergency calls and be dispatched. In this vacuum of police protection, you will be on your own. It would therefore be wise to organize with your neighbors, for mutual security. You will need a "Neighborhood Watch on Steroids." Coordinating such a watch 24 hours per day may be difficult, but in emergency circumstances it is likely to be essential to prevent houses in your neighborhood being picked off one by one, when families are sleeping.

### Communications

One key aspect of security is communications. Without reliable comms, you will essentially be on your own. It is only with robust and redundant communications that you will be able to contact neighbors beyond shouting distance. Do not plan on being able to rely on utility power or on existing telephone networks. Battery-operated systems will be effective—but you will need photovoltaic (PV) charging systems to maintain their batteries for these battery-operated radios to be effective in the long term.

**40%**

**THE ESTIMATED PERCENTAGE OF NEIGHBORHOODS PROTECTED BY A WATCH SYSTEM IN THE UNITED STATES.**

# BARTER

Of all the many categories of preparedness measures, bartering is one of the least understood and most often ignored. Being ready to barter requires both barterable goods and the requisite skill to confidently and competently barter. The latter comes only with experience. For that, I recommend visiting flea markets, swap meets, and gun shows. It takes time to learn how to dicker.

As for barter goods, your list of barterables will vary depending on your geography. If you live in an inland region, then salt might be quite important, but not so if you live on a coastline. And if you live in a cold climate, then heavy coats and sleeping bags will be at a premium—but obviously not if you live in the south of the United States or another warm climate.

To accomplish a barter exchange, five things have to align, as noted in the box to the right. If only four out of those five are true, then there is no deal.

1. You have an item
2. They want that item
3. You are willing to part with that item
4. They have something to give you in exchange for that item that you want
5. Both parties have agreed upon the valuations of both items

Keep most items reasonably small and easily divisible. I believe that .22 Long Rifle ammo will be the "nickels and dimes" of post-TEOTWAWKI barter. Be able to "make change," or you might have to settle for an unequal deal. Lower your risk by buying low. If it's a super deal, then it's hard to go wrong—but you must know the ins and outs of what you are buying, and the market pricing. Stick with what you know.

My blog reader "C.Y." put together an excellent guide for what criteria the best barter goods will meet:

## GUIDE FOR WHAT CRITERIA THE BEST BARTER GOODS WILL MEET

- Inexpensive to buy now, but will increase in value after collapse because they are not made or replaceable locally
- Stable over a few years in cool dry storage
- Provably in good condition at the time of trading, by demonstration
- Portable and robust; made out of durable materials like stainless steel
- Usable by the recipient for further exchange or for their original purpose
- Widely acceptable and recognizable; hard to counterfeit
- Not so expensive per indivisible unit (like guns) that it is hard to make a fair trade
- Impossible to use against you (avoid bartering large-caliber ammunition unless your trading partner is a trusted neighbor)
- Unlikely to arouse suspicion that you are a hoarder, a wholesale trader, or unusually well-prepared
- Usable by you in ordinary life so that they can be rotated like other stockpiled items
- Preferably packed in original containers to increase their perceived value, condition, and safety
- Containers, if reusable, will add to the value to the item. Don't forget to point this out as part of their value. This includes resealable bottles and boxes in glass, plastic, and metal.

## DURABLE GOODS SUITABLE TO STORE FOR BARTER

- Precision air-gun pellets and hunting arrows; slingshots and slingshot ammunition
- Candles and waterproof matches
- Small notebooks with pencils, eraser tops, and a small sharpener
- Resealable waterproof containers such as Ziploc bags, Tupperware, and small Mason jars
- Fishing line (that can be used for many things besides fishing) and galvanized wire
- Waterproof duct tape in dark neutral colors such as green, brown, or gray—not black, white, or orange
- Bicycle and bike-chain repair kits, sewing kits, and first-aid kits
- Plumbing and irrigation repair items such as hose clips, extenders, and plastic valves kept on their original store-display cards
- Stainless steel screws in common sizes; keep to Phillips (cross) or standard slot head versions. If they come in snap-top plastic containers, then so much the better.
- Strong hooks, bolts, and padlocks
- Small, good-quality pocket knives or multipurpose tools with can/bottle openers
- Small adjustable wrenches and stainless digging tools/camping knives
- Camping and travel supplies, like vacuum-packed space blankets and collapsible water containers
- LED flashlights, both battery and squeeze dynamo-powered
- 50-foot lengths of nylon cord or paracord with the ends heat-sealed so they don't fray, carabiners, and small books on knot-tying
- Salt and sugar; cubes are preferred over loose sugar because they can't be bulked out with fillers. They must be kept dry; sealed containers are your friends.
- Plastic-covered local street and regional maps or map books; colored chalk for marking buildings and routes; small compasses with measuring features
- Travel bars of soap and small bottles of rubbing alcohol
- Lightweight industrial-type fixings, such as long zip ties and tie-down straps
- 12-volt electrical-system components and light bulbs, particularly long-lasting and durable LEDs
- Paperback survival and repair guides—add value by packing them in waterproof bags

# CHARITY

During TEOTWAWKI, there will be millions without the basic necessities of food, shelter, water, and medicine. While you certainly can't be expected to care for everyone, you should plan to provide a bit of charity. Our family's personal chosen number is 10 percent; we store 10 percent more than we think we will need, which we can then give away as charity.

Your charity portion will have to be carefully disbursed so that you don't compromise your OPSEC, but you will fare better for having it. Charity can be neatly divided into two major classes: (1) charity for those you know but cannot take in; and (2) charity for those you don't know.

I'll be quite frank: Despite your best plans and your best conversations, there will be people you know but whom you did not invite that show up at your door looking for help. Having something in the charity bag to hand them while you politely shoo them on their way can both help them and ease your mind. Having something to give them allows you to keep your promise—"You can't come here!"—while fulfilling the implied promise of helping a friend in need.

There is a subcategory of those you do know but can't take in: those that you can take temporarily. Perhaps you can take them just overnight while they get a meal, shower, and wash their clothes before they move on. Or perhaps you can take them for a week, while they labor in your garden, cut firewood, or provide security. Whatever you decide, communication and setting proper expectations are paramount. Talk to them and make absolutely sure that they know your plans and parameters.

Then there are those strangers you don't know who may come knocking at your door for a handout. You need to avoid that happening when possible. One reason that might cause it is developing a local reputation as a charitable giver. In a lawless situation, that could be very dangerous. My often-repeated advice is to dispense most of your charity at arm's length. This is best accomplished by passing charity items through the hands of a third party, such as your local church or synagogue. Let the leaders know that you have a little available to share, but insist that your name is never mentioned to the recipients.

Making donations anonymously will be vitally important for your safety. Charity is desirable, but do not let it endanger you and your family.

**10%**

**OUR RECOMMENDED CHARITY EXCESS.**

# OPSEC

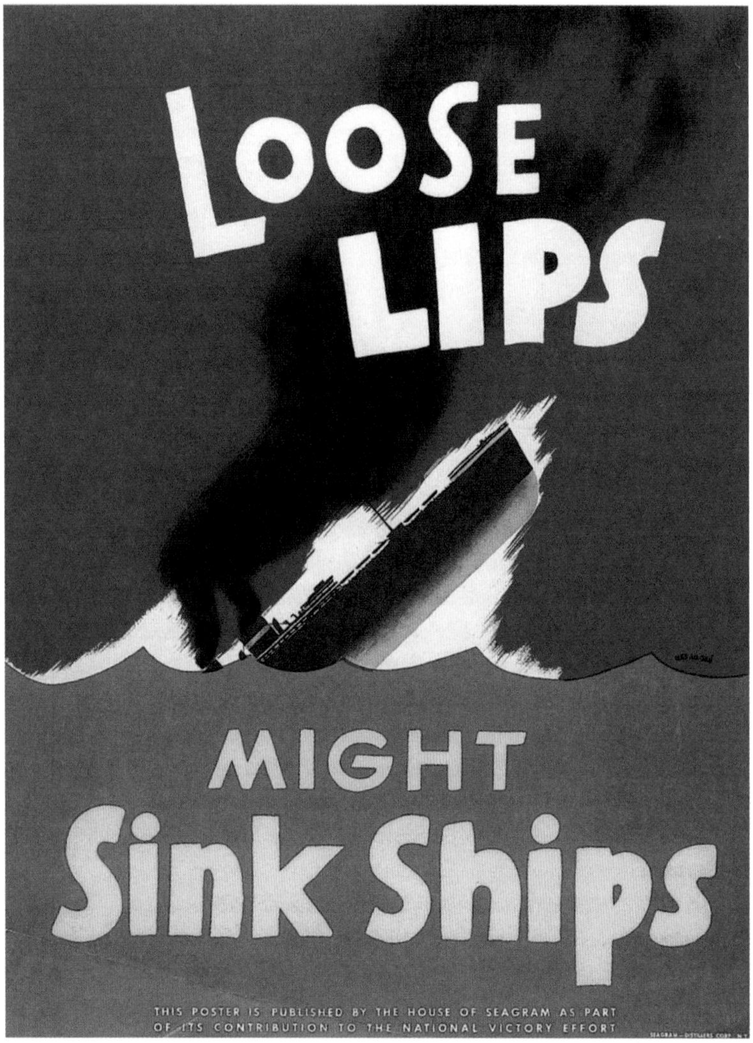


A World War II poster, the message of which is still relevant today.

The importance of operational security (OPSEC), both before and during a crisis, cannot be overstated. The old saying "loose lips sink ships" should dominate your mindset and your conversation. Always apply the "need to know" rule. If someone doesn't have a true need to know about your locale, logistics, capabilities, intentions, contingency plans, or security measures, then simply do not tell them. It is quite simple, but many people have never operated that way, and this is difficult for them. To illustrate the importance, I have a little question-and-answer session for you:

1. **Q**: How do you keep a rumor from spreading?
   **A**: Don't start it in the first place.

2. **Q**: If someone that you are bartering with, or dispensing charity to, happens to ask you how much more you have, how do you respond?
   **A**: "Just barely enough for my own family."

3. **Q**: How many vehicles at your retreat should be visible from public roads?
   **A**: As few as possible. Unless it is a genuine "show of force" situation, then always keep people guessing about your manpower and capabilities.

4. **Q**: How many lights should be visible at your home at night?
   **A**: None! You want to be seen as too poor to be able to afford candles or kerosene, and certainly not the guy who has a fancy PV power system.

5. **Q**: If you are sending out a security patrol, then which neighbors need to be told?
   **A**: Perhaps only one, and at the last possible minute. That one neighbor is the one through which your patrol must transit.

6. **Q**: What is the most effective ambush arrangement?
   **A**: The one that attackers cannot see, and that they weren't told about.

## Red List and Blue List

Since I have intended this book to be an advanced "thinking about the unthinkable" text, it would be remiss of me if I neglected

**$28.7 BILLION**

**FEMA'S 2020 BUDGET**

to discuss how to survive a change of government, where a new regime comes to power and begins asserting draconian measures, or rounding up those individuals that they deem to be enemies of the state. This may seem like a leap to those living in the United States, but you need only examine the collapse in democratic freedoms and norms in a country such as Turkey to see how quickly this can happen in even "modern" or Western countries, let alone those without a strong history in individual freedoms.

There has been a lot of conjecture in the past forty years about the existence of government round-up lists. Large-scale disaster and war planning exercises, like REX-84 (Readiness Exercise-1984) and Jade Helm 2015, have stimulated endless discourse about whether or not the government maintains a so-called red list and blue list of people that they deem to be dissidents who they might target for harassment, travel restrictions, or even detention without due process of law. Because any such lists would presumably be developed and updated under the wraps of a security classification—and the "need to know" rule—this topic is understandably rife with conjecture, speculation, and even downright fabrication. Therefore, I will do my best to just stick to the facts with a bit of well-reasoned extrapolation, based on known technological trends.

## The Real Face of FEMA

The centerpiece of the conspiracy speculation in the United States is the Federal Emergency Management Agency (FEMA). In my estimation, most of the chitchat on the Internet about "secret FEMA camps" is highly sensationalized. Civil internment is probably the lowest priority of any of FEMA's contingency missions, and some would describe it as an almost hypothetical contingency.

Most Americans don't realize it, but FEMA's key mission is not disaster relief to the general public. Rather, their highest priority mission is assuring "continuity of government" (COG) following an external attack or following a widespread disaster that disrupts command, control, communications, and intelligence (C3I) assets and processes. If FEMA's budget were ever drastically slashed, then the very last of their missions to be defunded would be COG. In FEMA-speak, the COG part of their mission is listed under "National Continuity Programs." They prefer to use the term "Continuity of Operations" (COOP), and that same term is used by the Department of Homeland Security (DHS). These tasks fall under the purview of FEMA's National Continuity Programs Directorate and are organized per the National Continuity Policy Implementation Plan (NCPIP).

A demonstrator raises her symbolically chained hands during a protest against the arrest of journalists Can Dundar and Erdem Gul, in Ankara, Turkey, in November 2015.

The COG/COOP mission was further clarified in 2007, under the National Security and Homeland Security Presidential Directive (National Security Presidential Directive NSPD 51/Homeland Security Presidential Directive HSPD-20). Therein, the term COG morphed into "Enduring Constitutional Government" (ECG).

At the time, various conservative activists argued that NSPD 51 was a violation of the Constitution, in that the three branches of government should be separate and equal, with no single branch coordinating the others. However, the executive was clearly here taking on the leading role.

A 2009 document prepared for the transition of the executive branch of government to the incoming Obama administration used the following euphemistic wording to describe FEMA's COG/COOP mission:

> **"FEMA provides continuity services, not only for FEMA, but also for the entire federal government, across the nation, for common and asymmetric threats alike. It is essential for FEMA to maintain high-performance continuity services in the form of exercises, planning, standards, training, communications, and resiliency measures."**

In the same briefing binder, there are also some more concrete but still slightly obtuse descriptions of FEMA's COG/COOP responsibilities:

> **"The criticality of continuity programs can be traced to three foundations. First, continuity programs, led by NCP, directly reflect the first of eight National Essential Functions (NEFs), 'Ensuring the continued functioning of our form of government under the Constitution [...].' Second, continuity programs form the foundation of the seven remaining NEFs by ensuring that the government structures are in place to govern and support the economic, defensive, and social well-being of the nation. Third, continuity programs form the foundation of the National Response Framework (NRF), ensuring government structures at each tier (local, state, and federal) are in place under all circumstances to sustain their essential functions, deliver essential services, and accept the assistance provided under the NRF. When government departments and agencies are inoperable and their continuity programs fail, the NRF will also fail."**

In a subsection, there is also this description:

> **"The Mount Weather Emergency Operation Center (MWEOC) located in Berryville, Virginia, is a continuity of operations relocation site for several aspects of DHS and FEMA. The facility provides operational space for FEMA and DHS Emergency Relocation Group members to perform Departmental and Agency mission essential functions."**

## A Billion Here, a Billion There...

In recent federal budgets, FEMA's Disaster Relief Fund has ballooned. In 2018, it rose to around $7 billion, but that came out of a more

An entrance portal into Raven Rock Mountain Complex, a massive, 650-acre nuclear bunker and national security site built inside a hollowed-out mountain near Blue Ridge Summit, Pennsylvania, pictured in 2018. Constructed during the Cold War, the facility was conceived as a backup for the Pentagon and built to house military leadership, as well as the president, in the event of a nuclear disaster. Entry is through one of four portals, each protected by a 34-ton blast door.

than $10 billion annual budget. So where was the other $3 billion spent? It was spent on a whole lot of things, and many of them fall into categories like "administration, training, and interagency liaison." Even though the big long-term bunkers were built decades ago, still included in FEMA's budget are many line items that relate to intelligence fusion, "national continuity," and "continuity of operations."

When FEMA Administrator Craig Fugate testified before the congressional Subcommittee on Disaster Preparedness about his agency's 2015 $10.38 billion budget request, he pointed out that FEMA is now working more closely with the DHS. Another key point that came up in the hearings was that 2015 was the first year that 25 percent of the agency's budget was not formally set aside for law enforcement/terrorism preventions.

What this all shows is that, with its traditionally strong COG/COOP emphasis, FEMA has invested—and crucially is still investing—many billions of dollars to ensure continuity of the executive branch of the federal government. The Mount Weather complex is reportedly just one of several redundant deep underground bunkers. Some of these facilities were developed by other government organizations, partly for the sake of redundancy. Although they have established deep hardened bunker facilities with accommodations for federal legislators and some federal judges, their main focus is directed toward sheltering the White House staff and the directors and key staff of all of the federal law enforcement agencies. Meanwhile, the U.S. military organizations each have their own infrastructures in place for protecting both their C3I networks and safely housing their general staff and related personnel.

Because of security classifications, it is difficult to know exactly how FEMA's budget is being spent and how much of that might be directed toward contingency plans for housing of "displaced persons." A lot could be hidden under that guise. Essentially the only difference between building a temporary city to house natural-disaster refugees and one that is built to house detainees is the presence or absence of concertina-wire perimeter fences.

Parenthetically, I'd be curious to know if FEMA has ever put out requests for quotation (RFQs) for the manufacturers of concertina wire or razor wire, as measured in miles. However, here, I'm straying into speculation. Let's return to the facts at hand.

## The J. Edgar Days

In the late 1930s, the FBI developed lists of individuals on cardstock index cards. One of these was the Custodial Detention Index, also known as the Custodial Detention List. This list was compiled between 1939 and 1941 under the "Alien Enemy Control" program. According to one published report:

> **"The Custodial Detention Index was a list of suspects and potential subversives, classified as 'A,' 'B' and 'C'; the ones classified as 'A' were destined to be immediately arrested and interned at the outbreak of war. Category A were leaders of Axis-related organizations, category B were members deemed 'less dangerous' and category C were 'sympathizers.'"**

After the United States entered World War II in 1941, these card-file lists were put into operation. Large numbers of German, Italian and Japanese nationals were rounded up and questioned. However, a disproportionately large number of Japanese were actually put in long-term detention—including thousands who were U.S. citizens living in coastal areas, ostensibly because the government "didn't want to break up families." This was a gross violation of civil rights, but given wartime exigencies it was hardly even questioned by most Americans until after the war was over.

According to research by the Federation of American Scientists, the FBI's habit of building card catalogs of people did not end with World War II. In the 1950s, they moved on to building lists of communist agents, subversives, and their fellow travelers. After the shocking revelations about Julius and Ethel Rosenberg, Klaus Fuchs, and other alleged spies targeting nuclear weapons technology, this record-keeping again seemed justified to many people.

By the late 1960s, when anti-draft protesters were a big concern for the executive branch, the FBI moved on to develop yet another list (actually a group of lists) called the Administrative Index (ADEX). This was before the FBI computerized their operations, and so this was still a paper list on index cards. It was perhaps later supplemented by Hollerith computer-punched cards. Additions to the ADEX were reportedly suspended in early 1978. However, before it was discontinued and moved to their inactive files storage, the ADEX cards had merged several sublists, including the "Agitator Index" and the "Reserve Index."

Majdanek concentration camp on the outskirts of Lublin, Poland. More than 79,000 people were killed at Majdanek during the thirty-four months of its operation.

## Automating the Lists

In the 1980s, following the lead of the early adopters at the NSA, Atomic Energy Commission (AEC), and NASA, the FBI moved into the computing age. Other than a few revelations about REX-84, very little has been revealed about any lists of enemies that were developed in the 1980s and 1990s. Even REX-84 itself would have been nothing more than an obscure code name, if it were not for the much publicized Iran–Contra hearings that captivated the American public through what would have otherwise been a boring summer.

The following transcript of the hearing appeared in the *New York Times* in July 1987. It records the dialogue between Congressman Jack Brooks, NSC miliatary aide Oliver North's attorney Brendan Sullivan, and Senator Daniel Inouye, the Democratic chairman of the joint Senate Select Committee:

> **[Congressman Jack] Brooks:**
> **Colonel North, in your work at the NSC were you not assigned, at one time, to work on plans for the continuity of government in the event of a major disaster?**
> **Brendan Sullivan [North's counsel, agitatedly]:**
> **Mr. Chairman?**
> **[Senator Daniel] Inouye:**
> **I believe that question touches upon a highly sensitive and classified area so may I request that you not touch upon that?**
> **Brooks:**
> **I was particularly concerned, Mr. Chairman, because I read in Miami papers, and several others, that there had been a plan developed, by that same agency, a contingency plan in the event of emergency, that would suspend the American Constitution. And I was deeply concerned about it and wondered if that was an area in which he had worked. I believe that it was and I wanted to get his confirmation.**
> **Inouye:**
> **May I most respectfully request that that matter not be touched upon at this stage. If we wish to get into this, I'm certain arrangements can be made for an executive session.**

Oliver North is sworn in before the House Foreign Affairs Committee on Capitol Hill in Washington. North cited his Fifth Amendment rights and refused to answer many of the committee's questions on the Iran-Contra arms deals. His mention of the REX-84 exercise was controversial.

Closely associated with REX-84 was Inslaw's Prosecutor's Management Information System (PROMIS) people-tracking software. For the sake of brevity, I won't delve into that. But suffice it to say, PROMIS was fairly simplistic old technology that has been supplanted by much more sophisticated database-search software and AI.

## Main Core

According to an article written for *Salon* magazine by Tim Shorrock in 2008, the NSA was the lead agency in developing a comprehensive personalities database called Main Core. This is the code name of a database containing personal and financial data of millions of U.S. citizens who are believed to be "threats to national security." The Main Core data is compiled by the NSA, FBI, CIA, and other agencies. It is believed that this database (or we can safely assume its successor, under a different name) is still active and growing.

The latest conjecture is that, in recent years, the Main Core successor program has moved into social media sites, such as Facebook, using them as veritable vacuum cleaners that sweep up personal information. By applying some sophisticated algorithms, the Main Core apparatus determines threat levels and builds extensive "contacts webs" of familial ties and social relationships in an attempt to piece together organizational structures—both formal and informal.

## Through a PRISM, Darkly

When taken in the light of the public revelations about the PRISM surveillance system that collates private communications on the Internet, the implications of Main Core now go well beyond just "list keeping." The presumed fusion of intelligence data that is going on has undoubtedly resulted in the creation of nested and prioritized lists of individuals to be tracked, questioned, detained, or have their travel restricted in a variety of crises.

Given the well-documented flaws in the FAA's No Fly List, the errors that can be assumed to exist in Main Core's successor databases could very well lead to the arrest of hundreds or even thousands of innocent people. Furthermore, if these databases were misused and applied for political reasons rather than legitimate counterterrorism investigations, it would open a Pandora's Box for tyrannical abuse.

Again, I discount the claims that there are "FEMA camps" that have already been specially constructed to keep teeming masses behind razor wire. To the best of my knowledge, all that FEMA has done thus far is to study and designate existing federal military reservations as potential detention facilities.

However, there are almost certainly some very lengthy round-up lists of immigrants with ties to terrorist organizations. That in itself is perfectly justifiable, given the nature of twenty-first-century transnational terrorism. However, I fear that the names of tens of thousands of outspoken native-born American citizens with high profiles have been listed in one or more databases as "persons of interest" by various agencies.

The fairly safe presumption of well-established "bad boy" lists that include native-born American citizens troubles me, on several levels. Perhaps my biggest concern is that any such lists represent the intent of federal officials to impose prior restraint or, worse yet, their intent to flag "pre-crime" tendencies of law-abiding American citizens. This sort of segregation and prioritization forms the basis of a future "shopping list" for tyrannical bully boys, in the event of a national crisis—a crisis that could be triggered by any number of events, including a natural disaster, a foreign or domestic terrorist attack, an unattributable or misattributed cyber attack, a banking/equities market panic, a rigged/contested election (or a suspension of elections), etc.

**8,000,000**

**THE ALLEGED NUMBER OF AMERICAN CITIZENS ON THE MAIN CORE LIST IN 2008.**

**RIGHT** Granada War Relocation Center was the official name of an internment camp for Japanese-Americans. During World War II, the Colorado barracks complex was surrounded by barbed-wire fencing.

## Black List

Of course, list-making such as this is by no means solely an American phenomenon. In some countries, lists such as these are relatively openly known, and their use common. They have helped to cause some of the greatest societal breakdowns of the twenty-first century: one of the early flashpoints leading to the outbreak of the ongoing Syrian civil war was the labeling as "terrorists" and rounding up of many prominent activists and human-rights campaigners in early 2011, long before any widespread violence had begun.

If you are politically active, no matter where you are, and an outspoken champion of personal liberty, then it is probably safe

Syrian demonstrators shout slogans and wave flags during a protest against Israel's military operation in the Gaza Strip on January 16, 2009.

to assume that you are already on at least a "watch list." You might also be on a cyber black list, targeting you for disinformation/discrediting campaigns, or perhaps for DDOS ping-attack hacking. It is no coincidence that DDOS ping floods are more frequently directed at politically outspoken blogs and websites. The key question is: what is your priority on those lists? If someone is a high priority for travel restrictions or detention, then their passport would be immediately flagged and they might not have the opportunity to leave the country via conventional means through normal passport controls.

The events in 2016 at the Malheur Wildlife Refuge in Harney County, Oregon, illustrated that quickly removing the leadership of any political organization through targeted arrests can render it impotent, or at least mute it in the court of public opinion.

Think this through: leaderless groups with redundant, secure means of communication are the wave of the future. Activist groups like the Black Panthers were the twentieth-century norm. Groups like Anonymous will be the twenty-first-century norm. But beware that the use of social media and nonsecure communications can be used by governments to build dossiers or even indictments against political organizers. Facebook was specifically mentioned several times in the recent Malheur indictments. It is best to avoid social media entirely, but if you must use it, then choose your words wisely!

## To Do List

As I have written before, it is important that all prepared families keep their passports updated. You should also have a plan B and a plan C. If you suspect that you are high on a priority list, then you might need a Von Trapp family (from the film *The Sound of Music*) "walk-out" escape plan. If you live near a coastline, then making the acquaintance of a deep-sea-trawler operator or a blue-water yachtsman might be something to put near the top of your "to-do" list.

**98%**

**FACEBOOK'S PERCENTAGE ACCURACY OF ITS FACIAL RECOGNITION SOFTWARE—BETTER THAN THE FBI'S.**

## Stay Vocal

I must urge you to not feel buffaloed into silence. If we allow ourselves to be frightened into political inactivity and "gray man" obscurity, then the tyrannical statist opponents of liberty will have won. Silence is tacit consent.

A friend of mine is fond of saying, "Never get on the bus..." and I consider that sage advice. Just consider the fact that there are as many unregistered firearms in this country as there are adult citizens. Armed Americans vastly outnumber those who might someday seek to enslave us. No attempt to round up a large segment of society will be successful if enough people refuse to register their guns, they keep their guns loaded, and they have the willingness to use them. We also have to commit ourselves to living through the angst of hiding any fellow citizens who come under persecution. This prayerful commitment must be made well in advance.

Keep in mind that the tech giants control the Internet, and that the Internet is now the linchpin of twenty-first-century public discourse. Cooperation between would-be tyrants in government with their counterparts in the tech industry could result in what I call outsourcing tyranny. This has already been demonstrated by Internet censorship, search keyword manipulation, defunding, and deplatforming. We can expect these trends to escalate in the 2020s and 2030s. Plan accordingly.

# CHAPTER 9
# BUGGING OUT OR STAYING PUT



**"But I will sing of thy power; yea, I will sing aloud of thy mercy in the morning: for thou hast been my defense and refuge in the day of my trouble. Unto thee, O my strength, will I sing: for God is my defense, and the God of my mercy."**

Psalm 59 (KJV)

Some potential contents of a bug-out bag. Your bag should be tailored to match the season, your locale, and your circumstances.

# A FUNDAMENTAL QUESTION

A fundamental question that you must ask yourself is this: in the midst of a disaster, shall I plan to stay, or shall I plan to go? If you can afford to own a rural retreat and can stock it in advance, then bugging out is the obvious choice. But for many folks with limited budgets, that is simply not within reach. Nor is relocating, when you are in a career with few opportunities in rural regions. Those folks need to stay where they can earn a good living.

Unless you have relatives who live in the country that are willing to shelter you and your family, then you are left in the position of bugging out with no certain destination. That is a difficult situation, because your supplies will be limited, and your range of travel may be limited to the fuel that you can carry on your vehicle—at least in "worst case" situations where fuel along your intended route is unobtainable or unaffordable. If you opt for this approach, then you will have to do a lot of research to find public lands (BLM or National Forest in the United States) in remote, lightly populated regions where you can camp for extended periods without fear of harassment. That will mean taking many scouting trips to find isolated primary and secondary destinations that are truly "out of the way" and that will be overlooked by the vast majority of refugees.

**In the midst of a disaster, shall I plan to stay, or shall I plan to go?**

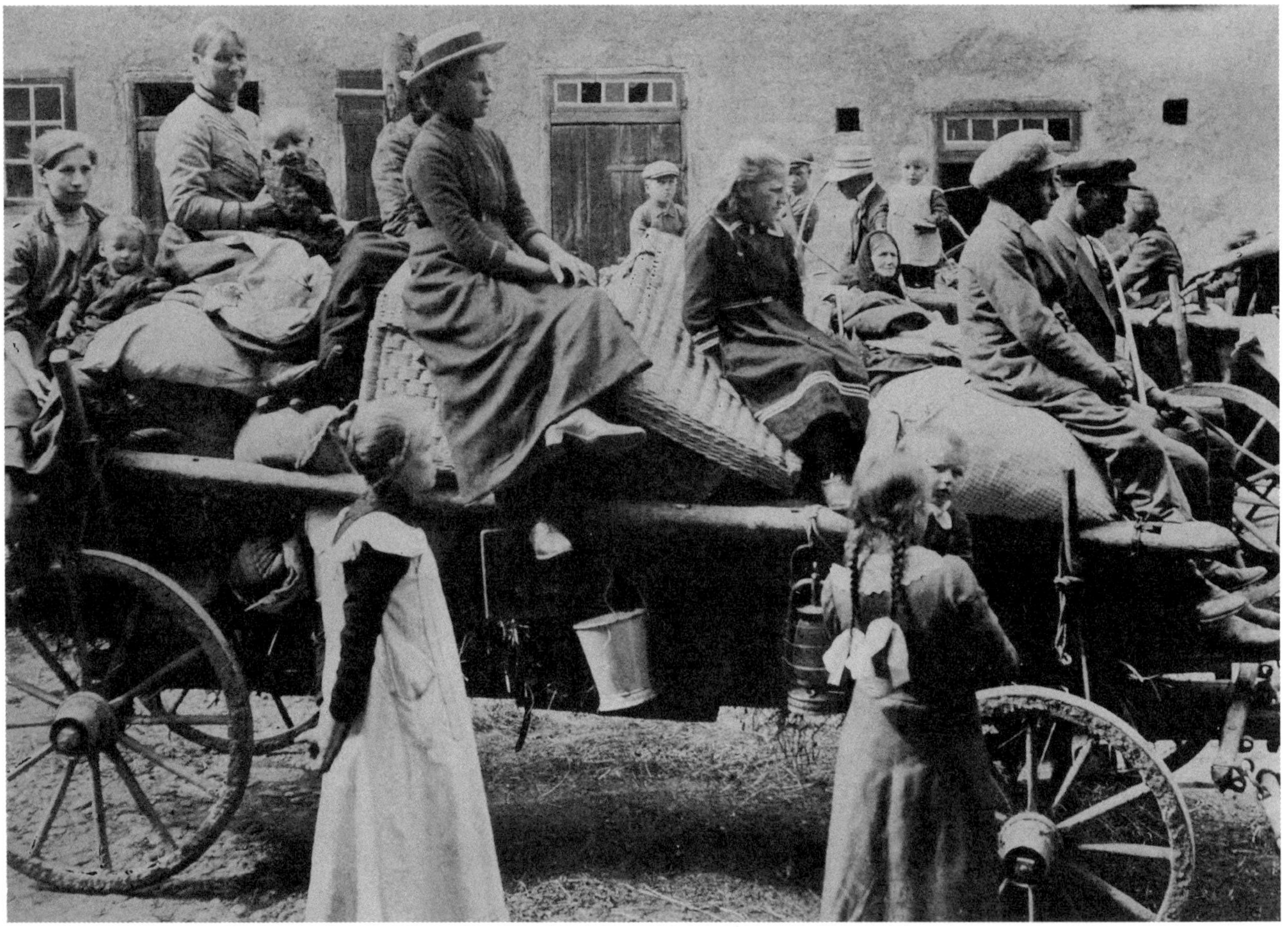

Refugees flee from advancing Russian troops in East Prussia in 1914.

# POPULATION DENSITY

I believe that no other factor will have as strong an actuarial correlation as population density. With some research using the 2000 United States census, I learned the following:

| Rank | State | Pop. Density per Sq. Mile |
|---|---|---|
| 1 | New Jersey | 1,185 |
| 2 | Rhode Island | 1,007 |
| 3 | Massachusetts | 835.2 |
| 4 | Connecticut | 737.7 |
| 5 | Maryland | 590.7 |
| 6 | Delaware | 459.6 |
| 7 | New York | 410.4 |
| 8 | Florida | 348.6 |
| 9 | Pennsylvania | 283.4 |
| 10 | Ohio | 281.7 |
| 11 | California | 238.9 |
| 12 | Illinois | 230.8 |
| 13 | Hawaii | 211.8 |
| 14 | Virginia | 202.1 |
| 15 | North Carolina | 195.8 |
| 16 | Indiana | 180.8 |
| 17 | Michigan | 174 |
| 18 | Georgia | 167.3 |
| 19 | Tennessee | 154 |
| 20 | South Carolina | 153.6 |
| 21 | New Hampshire | 146.8 |
| 22 | Kentucky | 109.2 |
| 23 | Wisconsin | 104.7 |
| 24 | Louisiana | 104.1 |
| 25 | Washington | 101.1 |
| 26 | Texas | 96.05 |
| 27 | Alabama | 94.19 |
| 28 | Missouri | 86.94 |
| 29 | West Virginia | 76.96 |
| 30 | Vermont | 67.65 |
| 31 | Minnesota | 66.62 |
| 32 | Mississippi | 63.26 |
| 33 | Arizona | 56.25 |
| 34 | Arkansas | 56 |
| 35 | Oklahoma | 54.63 |
| 36 | Iowa | 54.53 |
| 37 | Colorado | 48.49 |
| 38 | Maine | 43.04 |
| 39 | Oregon | 39.91 |
| 40 | Kansas | 34.87 |
| 41 | Utah | 33.65 |
| 42 | Nevada | 24.59 |
| 43 | Nebraska | 23.76 |
| 44 | Idaho | 18.94 |
| 45 | New Mexico | 16.97 |
| 46 | South Dakota | 10.73 |
| 47 | North Dakota | 9.75 |
| 48 | Montana | 6.79 |
| 49 | Wyoming | 5.80 |
| 50 | Alaska | 1.24 |

## Population Density of the Great Basin

The term "Great Basin" was coined by explorer John C. Frémont. It has also been called "America's Empty Quarter." This arid region stretches from southern Nevada to southern Idaho and southern Oregon. Its eastern limit is the Wasatch Front of Utah. Except in a few scattered cities, the population density of the Great Basin is incredibly low—averaging just a few people per square mile. This low density is best seen in the lights of U.S. satellite photo montages. Anyone who has not explored the area—especially via the smaller roads—can have no appreciation of just how incredibly sparse the population truly is.

I generally don't recommend the Great Basin for retreats. But for some—especially Californians—its proximity represents a tempting possibility. For anyone considering a rural retreat in the Great Basin, I'd suggest buying land that is far removed from cities, and that is way back on "a side road of a side road." That isolation, and a plentiful water source, will be your two key considerations. Once there, build your structures and photovoltaic systems with light discipline in mind, lest your retreat be spotted from a distance. An isolated valley that is not within line of sight of any settlement would be best. There are also a few isolated hamlets that have plentiful gravity-fed water—an example to explore is Unionville, Nevada.

Not every country around the world has the natural space that the United States has, but the principles noted above hold true. Make sure you research potential locations *before* any catastrophe.

A montage of satellite images showing North America at night, clearly delineating urban from rural areas.

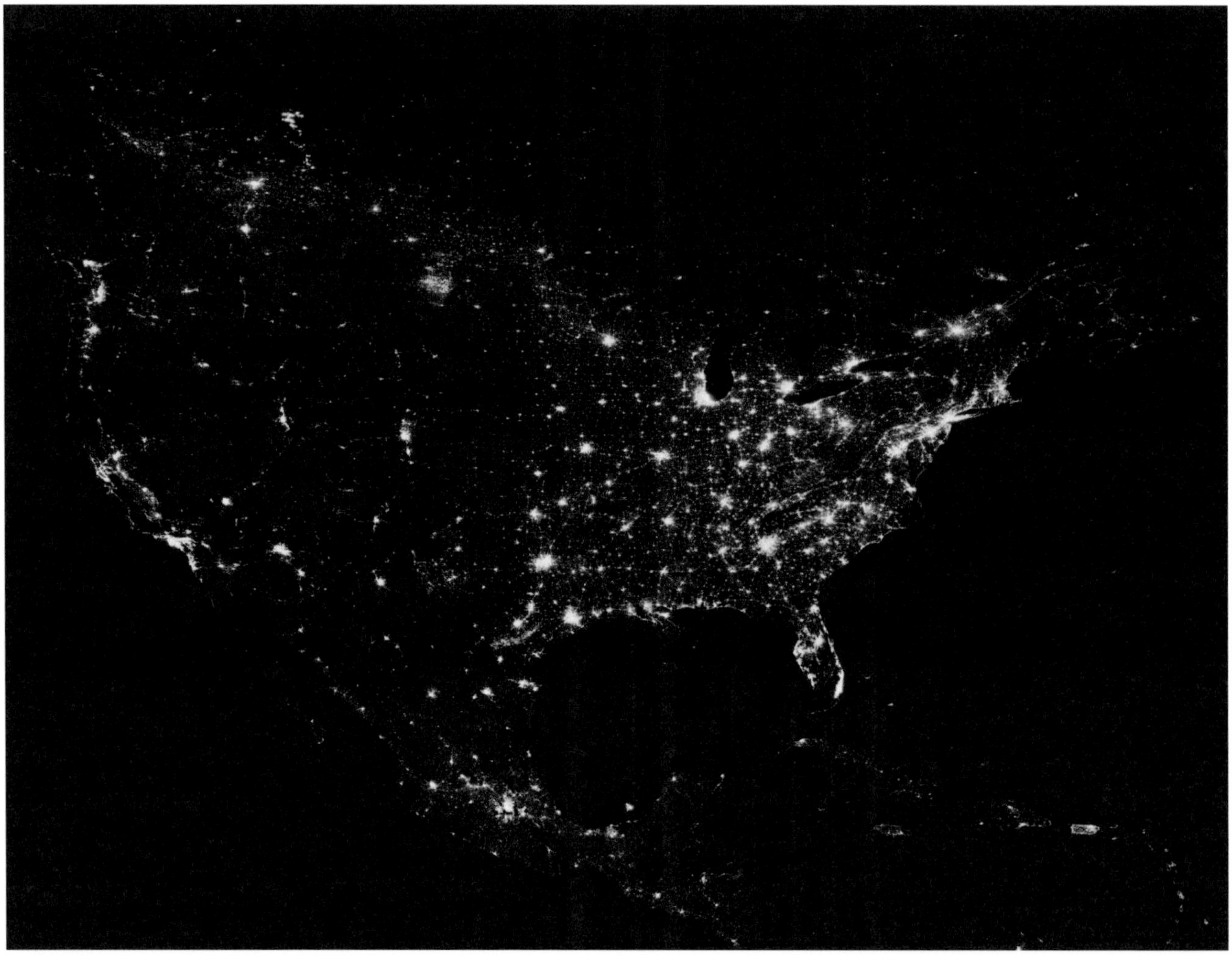

# ACTUARIAL THINKING

When assessing potential retreat locales, I recommend that you use the cold, dispassionate logic of an actuarial accountant. These are the specialists that calculate risks for insurance companies. Rather than dealing with subjective standards and emotions, they use data—such as crime statistics—to assign risk ratings.

If you use actuarial thinking rather than "feel-good" thinking, then you will have a longer, safer life. Forget things like "majestic views" and "charm" when looking at real-estate listings. Instead, examine factors like residential burglary rates, topsoil fertility figures, and both recorded well depths and gallons produced per minute.

# G.O.O.D. OPTIONS

It was my old friend "Scott T." who coined the acronym G.O.O.D., which stands for "Get Out Of Dodge." This is a reference to an oft-repeated line from *Gunsmoke*, the television series set in Dodge City, Kansas, in the 1870s: "I'll give you until dawn to get out of Dodge City."

Of course, knowing when to flee is of paramount importance. Fleeing too early or on a false alarm might mean losing a job. But fleeing just an hour too late could mean getting trapped in a traffic jam, without even the opportunity to back up and take a different route. Once you are boxed in and cars begin to run out of fuel, you will be stuck in a linear parking lot. That would mean abandoning the vital supplies that you have in your car, and perhaps continuing on foot. That would surely be a very vulnerable situation for you and your family!

Getting boxed in is one reason why I do not recommend towing a trailer for a G.O.O.D. evacuation. Your chances of being able to turn around are much smaller, and I must also mention that towing a trailer is also a symptom of poor planning. Any serious preppers will have the vast majority of their supplies already positioned at their intended retreat. If they need to carry more than what can fit in their personal car or truck, then they need to do more logistical shifting, in advance of any crisis!

The ideal G.O.O.D. vehicle would be a heavy-duty four-wheel drive pickup with a crash bumper mounted in the front, and a bicycle or motorcycle rack in the back. If you were to get irretrievably boxed in, then you would probably be able to revert to riding the bike or motorcycle. Either of those would be vastly superior to simply "bugging out" on foot. The average life expectancy of urban refugees on foot in a worst-case collapse could be measured in hours—not days.

A four-wheel-drive vehicle can provide great mobility. There is, of course, a trade-off between cargo capacity and fuel economy. Most preppers opt for a vehicle larger than a Jeep.

# HUNKERING DOWN: PRACTICALITIES

Undoubtedly, in a total societal collapse there will be some stay-put urbanites who survive on their wits, supplemented by plenty of providential fortune. The vast majority, though, would perish. I wouldn't want to play those odds. There are many drawbacks to a "hunker down" plan, any one of which could attract notice (to be followed soon after by a pack of goblins with a battering ram).

With the recognition that the majority of people reading this book are likely to be either urban or suburban and do not own a wilderness cabin or have "country cousins," I'll discuss a few complexities that must be fully considered if you opt to hunker down, right where you presently live, to wait out a population crash.

**Water**: Even with extreme conservation measures, you will need at least one gallon of water per day. That one gallon of water will provide just enough water for one adult for drinking and cooking—none for washing. If you run out of water before the rioting ends, then you will be forced to go out and forage for more, putting yourself at enormous risk. And, even then, you will have to treat the water that you find with chlorine, iodine (such as Polar Pure), or with a top-quality water filter such as a Katadyn Pocket water filter.

**Food**: For a six-month stay, you will need far more than just 50 pounds of rice! Work out a daily menu and budget for an honest six-month supply of food with a decent variety and sufficient caloric intake. Don't overlook vitamin supplements to make up for the lack of fresh fruit and vegetables. Sprouting is also a great option to provide vitamins and minerals, and it aids digestion. Speaking of digestion, depending on how your body reacts to the change in diet (to your storage food), you may need a natural laxative, such as bran, in your diet, or perhaps even a bulk laxative, such as Metamucil.

Protesters burn tires to stop riot police in Kiev, Ukraine, in January 2014.

**Sanitation**: Without water for flushing toilets, odds are that people in neighboring apartments will dump raw sewage out their windows, causing a public-health nightmare on the ground floor. Since you will not want to alert others to your presence by opening your window, and no doubt the apartment building's septic system stack will be clogged in short order, you will need to make plans to store your waste in your apartment. I suggest five-gallon buckets. A bucket-type camping toilet seat—a seat that attaches to a standard five- or six-gallon plastic pail—would be ideal. You should also get a large supply of powdered lime to cut down on the stench before each bucket is sealed. You must also consider the sheer number of storage containers required for six months of accumulated human waste. Perhaps a dozen 5-gallon buckets with tight-fitting O-ring-seal lids would be sufficient. Since you won't have water available for washing, you should also lay in a supply of diaper wipes.

**1 GALLON / ADULT / DAY**

**A MINIMUM AMOUNT OF WATER FOR YOU.**

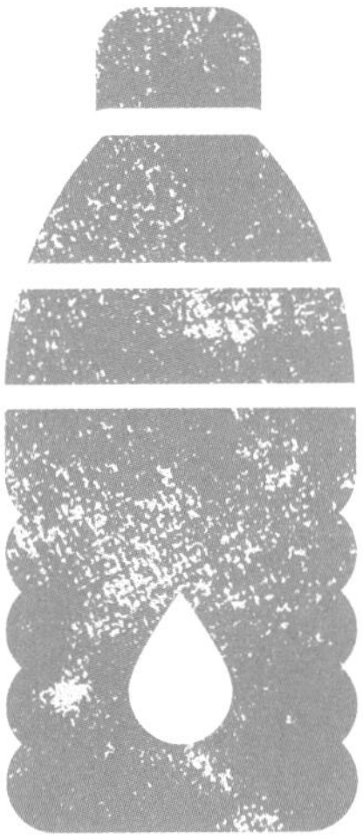

**Space heating**: In midwinter, you could freeze to death in your apartment without supplemental heat. As I discuss elsewhere, a small heater or just a few candles can keep the air temperature above freezing. This is addressed in more detail in chapter 4.

**Ventilation**: If you are going to use any source of open flame, you will need lots of additional ventilation. Asphyxiation from lack of oxygen or slow carbon monoxide (CO) poisoning are the grim alternatives. Unfortunately, in the circumstances that we are envisioning, the increased ventilation required to mitigate these hazards will be a security risk—as a conduit for the smell of food or fuel, as a source of light that can be seen from outside the apartment, and as an additional point of entry for robbers.

**Security**: The main point of entry for miscreants will probably be your apartment door. Depending on the age of your apartment, odds are that you have a traditional solid-core wooded door. In a situation in which law and order has evaporated, the intruders will be able to take their time and break through doors with fire axes, crowbars, and improvised battering rams. It is best to replace wooden apartment doors with steel ones.

Unless you own a condo rather than lease an apartment, approval for a door retrofit is unlikely. However, your apartment manager might approve of this if you pay for all the work yourself and you have it painted to match the existing doors. Merely bracing a wood door will not suffice. Furthermore, if you have an exterior window with a fire escape, or your apartment has a shared balcony, then those are also points of entry for the bad guys. How could you effectively barricade a large expanse of windows?

If you live in a ground-floor apartment or an older apartment with exterior metal fire escapes, then I recommend that you move as soon as possible to a third floor or higher apartment that is in a modern apartment building of concrete construction, preferably without balconies, with steel entry doors, and with interior fire-escape stairwells.

**Fire detection and contingency bug-out**: A battery-powered smoke detector is an absolute must. Even if you are careful with candles, lanterns, and cook stoves, your neighbors may not be. There is a considerable risk that your apartment building will catch fire, either intentionally or unintentionally. Therefore, you need to have a bug-out backpack ready to grab at a moment's notice. Although they are no proper substitute for a fireman's compressed-air breathing rig, a commercially made egress smoke hood or a military surplus gas mask might allow you to escape your building in time.

But even if you escape the smoke and flames, then where will that leave you? Outdoors, at an unplanned hour (day or night), in a hostile big city that is blacked out, with no safe means of escape. (This might prove far too reminiscent of the 1980s Kurt Russell movie *Escape from New York*.) By the time this happens, the mobs may not want just the contents of your backpack. They may be sizing you up for a meal!

**Fuel storage**: Bulk fuel storage has three problematic issues:

- As a safety issue (fire hazard);
- As a security issue (odors that could attract robbers); and
- As a legal issue (fire code or tenant contract restrictions).

I suspect that New York City's fire code, for example, would not allow you to have more than a week's worth of propane on hand, and completely prohibit keeping more than just one small container of kerosene or Coleman fuel. From the standpoint of both safety and minimizing detectable odors, propane is probably the best option. The odors of kerosene and chafing dish alcohol gel ("Sterno") are both quite discernable. Of course, consult both your local fire code and your apartment lease agreement before determining the maximum allowable quantity to keep on hand.

The odds are that there will be no limit on the number of candles that you can store. If

The destruction of the Warsaw ghetto by the German army, April 19, 1943.

that is the case, then lay in a large supply of unscented jar candles designed for long burn times (formulated to be high in stearic acid). I suggest the tall, clear-glass "devotional" candles manufactured in large numbers for the Catholic market. You can even heat individual servings of food over these if you construct a stand with a wide base out of stout wire. Watch for these candles at discount and close-out stores. We have found that the large adhesive labels slip off easily if you soak the jars in water for an hour. Since their burning time is approximately 24 hours, and since you might need two of them burning simultaneously for sufficient light and heat, that would necessitate laying in a supply of 360 candles! This assumes the worst case, with the outset of a crisis in October, and you having to hunker down for a full six months.

**Firefighting**: Buy at least two large multipurpose ("A-B-C") chemical fire extinguishers.

**Cooking odors**: In addition to the smell of fuel, cooking food will produce odors. I recommend that you store only foods with minimal spices. In situations where you are surrounded by starving people, just frying foods with grease or heating up a can of spicy chili con carne could be a death warrant.

**Noise discipline**: Just the sound of moving around in your apartment could reveal your presence. For some useful background, I recommend the best-selling memoir *The Pianist* by Władysław Szpilman. The book describes the harrowing experiences of a Jewish musician in hiding in Warsaw, Poland, during World War II. Following the 1943 Warsaw Ghetto uprising and forced deportation, Szpilman spent many months locked in a Warsaw apartment, receiving just a few parcels of food from some gentile friends. In his situation, the power and water utilities were still operating most of the time, but he suffered from slow starvation and lived in absolute fear of making any noise. His survival absolutely defied the odds. There was also an excellent 2002 movie based on Szpilman's book, but the memoir provides greater detail than the film.

**Light discipline**: If you have any source of light in your apartment, it could reveal your presence. In an extended power blackout, it will become obvious to looters within a couple of weeks who has lanterns or large supplies of candles and/or flashlight batteries. (Everyone else will run out within a few weeks.) And I predict that it will be the apartments with lights that will be deemed the ones worth robbing. So, if you have a light source, you must systematically black out all of your windows. Sadly, these efforts will be in direct conflict with your need for ventilation for your heating and/or cooking—trade-offs will need to be made.

**A warm bed**: With the aforementioned restrictions on fuel storage, heating your apartment for more than just a few days will probably be impossible. Buy an expedition-quality sleeping bag—preferably a two-bag system such as a Wiggy's brand FTRSS. Under the circumstances, don't attempt to heat your entire apartment. Instead, construct a small room-within-a-room (perhaps under a large dining-room table with corner legs, or by setting up a camping tent inside your apartment to hoard heat). Even if the rest of the apartment drops to 25 or 30 degrees Fahrenheit, your body heat alone will keep your demi-room in the 40s. Burning just one candle or a kerosene lantern will raise the temperature another 5 or 10 degrees. But, of course, you will need to take appropriate fire-safety and ventilation precautions. For the greatest efficiency at retaining heat, your demi-room should be draped with two layers of Mylar space blankets. There is additional detail on this topic in chapter 4, where I discussed buying or constructing box beds.

**Exercise**: You will need to maintain muscle tone while you are hunkered down. Get some quiet exercise equipment, such as a pull-up bar and some large elastic straps. Perhaps, if your budget allows in the future, also purchase or construct your own quiet stationary bicycle-powered generator. This would provide both exercise and battery charging.

**Sanity**: Hunkering down solo in silence for six months would be a supreme challenge, both physically and mentally. Assuming that you can somehow tackle all of the aforementioned problems, you also need to plan to stay sane. So have lots of reading material on hand.

A homemade stationary bike DC generator.

CHAPTER 10

# PLAN A OR PLAN B?

Priorities

For the Duration

Pulling Through

"I do love a good tree. There it stands so strong and sturdy, and yet so beautiful, a very type of the best sort of man. How proudly it lifts its bare head to the winter storms, and with what a full heart it rejoices when the spring has come again! How grand its voice is, too, when it talks with the wind: a thousand Aeolian harps cannot equal the beauty of the sighing of a great tree in leaf. All day it points to the sunshine and all night to the stars, and thus passionless, and yet full of life, it endures through the centuries, come storm, come shine, drawing its sustenance from the cool bosom of its mother earth, and as the slow years roll by, learning the great mysteries of growth and of decay. And so on and on through generations, outliving individuals, customs, dynasties—all save the landscape it adorns and human nature—till the appointed day when the wind wins the long battle and rejoices over a reclaimed space, or decay puts the last stroke to his fungus-fingered work. Ah, one should always think twice before one cuts down a tree!"

*Allan Quatermain* by H. Rider Haggard

A traditional red Swedish cottage house, near Uppsala, Sweden. It has been retrofitted with modern photovoltaic (PV) power panels.

# PRIORITIES

PV power costs have plummeted in recent years. I recommend standalone systems, rather than grid-tied systems.

As societal disintegration increases, you will surely be faced with some dire circumstances and some tough decisions. Knowing who you can trust will be difficult. And with no end in sight, knowing how much of your stored food and fuel you can spare for charity may be even more difficult. As a Christian, I approach all such decisions by keeping faith in God's word in the Bible, and in regular prayer for God's guidance and protection. I've also resolved to "give until it hurts." Charity is my Christian duty. But as a man with a family, I recognize that the biblical law of Tzedakah begins with providing for my own immediate family. I will always retain a substantial quantity of storage food and gardening seed for my own family's needs. Everyone must make their own decisions.

To reiterate what has been said before, your top priorities in family preparedness should be:

**A.** Water (see chapter 3)
**B.** Food (see chapter 5)
**C.** Self-defense (see chapter 6)
**D.** Heating (see chapter 4)
**E.** Communications (see chapter 7)
**F.** Power

## Power

Here, I would like to discuss alternative power systems in greater detail. For true self-sufficiency, I am not a proponent of home backup AC generators. They are noisy, high maintenance, and guzzle an alarming quantity of fuel very quickly. I instead advocate for installing a true off-grid power system—either photovoltaic (PV) or micro-hydro. Only hillside properties with a year-round creek, large spring, or artesian well are suitable for micro-hydro. But the vast majority of properties are quite well suited

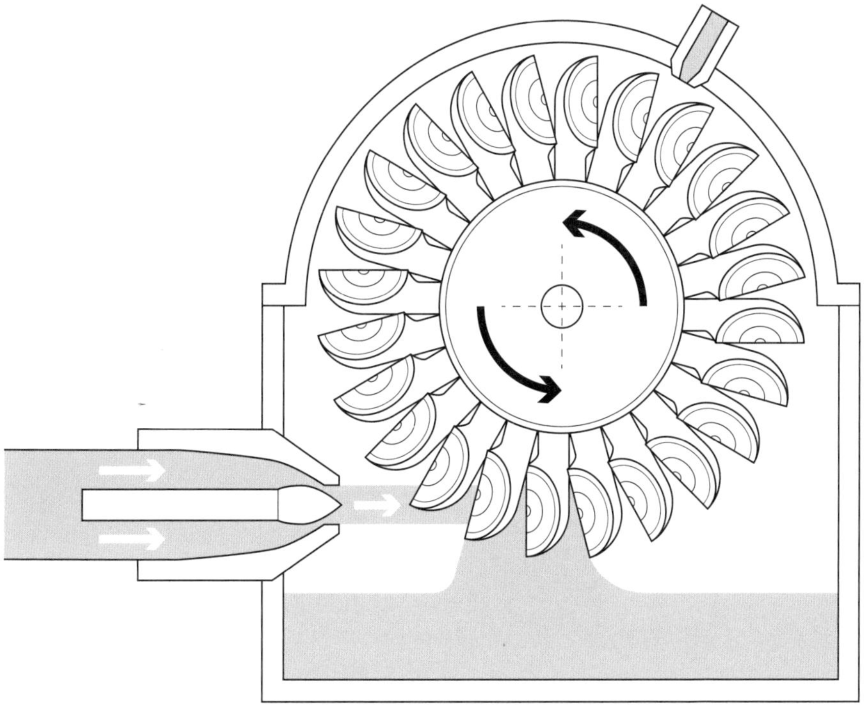

Diagram of the "wet side" of a Pelton Wheel micro-hydro power system.

to installing a PV system. The only exceptions would be for homes that are north of 60 degrees latitude or that are situated on a northern-facing ridge with little or no direct solar exposure.

I am also not a proponent of wind generators. This is because the cost of PV panels has dropped dramatically in the past 15 years. PV panels are low cost (per watt produced) and also nearly maintenance free—aside from a bit of glass cleaner and lubricants for passive trackers. In contrast, wind generators are both high cost per watt, and high maintenance. Furthermore, I wouldn't want to take the risk of climbing a wind-generator tower in the midst of a crisis when emergency medical services are sparse. PV power makes much more sense!

### First things first: home power prerequisites

One important foundation of a cost-effective, sustainable home-energy system is energy efficiency and conservation. The savings one can realize by applying the economies of ideas like these can make the difference between a viable system for your budget and/or location... or a perceived "no go" conclusion given current rates of energy consumption. It does require a bit of discipline, research, and care in analyzing current and proposed future energy usage, but it can pay off handsomely if, for example, you end up with a system for half the usual cost (or even less) by judicious selection of appliances, other electrical loads, and lifestyle choices. It's always a good idea to add in some "wiggle room" to account for extended periods without sun (solar), wind, and/or stream flow (micro-hydro), but overdesigning a system beyond this can be a waste of your financial resources.

This is an ideal time for a reminder that a total do-it-yourself (DIY) approach is not advised. While renewable energy systems have evolved tremendously over the past few decades, and integrated (mostly "turnkey") systems are much farther away from rocket science and closer to "appliance" status, there are still way too many variables and considerations to advise doing it all by yourself. Experienced renewable-energy (RE) system designers and installers serve a critically important role to help home-energy system owners avoid many other common design mistakes, safety pitfalls, and needless expenditures. It would be an expensive, time-consuming, and even potentially dangerous choice to not work closely with a local RE professional.

# 17%

**OF THE TOTAL ENERGY USED IN THE U.S. IN 2018 WAS RENEWABLE.**

While it might seem more costly than a stubbornly pure-DIY approach, buying a battery bank twice—before its typical life span is up—because of poor design or incorrect installation is far more expensive. Rely on the experience of a local professional; you'll learn more, save more, and benefit from their experience while helping to strengthen the RE industry. If you haven't already done an energy conservation audit, find a local RE professional and ask what they recommend as early in the design phase as possible. Sizing your battery system based on a realistic assessment of both sources and loads will make your project viable and economical. Ask around locally and online among neighbors, nearby friends, etc., to find an RE installer with the right expertise, credentials, and references to serve your needs.

A battery bank of 2V batteries charged from a PV panel power system.

## Battery Basics

Common to all off-grid systems that use batteries to store energy—from sun, wind, water, or whatever source (stationary bicycle generators, anyone?)—are a few key ideas and definitions. You might need to refer to a glossary of fundamental battery terms here. Batteries consist of one or more internal compartments, called cells, in a given enclosure, and each cell—depending on the chemistry and technology—has a typical nominal voltage. For example, a lead-acid cell produces about 2 volts, so a 12-volt (12V) battery internally has six cells wired in series, so that their voltages add up to 12V.

Batteries are typically wired in series, as is done, for example, in a typical flashlight, with the positive terminal of one battery connected to the negative terminal of the next in a daisy-chain fashion. This provides higher voltages to match inverters and loads, since most inverters designed for home usage have inputs of 12 or 24 volts. A typical system with 6V batteries will require four (or multiples of four) batteries wired together to provide the nominal 24-volt DC input that an inverter might require.

To provide more power for longer periods of time, strings of series-wired batteries can be wired in parallel, thus extending the time the system can keep loads powered during times when no new source of power (sun, wind, or water-generated electricity) is present. The practical limit is three parallel strings in a system, due to slight voltage imbalances between series strings that cause uneven performance and can cause premature system failure. The size of the battery bank, inverter, and energy sources (PV panels, wind generators, and/or water

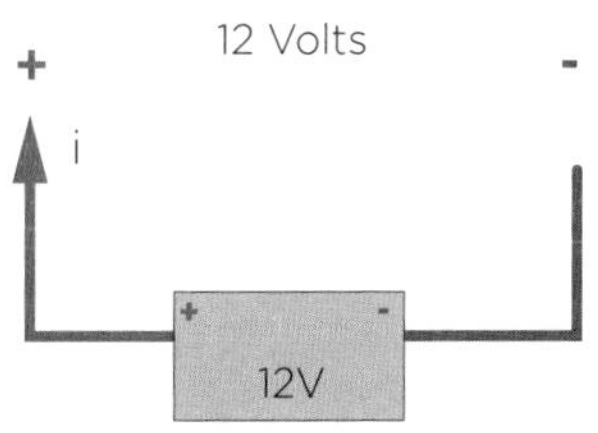


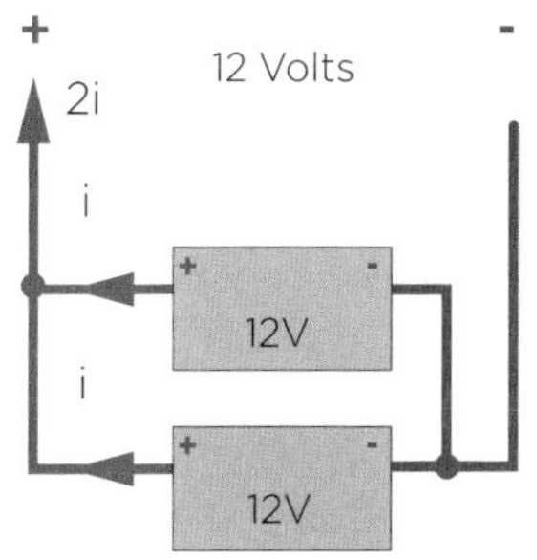


Parallel

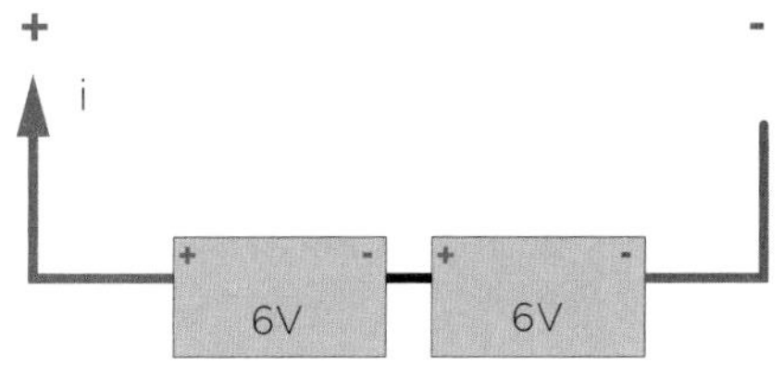


Series

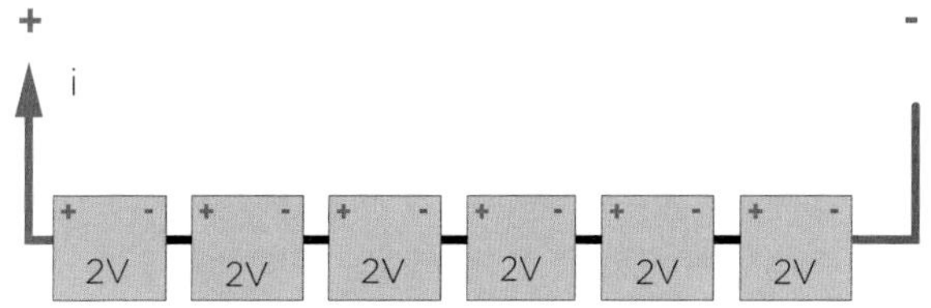


Series

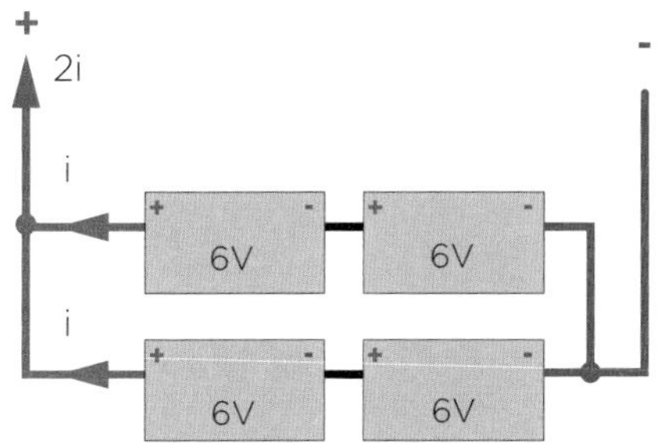


Series/Parallel

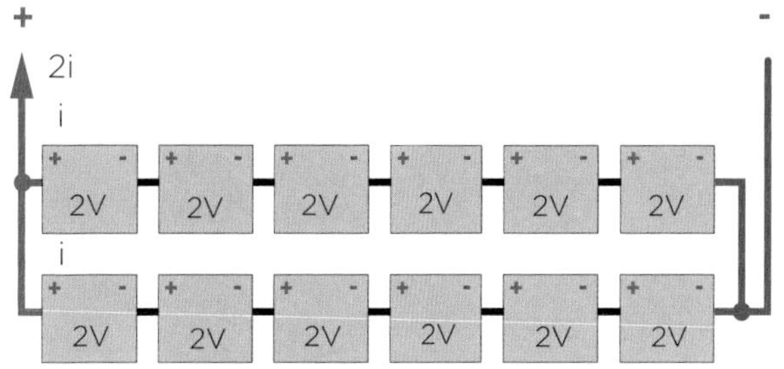


Series/Parallel

turbines) are all carefully matched and configured to provide optimum performance, with particular emphasis on optimizing the useful life of the battery system.

To get the most life out of a battery—and they all eventually do need replacement, just like any other battery—it is best to use identical new batteries made by the same manufacturer, using the same process, materials, chemistry, etc. You should even ask if it's possible to get all identical batteries with the same date code, if they are available. This tends to minimize uneven voltages and countercurrents (due to those uneven voltages) internal to the batteries that work against optimum efficiency and battery life. Using similar logic to replacing all tires on a car at the same time, replacing all the batteries in a system at once is the best way to get more "mileage" out of a home-power battery bank.

Battery capacity generally depends on the volume of the battery, so larger batteries of the same technology tend to have greater capacity in amp-hours (Ah), a term for specifying for how long a battery can supply that amount of current for an hour at the rated voltage. As an example, a 200 Ah battery delivers 10 amps for 20 hours. The generally accepted time rating for most manufacturers is 20 hours. A more important specification is the kilowatt-hour (kWh) capacity of a bank of batteries; multiply the nominal voltage of the bank by the Ah rating and then divide by 1,000 to get the kWh figure (e.g., 24V x 200Ah = 4,800Wh, then 4,800Wh / 1000 = 4.8kWh).

Two other terms that describe a battery's state are state of charge (SOC) and depth of discharge (DOD). These provide numbers, usually as a percentage, of how charged or discharged a battery bank or cell is at any given time. The sum of SOC and DOD is always 100 percent. For example, a system that is almost fully charged might have a 98 percent SOC and a 2 percent DOD.

There is no direct way to measure a battery's SOC, but there are several ways to indirectly get a useful approximation, each with its own level of accuracy. One way is measuring the voltage and comparing it to a standardized chart. This is the least accurate method, but also one of the least expensive, since it only involves an inexpensive digital meter, and often is part of an integrated inverter-battery system. One other method of estimating battery SOC is measuring the density or specific gravity of the electrolyte. (This involves accessing the sulfuric acid in the battery, which is quite caustic, so safety precautions are essential.) This is the most accurate test, yet it is only applicable to flooded batteries. It involves measuring the cell's electrolyte density with a battery hydrometer. Electrolyte density is lower when batteries are discharged and higher as the cells are charged. Chemical reactions in the battery affect the electrolyte's density at a predictable constant rate that affords a good indication of the SOC. An amp-hour meter can also accurately gauge the SOC. Amp-hour meters track all power going in and out of the battery over time. Thus, comparing flow rates determines the SOC.

## Battery Technology

Some of the newest battery technology tends to find practical application first in lightweight portable devices of all sorts, often in transportation (e.g., lithium iron phosphate batteries for electric vehicles). In even smaller devices, using exotic materials and processes in tiny amounts isn't a major concern, while extending useful charge, reducing weight, and optimizing portability are huge issues. However, on the other end of the size spectrum, battery technology for home-power applications tends to evolve more slowly over time, due to the vastly different concerns. Unlike cell phones, tablets, etc., a home-battery system doesn't need portability, small size, or weight. It does, on the other hand, require massive energy reserves. For that reason, the de facto battery standard for cost-effective domestic alternative/remote-energy systems is still the tried-and-true lead-acid technology. Lead-acid batteries are heavy, but relatively inexpensive both to manufacture and maintain. Timeframes between installations and replacements of well-maintained lead-acid systems are typically measured in years, so transportation and installation costs, while high compared to their small counterparts in modern electronic gizmos, are infrequent, and small compared to the system life.

Within the lead-acid battery category, there are a few variations. The most important one, as early adopters two or three decades ago discovered, is the difference between deep-cycle (e.g., those historically used on forklifts or other applications where it was expected that the batteries would use up a significant portion of their capacity before being recharged) and shallow-cycle batteries like a conventional car battery, which is designed to be charged almost continuously by an alternator. The thin plates within a car battery allow for a quick high-current surge during ignition, but, as many of us have learned, leaving headlights on without the alternator "topping off" the charge can result in a dead battery overnight. It doesn't take too many full discharges of a shallow-cycle system like that to require a new car battery. Even deep-cycle batteries should not be overly discharged. Too many discharges beyond 50 percent will decrease battery life.

2,000 amp-hours generated for UPS backup power from two banks of 2V batteries cabled in series.

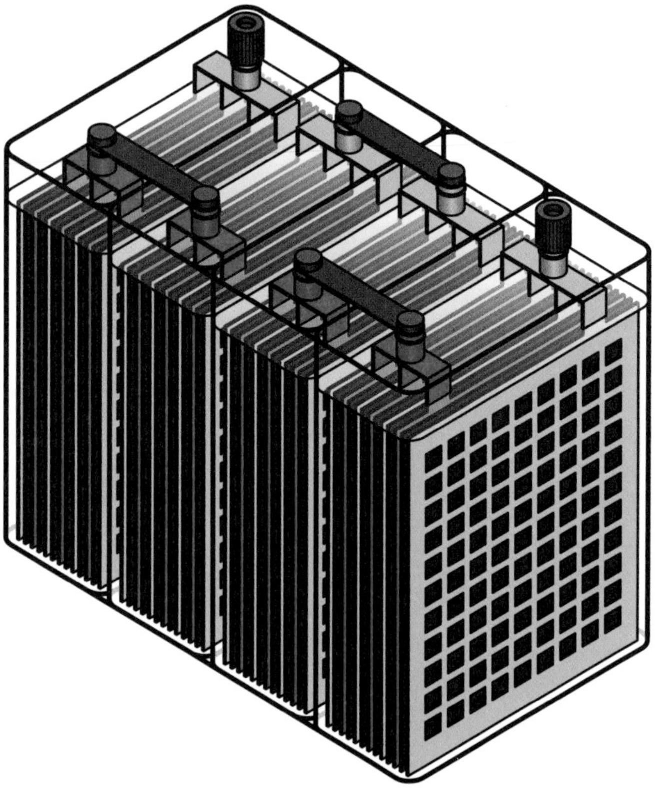

Diagram of a typical lead-acid marine or vehicle battery.

The thick plates of a deep-cycle battery, on the other hand, are designed to deplete a significant portion (but not all) of the available current with hundreds of deep discharges, but not too many significant high-current surges. The heavy plates and bulky design of deep-cycle batteries allow for these deep discharges over extended periods, thus affording an effective home-energy battery solution during multiple consecutive cloudy or windless days—assuming judicious conservation is in effect during these times (another example of how conservation measures resulting in an energy-mindful lifestyle and component choices pay off handsomely). Most deep-cycle batteries use a "flooded" or "wet" lead-acid design, meaning that their internal structure has sulfuric acid (liquid) and a water electrolyte into which submerged lead plates are suspended. Thick plates also maximize the lifespan of a battery that can be decreased by "positive grid corrosion," where the positive lead plate slowly wears away. Although plate thickness isn't the sole determining factor resulting in longer lifespan, it is perhaps the most critical variable, assuming batteries are properly maintained and used.

Another battery technology option to consider is sealed (developed in the 1970s) versus unsealed (relatively unchanged since their invention 1859 by French physicist Gaston Planté). For those who are interested, here is a little bit more on the history of batteries. Sealed batteries, also known as valve-regulated lead-acid (VRLA) cells, typically vent less gas and don't require regular addition of water. This can be a decided advantage for cabins and locations where less-than-full-time occupancy and/ or extended vacations are a concern. Sealed batteries use either a gel electrolyte to surround the lead plates or a fiberglass mat (such as an absorbed glass mat) to contain the electrolyte. When a gel electrolyte replaces a liquid, in some situations it can allow the battery to be used in different positions without leakage, although that's often not an issue, since once batteries are installed in home-power systems, they usually stay put for many years. There are varying opinions whether the pros outweigh the cons in these two types (gel or mat) of sealed batteries. Either will typically decrease the routine battery maintenance needed, since unsealed lead-acid cells require the periodic addition of distilled water and other maintenance. Because slow out-gassing depletes the electrolyte and exposes the lead plates above liquid levels—an unacceptable battery maintenance practice—it decreases battery life far more quickly than a carefully maintained battery.

When comparing sealed versus unsealed lead-acid batteries, there are considerations favoring both that generally hold true. Unsealed batteries usually have the longest life and the lowest cost per amp-hour of any of the other choices. These include the newer technologies, often for reasons of economies of scale and market saturation. The downside of unsealed battery systems is that they do require regular maintenance: watering, equalizing charges, and keeping their terminals clean.

## Other Battery Terms and Specifications

One of the most important battery specifications is the C-rate, which quantifies discharge rates and charge rates. To calculate the C-rate value, divide the cell's capacity by the number of hours it takes to either fully charge or discharge it. As an example, a 220 Ah capacity battery, discharged at 22 amps, is being discharged at a C/10 rate (220/22 = 10). If the same battery is charged back up by an 11-amp PV system, the charge rate is C/20 = (220/11 = 20).

The number of days of autonomy is another important specification for a renewable-energy system. An effective design ensures that the typical year-round daily charging from all available sources (wind, PV, hydro, generator, etc.) exceeds the typical daily discharging from all loads. A primary requirement for any viable system design is adequate storage between charging periods, including extended days without significant wind, sun or hydro power, as well as nighttime lulls in input power. The days of autonomy figure is a rating that gives the theoretical number of days the system will provide power for the average daily load without any new power input. This is also a useful number when estimating time for replacing major source components if there is a power-input subsystem failure.

Of course, each system is different and the selection and number of batteries, just as the sizing and number of PV panels, wind turbines, etc., will vary with each situation and location. Again, consult a local professional before making any cash outlays.

**100 GIGAWATTS** was generated by wind turbines in the U.S. in 2019.

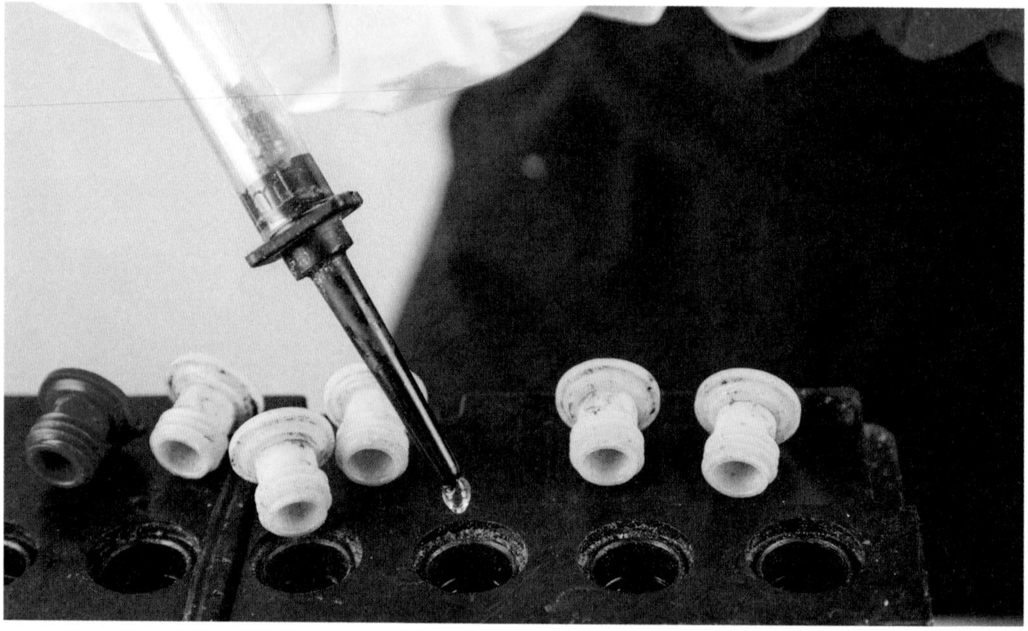

Lead-acid batteries require regular maintenance—with safety precautions for electric shock, shorting (sparks/explosions), and skin exposure to sulfuric acid.

## Best Practice for Storage and Access

Keep your batteries in a safe, easy-to-access spot. Most batteries require enclosures that are lockable, sealed, insulated, and vented to the outdoors. Sloped box covers keep things from being piled on top, making the battery system safer and more accessible. Clear viewing windows allow for easy inspection. A removable side of the battery box eases replacement.

Since batteries store considerable zapping power and contain acid and other toxic elements like lead, they are dangerous. They should be accessible only to mature family members trained in proper safety protocols. Keep battery boxes locked but accessible when they need maintenance. Make sure caps and terminals on flooded battery cells are easily reachable. Well-thought-out enclosure layout—ideally making all batteries easy to reach without having to lean over one battery to reach another—reduces the chance of accidental shorting, which could reduce the life span of both batteries and their owners.

In addition to the obvious overall environmental factors like protection from the elements, always consider the average and extreme temperatures (both daily and annual) of the battery housing, which should usually be a very short distance from the inverter to minimize power losses and inefficiency. Temperature extremes and averages affect battery capacity and are a crucial part of the design process. Keep batteries out of direct sunlight to avoid uneven heating of individual batteries. This could shorten life spans due to uneven currents. Battery manufacturers typically rate capacities at 77°F; name-plate-rated capacity decreases at lower temperatures and increases at higher temperatures.

## Battery Interconnections

Solid-metal bus bars come with some industrial batteries for making the series and parallel interconnections. However, most battery banks need cables for these interbattery connections, as well as cables to connect to an inverter or DC load center. Size battery cables big enough to handle their maximum rated continuous current. Protect them with fuses or circuit breakers rated for high amp-interrupt current. Determine cable size from inverter specifications and/or any DC loads that the battery bank powers directly—2/0 or 4/0 cable is common for residential-sized systems.

Don't use welding cable! This used to be a common practice for batteries, since listed cable was not available and welding cable was relatively inexpensive, flexible, and could handle ample current. However, welding cable is not designed for this application and is not listed by the National Electrical Code for battery-system use. Do use flexible, UL-listed, NEC-approved battery cable—now readily available—for all battery wiring. If you are hiring a consultant—highly recommended, regardless of your level of proficiency and expertise, even if only to double-check your work—you can ensure that your entire system, not just the battery subsystem, is safe, meets all applicable building and regulatory codes, and is the most cost-effective, energy-efficient, and long-lasting design possible.

## Wiring Best Practice

Equal charging and discharging across all cells keeps batteries healthy; resistance differences within a battery bank can lead to premature failure. Poor lug crimps, loose terminal connections, unequal parallel cable lengths, and too small a wire gauge can all affect the equal treatment of cells, thereby shortening battery and system life span.

It is important to minimize the number of parallel connections and ensure their lengths are equal. When wiring parallel strings, always make series connections first. Then parallel the positive ends of the strings, and finally connect the negative terminals. Connect inverter cables to opposite corners of the battery bank to keep electrical paths between strings as equal in length as possible.

## Ongoing Battery Maintenance and Operation

In the excellent *Home Power Magazine* article titled "Managing Your Batteries," author Dan Fink says:

> **"Take the initial cost of your battery bank, and divide by the number of years until it needs replacement. That's your annual 'battery bill.' If you can stretch battery life to eight or ten years, the bill is minimal. If you ruin them in a year, that's a big bill, and you probably were not paying much attention to them. Overcharging, undercharging, and high and low temperatures can all count as 'abuse.'"**

As indicated, careful maintenance of batteries can make a huge difference in their life span, and thus the effective prorated cost of this highly variable component in the overall renewable-energy system.

Before doing battery maintenance, remember that you're dealing with strong acid. First put on protective eyewear, rubber gloves, old clothes, and/or a protective apron. As noted above, monitoring the SOC is not a simple process, but there are viable approaches, such as using temperature-compensated hydrometers (the most accurate but most complicated method). Other methods, best used in combination with hydrometer readings, are voltage measurements taken after a rest period (with no incoming or outgoing currents for two hours to allow the electrolyte to stabilize), and coulomb counting, which calculates Ah by measuring accumulated charge or discharge amounts, typically by use of highly accurate shunts (precisely chosen low-resistance elements in a circuit whose purpose is to measure current with sensitive volt meters). Meter choices include internal meters (built into modern inverters), system-integrated meters (for networked systems), and stand-alone meters. Many monitoring systems are integrated with computer interfaces for logging and analysis to automate some of the tedious aspect.

This section has just been a general guide, and doesn't cover all aspects of setting up an off-grid power system by any means. But, if nothing else, it has shown how thoroughly you will need to research the whole subject.

## Wildfires

If you have a rural retreat, being prepared for wildfires is important, particularly in dry climates such as the western United States or Australia.

The goal is to prevent a forest fire from reaching your house by reducing the amount of fuel for a fire near your home. When forest fires lack fuel, crown fires drop down a level to ground fires. Ground fires burn slower and are easier to contain. My recommended defensive space plan divides the area around your house into three zones.

**Zone one:** Up to 15 feet all around your home. It is recommended that you have no trees and no large shrubs in this zone if you live in an area prone to wildfires. If you do have landscaping close to your house, then it should be a plant species that is not readily combustible. Succulent groundcover plants are recommended. Decorative rocks would be better yet. The idea is that there should be no organic fuel within 15 feet of your home.

**Zone two**: 15 to 75+ feet around your home. In this area, it is recommended that trees are spaced so that there is a 10-foot space between the outermost edges of the branches of each tree. This means large trees might need to be spaced 30 or 40 feet between the trunks of the trees. The purpose of this is so that a crown fire would not be able to jump from crown to crown within your defensive space. You do not want to give a ground fire a "ladder" to climb into the tops of your trees, so it is recommended that you remove all the limbs that are within 10 feet of the ground. You should also not allow thick underbrush to

The fire protection zones surrounding a house.

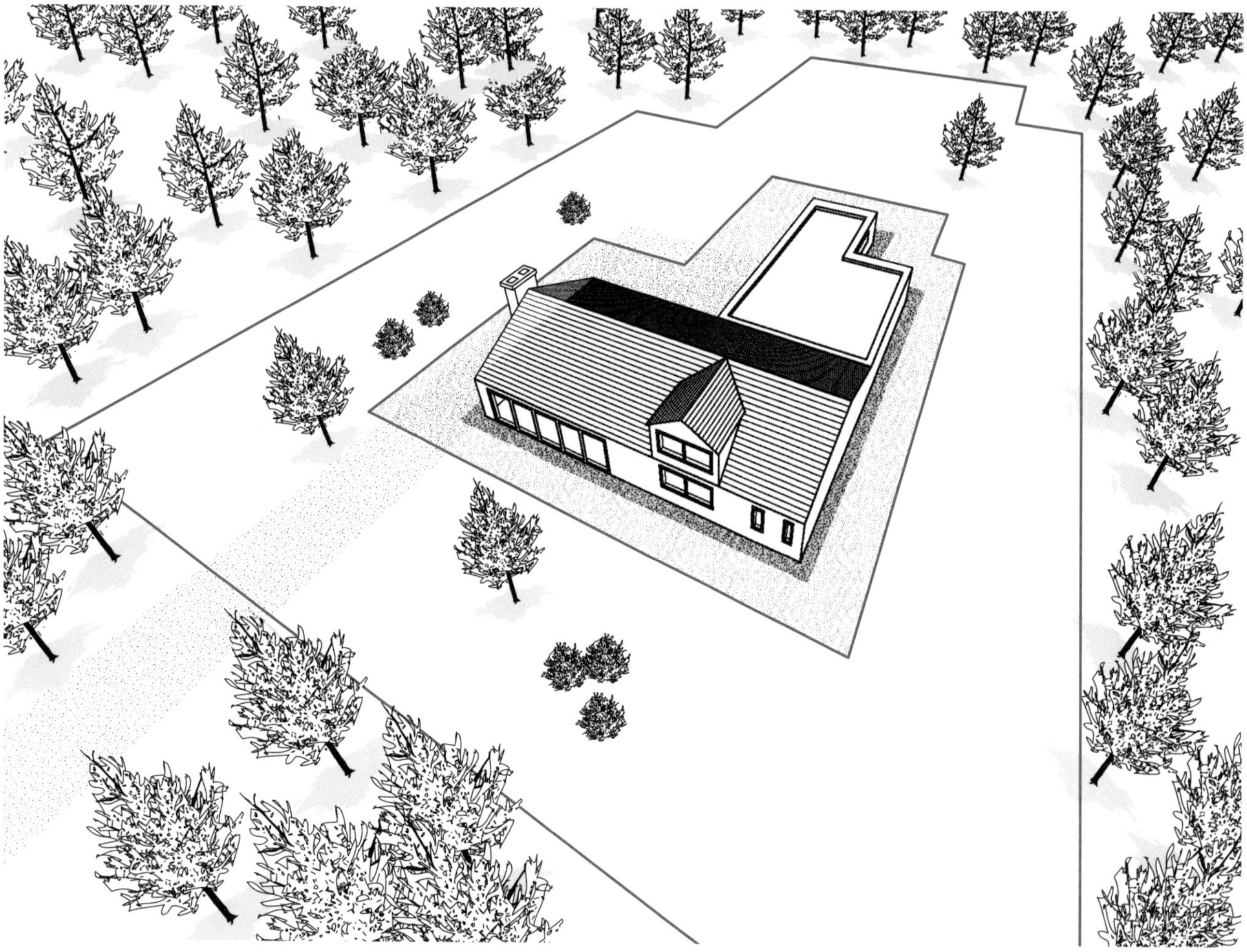

grow around your trees that could feed a fire and also serve as a ladder. Note that if your house is on a hillside, then zone two might be as far as 125 feet downhill.

**Zone three**: From the outer edge of zone two to the edge of your property. (Zone three is described by one web page as "an area of traditional forest management and is of no particular size. It extends from the edge of your defensible space to your property boundaries.")

By the time you have created a proper defensive space around your home, the landscaping is not going to look too natural, I'm afraid. It will be much more like a town park than a natural habitat. But that is a sacrifice you must be willing to make in order to defend your home against forest fires.

**8.8 MILLION ACRES**

**THE TOTAL AREA BURNED BY WILDFIRES IN THE U.S. IN 2018.**

A house threatened by the Holy Fire in California in 2018.

# FOR THE DURATION

## The more that you can do now, to plan for such times, the better.

Remember that your preparations will need to carry you and your family through the duration of a crisis. And in the case of a deep economic depression, that could mean a period of up to a decade. As your supplies start to run out, you will have to increasingly rely on barter and the food that you grow, or livestock that you raise.

The more than you can do now to plan for such times, the better. By stockpiling now, you will position yourself to weather any storm. Be prepared to survive a collapse for the duration. You owe it to your children.

**BELOW** A variety of goods that would be useful to stockpile to be used as barter.

**MEAL, READY-TO-EAT**

**CANNED GOODS**

**BAGS OF RICE**

# PULLING THROUGH

Successfully pulling through any future disaster will take plenty of planning, faith, and a bit of luck. The fact that you have read though this book to this point illustrates that you have a willingness to learn, and a desire to provide for your family. So you've already taken the first step. Now, you just need to carry through, reprioritize your budget, and prepare. The phrase "beans, bullets and Band-Aids" should be part of your psyche. So should be the phrase "two is one, and one is none." It is that mindset that will greatly increase your chances of survival.

The future is a mystery. The only way to ensure your family's safety is to prepare for the worst case now.

**"BEANS, BULLETS, AND BAND-AIDS"**

# CHAPTER 11
# THE YEAR AFTER

- **Inevitabilities**
- **Emigration?**
- **Prayer**

"Our government... teaches the whole people by its example. If the government becomes the lawbreaker, it breeds contempt for law; it invites every man to become a law unto himself; it invites anarchy."

*Louis Brandeis*

A demonstrator throws a tear-gas canister back at riot police during clashes in Caracas, Venezuela, on January 22, 2018.

# INEVITABILITIES

A Venezuelan anti-government rally in January 2019.

Nature abhors a vacuum. If the stock markets collapse and currencies tumble, there will certainly be other structures that spring up, quite rapidly. In the context of the twenty-first century, that may very likely be a rapid switch to cryptocurrencies—at least in situations where mobile phones are still operational.

It is difficult to predict what our world will be like the year after a major disaster that triggers an economic collapse or a die-off. But some things are inevitable: after seeing a failure in their ability to cope, trust in governments will decline; and after facing shortages, the citizenry will surely show more interest in food storage, gardening, and self-sufficiency. But given human nature, that interest will soon wane, and people will slip back into their old habits of dependency and poor provisioning. Seeing the chaos that will accompany a collapse will surely inspire many to arm themselves. However, that too will slip away, over time. The closing chapter of my first novel, *Patriots*, is illustrative of this.

Human nature has some constants. One of those is normalcy bias. This is where people get into the habit of expecting tomorrow to be just like today. That is, until a strikingly different day dawns, and shatters their normalcy bias. Then, just a few years later as normal commerce returns, people slip back into their old routines, and their normalcy bias resumes. We've seen this pattern repeat throughout human history. Most people never really learn. I'm hopeful that my readers are exceptions to that rule.

## Good Government

Governments have a tendency to centralize power over time. In democratically ruled republics, there is the chance that this trend can be checked, and good government can be restored. But sadly, this is not the norm. More frequently, governments simply become bloated and totalitarian. At some point, it takes a revolution to replace them. But revolutions require both collective willpower and the means to conduct a revolution. In nations where the citizenries are disarmed, the will may exist, but the means are lacking. The recent mass protests in Venezuela and Hong Kong both clearly illustrate that situation.

# EMIGRATION?

I often have consulting clients who bring up the topic of emigration. For those of you who are libertarians, I must warn you: if you plan to emigrate in search of more personal freedom, then you may be simply trading one form of oppression for another.

Where to go? Many American survivalists often mention Canada, but Canada's gun laws have a stench. There, unless you fall under an exemption for law enforcement or are a member of a competitive shooting team, it is illegal to possess a magazine for a semi-auto center-fire rifle that holds more than five rounds or any magazine for a handgun that holds more than ten rounds. Their magazine ban has no "grandfather" clause. If Canada's gun laws were more lax, then a lot more people would consider emigrating there, but they are much more restrictive than here in the United States. Plus, their income-tax rates are only slightly lower than in the United States. Therefore, unless you are a pacifist with no interest in owning a gun, I frankly cannot see any substantive advantage gained by relocating to Canada.

As for the TSA's X-rays and searchers, I have greatly curtailed taking commercial flights. For the few that I do take, I have scheduled flights that originate from small regional airports. My connecting flights are at larger airports, but by then, I'm already inside the security cordon. I drive most places in my SUV. If I ever fly internationally again, it will be out of a Canadian airport.

All people seem to have differing views of what they consider acceptable, comfortable, and "right." For example, I once had a long conversation with a friend visiting from England who considered the patchwork of laws in the fifty United States confusing and "chaotic." His comment was prompted when I was driving him to a tourist destination and I pulled over before reaching a state line to unload my pistol. He was astonished to hear that the gun laws in the United States weren't uniform. I personally consider it an advantage—in that Americans can vote with their feet and move from one state to another at will, to take advantage of differences in tax laws, gun laws, or homeschooling laws, for instance. On the other hand, he saw it as confusing and somehow "unfair." In his estimation, he'd rather see everyone living under identical laws, even if that meant some of them had to give up part of their freedom.

## The Key Liberty?

In terms of freedom from government surveillance, many Third World countries have the edge, but property crime and murder rates are generally higher—sometimes much higher. If firearms freedom is your concern, then countries like the United States, Finland, Switzerland, and the Philippines are some of the best, at least for full citizens. Yes, I know that firearms freedom is even greater in Yemen, Pakistan, or Somalia—where you can buy machine guns and hand grenades at the local souk—but who would want to actually move there, given their high crime rates and their dislike of Westerners?

Trade-offs are part of the human condition, and emigration decisions are always a collection of trade-offs. Facebook cofounder Eduardo Saverin recently moved to Singapore for tax reasons, but that nation has perhaps the nosiest police on the planet and stiff penalties for violating their strict gun laws. McAfee Software founder John McAfee chose Belize as his hidey-hole, but despite lavishing millions of dollars on the local gendarmerie, he still ran afoul of local gun laws. It is also noteworthy that multimillionaire actor Mel Gibson bought an island all to himself in Fiji, but he will still be taxed as part of the 1 percent.

Furthermore, there are no guarantees that laws won't change after you have moved to a perceived safe haven. (For example, Vanuatu is discussing adding an income tax.) The bottom

**ABOVE** Yemen might have very lax gun laws, but I would not recommend this as an ideal place to live.

line is that there is no single "perfect" country. Perhaps the perpetual traveler crowd has it right. But then, that approach doesn't usually provide a well-secured deep larder in the event of a global economic collapse or other widespread disaster!

I've decided that I'm staying put in the United States, fighting for my freedom. Of course, I'll always have a plan B and plan C, but for me, freedom of religion, freedom of the press, and the right to keep and bear arms are my priorities. If any of those three key liberties are substantially degraded here in the United States and if I see no way of fighting to regain them without ending up behind barbed wire, then I will definitely consider voting with my feet. But my situation is unusual. As an international journalist and commentator, I can accomplish much more by agitating for change via my blog and books than I can as just one man with a rifle. So it will only be if and when the statists try to overtly censor me that it might be time to move.

But again, for now, I'm staying.

# PRAYER

I've often written that it takes faith and friends to survive. I stand by that. Without faith in a higher power to which even national governments are answerable, then we are lost. We now live in a world that is losing its moral absolutes and the original underpinnings of all modern societies. These are the common agreements in the right to personal property, freedom of contract, life, and liberty. My prayer for the Western world is that we return to faith. All else is proverbial sinking sand.

My prayer for the readers of this book is that they take my words seriously. Come to peace with your faith. Throw off your slovenly habits and dependency. Learn to be self-sufficient. Stock up, team up, and train up. Arm yourselves. With faith and friends that you can count on, chances are that you'll pull through.

**No matter where you live, a rural location with neighbors that share your mindset—forming a strong community—is your best bet for safety.**

# CHAPTER 12
# LIST OF LISTS

- **Barter and Charity**
- **Books**
- **Bug-out Bag**
- **Vehicle Bug-out Bag**
- **Food and Water**
- **Financial Preparation**
- **Gardening and Outdoors**
- **House and Home**
- **Hygiene and Sanitation**
- **Personal Preparations**
- **Security**

**Author's Note:** The following lists are intended just as starting points. Your own lists will vary depending on your locale, age, financial resources, health, occupation, your local firearms laws, et cetera. Start with these lists and tailor them for your family's goals and both your present-day and anticipated locale and circumstances.

I recommend creating your tailored lists as hard-copy pages with the following as page headings. Alternatively, you can modify the Excel spreadsheet available at SurvivalBlog.com, under the "Resources" tab.

# BARTER AND CHARITY LIST

Be ready to barter in the event of an economic collapse. National currencies may become hyperinflated and worthless, but practical barter items have intrinsic value that is almost universally recognized. These items can also be dispensed as charity.

Concentrate on items that are durable, nonperishable, and either in small packages or that are easily divisible. Give special consideration to the items that other people are likely to overlook storing, or that for unforeseen reasons will be in short supply. Some staple foods and consumer goods have remarkably shallow stocks, where the supply chain has adopted "just in time" inventory control and "lean manufacturing."

Here is just one example: water filters. Say that you live in a city of 100,000 people. It is safe to assume that there are only one or two stores there that keep an inventory of backpacking water filters. Go visit that store. See how many that they have on the shelf. Chances are that they will stock three brands, and perhaps five models. And they will only have an average of three of each model in inventory. That equates to a supply of just fifteen water filters for 100,000 people—and 98,000 of them do not presently own a filter.

**Some barter and charity items to consider stocking:**

- Common caliber ammunition (such as: .308 Winchester, .223 Remington, 7.62x39mm, 9mm, .45 ACP, .22 LR, 12 gauge, and .410 gauge long rifle)
- Feminine hygiene products
- Salt (both cattle blocks and 1-pound canisters of iodized table salt)
- Two-cycle engine oil (for chainsaw gas mixing—gas may still be available, but two-cycle oil will probably be scarce)
- Gas stabilizer
- Diesel antibacterial additive (sold under the trade name Pri-D)
- Water filters
- 50-pound sacks of lime (for outhouses)
- 1-ounce bottles of military rifle bore cleaner and Break Free (or similar) lubricant
- Waterproof duffel bags in earth-tone colors (whitewater rafting "dry bags")
- Thermal socks
- Military web gear (lots of folks will suddenly need pistol belts, holsters, magazine pouches, etc.)
- Pre-1965 silver dimes
- 1-gallon cans of kerosene
- Rolls of olive-drab parachute cord
- Rolls of olive-drab duct tape
- Spools of monofilament fishing line
- Strike-anywhere matches (dip the heads in paraffin to make them waterproof)
- Semi-waterproof matches (from military rations)
- Playing cards
- Cooking spices (do a web search for reasonably priced bulk spices from companies like Azure Standard, and some small, sturdy Ziploc bags for repacking for individual barter transactions)
- Rope and string
- Sewing supplies
- Candle wax and wicking

**Here are some key barter reference books. Be sure to get the latest editions:**

- *Flayderman's Guide to Antique American Firearms and Their Values,* by Norm Flayderman
- *Blue Book of Gun Values,* by S. P. Fjestad
- *The Official Red Book: A Guide Book of United States Coins,* by Richard S. Yeoman
- *Standard Catalog of World Coins 1901-2000,* by Thomas Michael, Tracy L. Schmidt
- *Standard Catalog of World Coins 2001-Date,* by Thomas Michael, Tracy L. Schmidt
- *Antique Trader; Antiques & Collectibles Price Guide,* by Eric Bradley
- *Wristwatch Annual: The Catalog of Producers, Prices, Models, and Specifications,* by Peter Braun
- *Jewelry & Gems the Buying Guide: How to Buy Diamonds, Pearls, Colored Gemstones, Gold & Jewelry with Confidence and Knowledge,* by Antoinette Matlins, Antonio C. Bonanno

# BOOKS LIST

**First-tier books—must-haves for every family**

- Holy Bible (King James Version with apocrypha)
- *First Aid: Responding to Emergencies* (American Red Cross Handbook)
- *Strategic Relocation: North American Guide to Safe Places*, by Joel and Andrew Skousen
- *Where There Is No Doctor: A Village Health Care Handbook*, by David Werner
- *Where There Is No Dentist*, by Murray Dickson
- *The Encyclopedia of Country Living (Tenth Edition)*, by Carla Emery
- *Making the Best of Basics: Family Preparedness Handbook*, by James Talmage Stevens
- *Ball Blue Book of Preserving*, by Judi Kingry
- *Cookin' with Home Storage*, by Vicki Tate
- *Nuclear War Survival Skills*, by Cresson H. Kearney
- *The Alpha Strategy*, by John Pugsley (out of print, but a PDF is available for free download)
- *Boston's Gun Bible*, by Boston T. Party
- *Survival Guns*, by Mel Tappan
- *Tappan on Survival*, by Mel Tappan

**Second-tier specialty titles (some of these may not be applicable to your locale)**

- *Root Cellaring: Natural Cold Storage of Fruits & Vegetables*, by Mike Bubel
- *Back to Basics: A Complete Guide to Traditional Skills (Third Edition)*, by Abigail R. Gehring
- *Putting Food By (Plume)*, by Janet Greene
- *Stocking Up: The Third Edition of America's Classic Preserving Guide*, by Carol Hupping
- *Emergency Food Storage & Survival Handbook*, by Peggy Layton
- *Gardening When It Counts: Growing Food in Hard Times*, by Steve Solomon
- *All New Square Foot Gardening*, by Mel Bartholomew
- *Seed to Seed: Seed Saving and Growing Techniques for Vegetable Gardeners*, by Suzanne Ashworth
- *Small-Scale Grain Raising*, by Gene Logsdon
- *How to Find Your Ideal Country Home: A Comprehensive Guide*, by Gene GeRue
- *Possum Living: How to Live Well Without a Job and with (Almost) No Money*, by Dolly Freed
- *Starting a New Life in Rural America: 21 Things You Need to Know Before You Make Your Move*, by Ragnar Benson
- *The Fifty Dollar and Up Underground House Book*, by Mike Oehler
- *Emergency War Surgery (NATO Handbook: Third United States Revision, 2004)*, by Dr. Martin Fackler, et al.
- *PDR for Nonprescription Drugs, Dietary Supplements, and Herbs*
- *Physician's Drug Handbook*
- *Physicians' Desk Reference* (2017 edition—later editions are available online only)
- *The Merck Veterinary Manual*
- *Where There Is No Vet*, by Bill Forse
- *The ARRL Operating Manual For Radio Amateurs*
- *Passport to World Band Radio (2009 Edition)*, by Lawrence Magne (sadly, this was the last edition published)
- *Outdoor Survival Skills*, by Larry Dean Olsen
- *Essential Bushcraft*, by Ray Mears
- *SAS Survival Handbook*, by John "Lofty" Wiseman
- *Ultimate Sniper 2006: An Advanced Training Manual for Military and Police Snipers (2006 Updated Edition)*, by Maj. John L. Plaster
- *Total Resistance*, by H. von Dach

**Books recommended by the late "Memsahib"**

- *Gardening When It Counts*, by Steve Solomon
- *How to Survive Without a Salary: Learning How to Live the Conserver Lifestyle*, by Charles Long
- *Small-Scale Grain Raising*, by Gene Lodgson
- *The Family Cow*, by Dirk van Loon
- *Raising a Calf for Beef*, by Phyllis Hobson
- *Small-Scale Pig Raising*, by Dirk van Loon
- *Raising Rabbits the Modern Way*, by Bob Bennett
- *Raising Sheep the Modern Way (Updated and Revised Edition)*, by Paula Simmons
- *Ducks and Geese in Your Backyard: A Beginner's Guide*, by Rick and Gail Luttmann
- *The Complete Medicinal*

*Herbal: A Practical Guide ot the Healing Properties of Herbs*, by Penelope Ody

**Note:** I recommend buying hard-copy books—and preferably with hardback bindings, for longevity. Keep in mind that e-books are only available for as long as you have both a working e-book reader and a continuing source of power.

Lastly, I recommend finding a hard-copy set of *The Encyclopedia Britannica*. The last hard copy edition was printed in 2012. Newer editions are only available online.

# BUG-OUT BAG LIST

Consider the following a "bare-bones basics" list:

- Backup battery for electronics
- Emergency radio
- Whistle
- Monocular
- Parachute cord
- Sharpening stone
- Headlamp
- Flashlight
- Multitool (I prefer the Leatherman Wave model)
- Water bottle
- Compact water filter
- Spare eyeglasses
- Fire-starting kit
- Two Mylar space blankets
- Two packages of Datrex rations
- $300 cash ($200 in twenties, $95 in fives and ones, and $5 in quarters, or equivalent in your local currency)
- Small sewing kit
- Small roll of duct tape
- Hatchet or Kukri knife
- Spare AAA and AA batteries for electronics
- Two full-size trash bags

Here are some items to consider for a more comprehensive (and weighty) bug-out bag that you can assemble more gradually, as your budget permits:

**Shelter**

A tent, bivy sack, hammock, bug netting, tarp, etc. Just make sure these match your climate and expected situation of use. Please don't be foolish and buy one of these and put it into your pack without ever practicing putting it together at home. Putting up a new tent, in the dark, while it's raining, miles away from your car, only to find out that your new tent did not come with stakes, the seams aren't sealed (water goes through the stitching), and the tent door zipper is broken makes for a memorable night.

**One Change of Clothing and Footwear**

This allows you to change out of wet clothing or add layers, if cold. If your daily work environment calls for inappropriate shoes (high heels or penny loafers), then make sure to pack shoes that will match your intended use that add adequate foot protection and medial and lateral support.

**Water Filter**

Tablets work, but having to wait more than twenty minutes before you can drink limits you. Boiling water is time consuming, plus the smoke from the fire may give away your position, it requires fuel, and some places/situations won't allow for a fire (for instance, while you are in a canoe). Additionally, having to wait for the water to cool down feels like forever in the hot summer heat. A water filter/purifier makes murky water clear, improves the taste, and removes odors and colors as well as a few chemicals. A good filter is the fastest safe method available. However, I would recommend a metal water bottle for boiling as a backup, or iodine tablets in case your filter gets lost, frozen, or broken. (Never use a filter after it has frozen!)

**Water Bottles**

Notice the plural: "bottles." Take two, just in case one

breaks or if water is sparse and sources are a great distance apart. I recommend 32-ounce, wide-mouth stainless-steel bottles.

**Knives**
I recommend a quality Kukri or large knife for wood processing, shelter-making, and defense. Additionally, for finesse tasks, such as bushcraft and food preparation, I recommend a smaller knife blade of 3 to 5 inches.

**Sleeping Bag and Pad**
These go hand-in-hand with your shelter system. Choose quality! When in doubt, opt for a warmer bag than you expect you'll need. Being cold in a sleeping bag that is not warm enough is miserable and makes for a long, stressful night. If you choose a bag that is too warm, then you can just unzip your bag or use it as a blanket. As for goose down versus synthetic insulation: this depends on your environment, budget, and type of intended use. However, I generally recommend Wiggy's brand Lamilite synthetic bags. Don't forget the pad, as it has many purposes beyond aiding in a comfortable night's sleep.

**Food**
Good food uplifts your spirits. Bad food can get you sick, constipated, or is an easy way to run out of toilet paper. Only bring food that you have tried out at home and that you enjoy. If you get an allergic reaction out in the backcountry, medical help might not be available. I don't recommend bringing heavy cans. MREs are heavily advertised in the prepping world. However, many don't realize how heavy they are and how much space they take up. Buy primarily freeze-dried and dehydrated foods. Backpackers Pantry and Mountain House are a great place to start. You simply boil water, pour it into the package, wait, and eat from the package. It is ideal for stressful disaster situations, but remember to check food expiration dates.

**First-aid Kit**
Do not buy a premade kit that you only open in an emergency. Most premade kits are inadequate, so you will need to add to them. Every route brings different risk factors, so your kit needs to be adapted to that intended route. Make sure it is in a waterproof container! Wet Band-Aids don't stick, and wet gauze can become moldy. Benadryl and EpiPens have both saved a lot of lives. Make sure to pack them, and don't forget to check expiration dates on any medications that you bring.

**Fire Starters**
Bring at least two different methods for starting a fire. My favorite combination to bring is a Bic lighter (they work), magnesium fire starter (works when wet), and a Fresnel lens (get the full-page size) for sunny days. Cotton balls with petroleum jelly do wonders, and those trick birthday candles that don't go out are great (and inexpensive) fire starters, too.

**Map and Compass**
Nothing more needs saying about these.

**Compact Bible**
This is the best reading material for inspiration, peace, instruction, and when you're in trouble.

**Toilet Paper**
This can be used as a fire starter, bandage, for note taking, as an emergency feminine pad, or napkins. It can help with chaffing or help wipe debris out of your eyes, as well as to wipe yourself.

**Water-resistant LED Headlamp**
Princeton Tec, Black Diamond, and Petzl all make good ones.

**Hiking Poles**

**Firearm and Extra Ammunition**
Please ensure you consult your local and state laws before making any purchases.

**Note:** As much as possible, buy items that are in flat, subdued, earth-tone colors—most importantly your pack, jacket, and poncho.

# VEHICLE BUG-OUT BAG LIST

Bugging out by vehicle allows you the luxury of carrying much more weight than carrying a pack. Most of the following items will fit in standard duffel bags. I use medium-sized zippered horizontal duffel bags rather than large, top-loading duffels. *Keep these duffel bags packed and all together in one place, so you're ready to bug out in a hurry.* Any items that must be kept dry should be stored in double thicknesses of Ziploc plastic bags.

Many of the following items may already be packed in your vehicle as utility/roadside emergency items. If so, then they can be omitted from your stored vehicle bug-out bag(s). However, if you switch vehicles, then all of those items must be retrieved and transferred. Buy items that are in flat, subdued, earth-tone colors—including your duffel bags.

**Three to ten days' worth of lightweight food**
- MRE (one meal each, three times a day)
- Datrex emergency food bars (one 2,400-calorie bar, once a day)
- Freeze-dried camping food (once a day for three days)

**Three days' worth of water**
- Water packets (one 4-ounce pack per person per day)
- Water bottles (one liter per day)
- Water gallon jugs (3.3-liter jugs—carry plenty!)

**Water purification**
- Water filter (the Katadyn Vario and Conbi filters are both excellent)
- Backup: military water-purification tablets

**Food prep equipment**
- Stove
- Stove fuel
- 1-quart pot
- Frying pan
- Stainless-steel mess kit
- Utensils
- Basic spices
- Bottle of bleach (in a double bag)
- Bottle of liquid dish soap (in a double bag)

**Water and food storage**
- Aluminum water bottle
- Clear hard-plastic water bottle
- Collapsible water jug
- Canteen with cup
- Canteen carrier ("cover") sleeve

**Shelter and sleeping**
- Tent
- Emergency tent
- Emergency blanket
- Tarp (earth tone)
- Sleeping bag/blankets
- Sleeping pad/bed roll
- 20 small nails
- 100 feet of parachute cord (550 cords)
- Garbage bags

**Clothing**
- Underwear (four pairs)
- Socks, cotton/wool (two pairs)
- Socks, hiking (two pairs)
- T-shirt (two cotton)
- T-shirt (two synthetic)
- Long-sleeve shirt (two)
- Fleece/wool sweater (earth tone)
- Water-resistant jacket (earth tone)
- Jeans (earth tone)
- Shorts
- Pants (earth tone)
- Thermal underwear (one set)
- Beanie (earth tone)
- Hat/cap (earth tone)
- Walking shoes or sneakers
- Hiking boots
- Water shoes
- Poncho (earth tone)
- Bandana (more than three)

**Tools**
- Leatherman multitool
- Folding knife (3–4 inch)
- Fixed blade (4–6 inch)
- Hatchet or camp axe
- Machete
- Leather gloves
- Compass
- LED flashlight
- Crank flashlight
- Light sticks (four)
- Solar/crank multiband radio
- Whistle
- Matches, waterproof/strike anywhere (50)
- Disposable lighters (three)
- Magnesium fire block
- Binoculars
- Entrenching tool
- Fishing line (50 feet)

- Fishing hooks (three to five)
- Fishing line sinkers (two)
- Duct tape (two)
- WD-40
- Super glue/cyanoacrylate glue
- Sunglasses (two)
- Waterproof watch
- Candles, long lasting (two)
- Manual can opener

**First aid and medical**
- First-aid kit
- Blister cream
- N95 masks (two)
- Exam gloves (four pairs)
- Ace bandages
- Gauze
- Spare contacts, glasses
- Prescription medications
- Lip balm (two)
- Petroleum jelly (one jar)
- Sunscreen
- Warmers, hand/feet (two)
- Coolers, hand/feet (two)
- Ibuprofen (50 pills)
- Aleve (50 pills)
- Benadryl (20 pills)
- EpiPen

**Personal hygiene**
- Comb/brush
- Toothbrush
- Toothpaste
- Floss
- Nail clippers
- Soap (solid or liquid)
- Washcloth
- Hand towel
- Bath towel
- 1–3 ounces of shampoo
- Antibacterial wash
- Disposable razor
- Sample-size shaving cream
- Toilet paper
- Feminine hygiene products

**Miscellaneous**
- Signal mirror
- Carabiner, climbing (two)
- Carabiner, non-climbing (four)
- Deck of cards
- Roll of quarters
- Cash ($300+)
- Waterproof box/bag
- Passport/ID
- Local city map
- State map
- Topography map
- Regional map
- Map with bug-out routes highlighted
- Paper
- Pen/pencil (two)
- Permanent marker (two)
- Two-way radio (one pair)

**Photocopies of important papers**
- Insurance
- Birth certificate
- Passport
- State/local ID
- House/land deed
- USB stick with a second set of document copies (encrypted)
- Fully packed individual bug-out bags (crucial, in case you must abandon your vehicle!)

**Firearms**
- Pump-action shotgun
  - Sling
  - Waterproof case (optional)
  - 00 buckshot shells (75)
  - Bird shot shells (25)
- Battle rifle (.308 or .223)
  - Sling
  - Scope, red dot sight (4x magnification)
  - Magazines, spare (eight)
  - Ammo (JHP/FMJ, 500 rounds)
  - Gun cleaning kit
  - Magazine pouches
- .22 Long rifle
  - Sling
  - Magazines, spare (four)
  - Ammo (500 rounds)
- Pistol, semiautomatic, .45 ACP or 9mm
  - Holster
  - Magazines, spare (four to six)
  - Ammo (200 rounds)
  - Magazine pouches
- Shooting glasses
- Night-vision device
- Body armor/load-bearing vest
- Ballistic helmet
- Waterproof GPS
- Portable solar panel with battery charger
- Rechargeable batteries (four AA, two AAA)

# FOOD AND WATER LIST

## Food Preparation List

- The likelihood of having more people living under your roof will necessitate having an oversize skillet and a huge stew pot.
- Buy several large kettles, because without grid power or piped natural gas you will have to heat water on your wood stove for bathing, dish washing, and clothes washing.
- You will also need even more kettles, barrels, and 5- or 6-gallon PVC buckets for water hauling, rendering, soap making, and dyeing clothes. They will also make great barter or charity items.
- Don't overlook recipe books, skinning knives, gutbuckets, gambrels, and meat saws.

## Food Storage List

Although this topic is worthy of a full separate book, I will briefly summarize.

Start with the staple foods that you use every week, and stock up heavily. Buy mouse-proof containers, and repackage as necessary.

Next, supplement those staples with 5-gallon food-grade buckets or canned food cases of:

- Wheat
- Rice
- Beans
- Rolled oats
- Peanut butter
- Tuna fish
- Salt
- Sugar
- Powdered milk
- Honey

Note that if you buy whole wheat, as I suggest (which stores much longer than flour), then you will also need to get a wheat grinder. I recommend the Country Living brand grinder.

Also, stock up on multivitamins. Double-encapsulated ones have the longest shelf life.

As your budget and storage space allow, consider buying some commercially packaged dehydrated and freeze-dried foods in #10 cans. These have shelf lives of up to thirty years.

You should also buy some very lightweight backpacking foods or MREs for your bug-out bags.

## Water List

Your water preparations will vary greatly depending on your local average rainfall. Below are some things to consider.

**Collecting water**

- Outfit your house with downspout conversion sheet-metal work and barrels (this is another good reason to upgrade your house to a fireproof metal roof).
- For collecting water from open sources, get plenty of containers. Don't buy big barrels, since 5-gallon food grade buckets are the largest size that most people can handle without back strain.

**Transporting water**

- For transporting water if and when gas is too precious to waste, buy a couple of heavy-duty two-wheel garden carts—convert the wheels to foam-filled "no flats" tires. (You will find lots of other uses for those carts around your retreat, such as hauling hay, firewood, manure, fertilizer, etc.)

**Treating water**

- Buy plain Clorox hypochlorite bleach. A little goes a long way. Buy some extra half-gallon bottles for barter and charity.
- If you can afford it, buy a "Big Berkey" British Berkefeld ceramic water filter. These are available from the Berkey Guy, Ready Made Resources, and several other Internet vendors. Even if you have pure spring water at your retreat, you never know where you may end up, and a good filter could be a lifesaver.
- You should also buy a compact filter for your bug-out bag, but leave that one stored new and dry.

# FINANCIAL PREPARATION LIST

The following is my list of recommendations for the 2020s:

**Stocks**
Minimize. The 2020s will be a decade to get out of all but a few very safe "widows and orphans" stocks. Even with those, you should set stop loss orders. Precious metals mining stocks look like they will continue to be poor performers. Presently, buying a mining stock is not a good way to invest in precious metals.

**Precious Metals**
Hold. This may be a good opportunity to rebalance your personally held metals portfolio, but it is certainly not a time to reduce it! Your mileage may vary, but here is how I've allocated my personal metals portfolio:

1. Silver: 80 percent (mostly a mix of pre-1965 dimes and quarters, as well as some 1-ounce United States Mint Silver Eagles, and just a few serialized Engelhard 10-ounce bars)
2. Gold: 10 percent (I now have far more 1-ounce United States Mint Gold Eagles than I do numismatics)
3. Platinum: 10 percent (United States Mint Platinum Liberty 1/4-ounce and 1/2-ounce bullion coins)

**Base Metals**
Hold. I trust that if you live in the United States, you have long since bought some boxes of nickels at face value. Hang on to them. I also suggest closely watching the world supplies of cobalt, copper, lithium, and nickel. These are all key components of large batteries used for electric vehicles. If shortages of any of these loom up, then it would be a good time to invest in a few very carefully selected mining stocks. And, of these, nickel is compact enough to invest in, tangibly.

**Bank Deposits**
Diversify. The 2020s will be a decade of caution with banks. The Deutsche Bank fiasco has yet to reach full fruition. And it is indicative that some very poor decisions were made by some of the world's biggest banks. If you have more than $5,000 on deposit, then you should have it in at least two banks. Better yet, a bank and one or more credit unions.

**Cash/Currencies**
Diversify and be ready for a banking crisis. If possible, keep enough cash at home (preferably in $20 bills) to be able to pay all of your bills for at least two months. Whether or not you do any international travel, you should also consider buying some Swiss francs and British pounds.

**Cryptocurrencies**
Minimize. I expect the announcement of new sovereign (government-managed) cryptos in the next few years. So, in one nation after another, private cryptos will become closely scrutinized and either banned or heavily taxed. Sell at the peaks.

**Tangibles**
Increase. The 2020s will be a decade to increase your holdings of compact investment barterables, especially firearms and tools of your trade. There is a chance that in the future the private-party sales of modern (post-1898) guns will be banned.

**Collectibles**
Minimize. With the exception of guns, the nascent recession will be a poor time to have much invested in collectibles. So minimize your holdings of fine art, rare wines, stamps, classic cars, Swiss watches, or other collectibles.

**Land**
Sell your rentals. The real-estate market is showing signs of weakness. This is a good time to reduce your holdings of rental properties. But you should hold on to rural farm property that can double as a retreat. If you are liquidating land, rental houses, and any other assets, then this is a good juncture to pay down (or pay off) the mortgage on your personal residence. Make yourself debt-free. With a recession looming and redundancies very possible, being debt-free is important!

**Vechicles**
Get practical. Fancy, impractical cars don't gain value in a recession. So this is a good time to trade into the most practical and well-maintained used cars and trucks that you can find. Ideally, you should have both one big and very sturdy four-wheel-drive pickup, and one small, very economical runabout.

# GARDENING AND OUTDOORS LIST

## Farm Animals List

This list will vary considerably depending on your type of livestock, livestock guardians, and pets. As a starting point, consider:

- Hoof rasp
- Hoof nippers
- Hoof pick
- Horse brushes
- Hand sheep shears
- Styptic
- Wool carding combs
- Goat-milking stand
- Teat dip
- Udder wash
- Bag balm ointment
- Elastrator and bands
- SWAT fly repellent
- Nail clippers (various sizes)
- Kopertox
- Livestock leads, leashes, collars, and halters
- Hay hooks
- Hay fork
- Manure shovel
- Feed and water buckets
- Bulk grain and C-O-B sweet feed (store in galvanized trash cans with tight-fitting lids to keep the mice out)
- Various tack and saddles
- Tack repair tools and hardware
- Any breed-specific tack, tools, supplies, and medicines

If your region has selenium-deficient soil (ask your local agricultural extension office), then be sure to get selenium-fortified salt blocks rather than plain white salt blocks for those that you are going to set aside strictly for your livestock.

## Gardening List

One important item for your gardening list is the construction of a very tall deer- and rabbit-proof fence. Under current circumstances, a raid by deer on your garden is probably just an inconvenience. After the balloon goes up, it could mean the difference between eating well and starvation.

- Top soil/amendments/ fertilizers
- Gardening tools and work gloves (any extras will serve for barter/charity)
- Long-term storage non-hybrid (or open pollinated) seed (non-hybrid "heirloom" seed assortments are available from seedforsecurity.com and several other vendors)

## Hunting/Fishing/ Trapping List

- Night-vision gear, spare batteries, and battery charging
- Salt (post-TEOTWAWKI, it would be a waste of effort to "go hunting"—have the game come to you by puchasing twenty or more salt blocks; they will also make very valuable barter items)
- Sell your fly-fishing gear (all but perhaps a few flies) and buy practical spin-casting equipment
- Extra tackle may be useful for barter, but probably only in a very long-term crunch
- Buy some frog gigs if you have bullfrogs in your area, or crawfish traps if you have crawfish in your area
- Learn how to rig trotlines and make fish traps for non-labor-intensive fishing

## Medicinal Herbs and Plants List

Some medicinal herbs are fairly easy to grow. Many are perennial and can be grown indoors. Some to consider, as a starting point:

- Aloe vera (for burns)
- Echinacea (purple cone flower)
- Valerian (the root is a natural sleep aid)

## Tools List

- Gardening tools
- Auto mechanics tools
- Welding tools and gases
- Bolt cutters (the indispensable "universal key")
- Woodworking tools
- Gunsmithing tools
- Put an emphasis on hand-powered tools
- Hand- or treadle-powered grinding wheel
- Hand- or treadle-powered sewing machine
- Plenty of extra work gloves (in earth-tone colors)

# HOUSE AND HOME LIST

## Fuels and Petroleum Products List

- 1-gallon cans of Coleman stove/lantern fuel
- Standard propane cylinders (the size used for torches and camp stoves)
- 1-gallon cans of kerosene
- Extra welding cylinders (oxygen and acetylene), if you have a cutting/welding rig

Buy the biggest propane, home heating oil, gas, and/or diesel tanks that your local ordinances permit and that you can afford. If your budget allows it, also install a 300- to 800-gallon underground gasoline tank and a 600- to 2,500-gallon underground diesel tank. (Of course, make sure that you have at least one diesel vehicle.) You should carefully camouflage the filler necks and hand pumps for those tanks.

Always keep your bulk fuel tanks at least two-thirds full.

For privacy, ballistic impact, and fire concerns, underground tanks are best if your local water table allows it. In any case, do not buy an aboveground fuel tank that would be visible from any public road or navigable waterway. Buy plenty of extra fuel for barter. Don't overlook buying plenty of kerosene. (For barter, you will want some in 1- or 2-gallon cans.)

Stock up on firewood or coal.

Get the best-quality chainsaw you can afford. I prefer Stihl or Husqvarna brand saws. If you can afford it, buy two of the same model. Buy extra chains, critical spare parts, and plenty of two-cycle oil. (Two-cycle oil will be great for barter!) Be sure to buy a pair of Kevlar chainsaw safety chaps, and always wear them when your chainsaw engine is running. They are expensive but they might save you a trip to the emergency room. Always wear gloves, goggles, earmuffs, and a helmet. (I prefer the helmets with integral face screen and earmuffs.) Our family's motto: "Wear all the gear, all the time."

Have someone who is well experienced teach you how to resharpen chains.

**Note:** Don't cut up your wood into rounds near any rocks or you will dull or destroy a chain in a hurry.

## Home Businesses List

I have often recommended having multiple income streams, to become recession-proof and layoff-proof. Some possible home-based businesses include:

- Mail order/Internet sales
- Sandblasting/beadblasting
- Leatherworking
- Kydex holster and sheath making
- Antique "picking" and resale
- Day care
- House/office cleaning
- Small-appliance repair
- Gunsmithing
- Locksmithing
- Security/web camera installation
- Graphic design/web page design
- Freelance video editing
- 3-D printing
- Battery pack refurbishing (rebuilding packs for power tools)

## Home Info List

For your own reference, or for that of your heirs, put together a binder (or several) containing:

- Product user manuals (staple purchase receipts into each, to confirm warranty eligibility)—group all of the major appliance information together
- Service manuals
- Warranty cards/sheets
- Utility contracts
- Storage tank lease information/contracts
- Covenants, Conditions & Restrictions and Homeowners Association contracts/correspondence
- Lien information
- Right of way agreements
- Receipts/contracts for major home repairs and improvements
- Correspondence, contracts, or signed agreements with neighbors regarding shared fences, gates, wells, or access lanes, including road maintenance, repairs, and snow plowing

## Household, Shop, and Sundries List

- Cleaning supplies
- Bulk paper products (primarily toilet paper and paper towels)
- Basic tool set
- Basic mechanic's tool set
- Sturdy workbench

To round out this list, make an inventory of what is in your house and then think through all of the items that you'd need if you must hunker down for six months or longer, without access to stores. This list will have things such as kitchen cleaners, trash bags, mousetraps, wire of various gauges, duct tape, reinforced strapping tape, chain, nails, nuts and bolts, weather stripping, abrasives, twine, white glue, super glue, cyanoacrylate glue, etc.

## Power, Light, Heat, and Batteries List

- Get a photovoltaic (PV) power system. Buy the biggest and best that you can afford.
- Install a 12V DC interior lighting system. One proviso: in the event of a "grid-down" situation, if you are the only family in the area with power, it could turn your house into a "come loot me" beacon at night. At the same time, your house lighting will ruin the night vision of your LP/OP pickets. Buy materials in advance for making blackout screens or fully opaque curtains for your windows.
- Kerosene lamps are important. Get plenty of extra wicks, mantles, and chimneys.
- Purchase some rechargeable batteries and both AC-to-DC and DC-to-DC battery charging trays.
- When possible, buy rechargeable nickel metal hydride (NiMH) batteries. But also carry a set of alkaline batteries for each device, in case your rechargeable batteries are discharged at a crucial time.
- Consider a whole-house backup generator. But recognize that for a long-term situation, your PV system will be your main source of power. If your home has propane appliances, get a "tri-fuel" generator—with a carburetor that is selectable between gasoline, propane, and natural gas.
- If you heat your home with home-heating oil, then get a diesel-engine generator (and plan on getting at least one diesel pickup and/or tractor). In a pinch, you can run your diesel generator and diesel vehicles on home-heating oil.

# HYGIENE AND SANITATION LIST

- Sacks of powdered lime for the outhouse (buy plenty!)
- Toilet paper in quantity (stores well if kept dry and away from vermin; it is lightweight but bulky, and is a good item to store in the attic (see my novel *Patriots* for information about stocking up on used phone books for use as toilet paper)
- Soap in quantity (hand soap, dish soap, laundry soap, cleansers, etc.)
- Bottled lye for soap making
- Feminine hygiene products
- Toothpaste (or powder) and toothbrushes
- Dental floss
- Fluoride rinse (unless you have health objections to the use of fluoride)
- Sunscreen

## First-Aid/Minor Surgery List

When tailoring this list, consider your neighborhood going for many months without power, the extensive use of open flames, and sentries standing picket shifts exposed to the elements. Then consider axes, chainsaws, and tractors being wielded by newbies, and a greater likelihood of gunshot wounds. Then factor in the lack of access to doctors or high-tech medical diagnostic equipment.

Put a strong emphasis on burn treatment in your first-aid supplies.

- Don't overlook do-it-yourself dentistry! (Oil of cloves, temporary filling kit, extraction tools, etc.)
- Buy a full minor surgery kit (inexpensive Pakistani stainless-steel instruments), even if you don't know how to use them all yet. You may have the opportunity to put them in the hands of someone experienced who needs them.

# PERSONAL PREPARATIONS LIST

## Personal ("You") List

Make a separate tailored list for each family member and individual expected to arrive at your retreat.

- Spare glasses
- Prescription and nonprescription medications
- Birth control
- Keep dentistry up to date
- Any elective surgery that you've been postponing
- Work off that gut
- Stay in shape
- Back strength and health (particularly important, given the heavy manual tasks required for self-sufficiency)
- Educate yourself on survival topics, and practice them (for example, even if you don't presently live at your retreat, you should plant a vegetable garden every year—it is better to learn through experience and make mistakes now, when the loss of crop is an annoyance rather than a crucial event)
- "Comfort" items to help get through high-stress times (books, games, CDs, chocolates, etc.)

## Training Courses List

Take as many of these courses as your time and budget allows:

- American Red Cross First Aid
- American Red Cross CPR
- Wilderness First Responder course
- Defensive Techniques: Walking Stick (a 40-minute training DVD produced by the Gunsite Academy)
- Project Appleseed marksmanship courses (great, inexpensive training for ages 10 and up)
- Gunsite Academy firearms training courses (Arizona)
- Thunder Ranch firearms training courses (Oregon)
- Front Sight firearms training courses (Nevada)

And to round out your training:

- Max Velocity Tactical small unit tactics live fire courses (based in Virginia, with some mobile training)

**For Your Children**

- Trail Life USA
- American Heritage Girls

# SECURITY LIST

## CBR and NBC Protection List

- Dosimeter, rate meter, and charger
- Radiac meter (handheld Geiger counter)
- Rolls of heavy-duty sheet plastic (for isolating airflow to air-filter inlets and for covering window frames in the event that windows are broken due to blast effects)
- Duct tape (crucial for sealing air gaps)
- HEPA filters (and spares) for your shelter
- Potassium iodate ($KIO_3$) tablets to prevent thyroid damage
- An outdoor bucket-shower rig for decontamination, just outside of your shelter entrance
- Fallout shelter reference books (*see* the *Books List*)

### Biological Warfare Defense

- Disinfectants
- Hand sanitizer
- Exam gloves
- N95 face masks
- Colloidal silver generator and spare supplies (distilled water and .999 fine silver rod)
- Natural antibiotics (echinacea, tea tree oil, etc.)

## Communications/ Monitoring List

- Police/public service bands scanner
- General coverage AM/ shortwave receiver (Sony and Grundig both make great compact models that have SSB demodulation)
- MURS band transceiver(s)
- 40-channel CB transceiver(s)

Optional:

- HF transceiver
- 2-meter band transceiver(s)
- Marine band VHF transceiver(s)

When selecting radios, try to find models that will run on 12-volt DC power or rechargeable nickel metal hydride battery packs (that can be recharged from your retreat's 12V DC power system without having to use an inverter). As a secondary purchasing goal, buy spare radios of each type if you can afford them.

Keep your spare radios in sealed all-metal boxes (such as popcorn tins) to protect them from EMP.

If you live in a far inland region, then I recommend buying two or more 12V DC marine-band radios. These frequencies will probably not be monitored in your region, leaving you an essentially private band to use. (But never assume that *any* radio communications are secure!)

## Firearms List

I recommend the following as minimums (check local gun laws, of course):

### Firearms

- One semi-auto battle rifle for each adult (e.g., AR-10 or AR-15/M4 series)
- One semi-auto pistol for each adult (e.g., Glock 30, Glock 19, or SIG P320)
- One scoped big-game hunting/countersniper rifle for every three adults (e.g., Ruger M77, Remington 700, or Winchester Model 70)
- One semi-auto .22 rifle for each adult (e.g., Ruger stainless-steel 10/22 takedown)
- One shotgun for every two adults (e.g., Remington 870 or Mossberg 500 series)

### Ammunition

- 2,000 rounds per battle rifle
- 2,000 rounds per centerfire pistol
- 400 rounds per hunting rifle
- 3,000 rounds per rimfire rifle or pistol
- 750 rounds per shotgun (or more, if you cannot own or don't yet own a battle rifle)

### Accessories

- Eye and ear protection for every family member!
- Cleaning kit for each gun
- 12 magazines for each battle rifle
- 8 magazines for each pistol

## Firefighting List

You will need to consider fighting fires without the aid of a fire department. In a major disaster or a societal collapse, fire departments may be unavailable or no longer functioning.

- Smoke and CO detectors (replace batteries annually, at end of Daylight Savings Time)
- Upgrade your retreat with a fireproof metal roof
- 2-inch water line from your gravity-fed storage tank (to provide large water volume for firefighting)
- Firefighting hose rig with an adjustable stream/mist head

## Security List

- Upgrade exterior doors and locks
- Dakota Alert and at least four passive infrared sensors
- Light amplification night-vision monocular (an autogated AN/PVS-14 would be ideal)
- Infrared exterior floodlights (for use only briefly, if your house comes under attack)
- Sandbags
- Concertina wire and stakes
- A gun vault/"panic room" (as a last bastion)

## Tactical Living List

- Adjust your wardrobe buying toward sturdy earth-tone clothing (frequent your local thrift store and buy extras for retreat newcomers, charity, and barter)
- Dyes (stock up on some boxes of green and brown cloth dye, with extra for barter; with dye, you can turn most light-colored clothes into semi-tactical clothing on short notice)
- 2-inch-wide burlap strip material in green and brown (available in large spools from Gun Parts Corp; even if you don't have time now, stock up so that you can make camouflage ghillie suits or capes post-TEOTWAWKI)
- Save those wine corks (burned cork makes quick and inexpensive face camouflage)
- Cold-weather and foul-weather gear (buy plenty, since you will be doing more outdoor chores, hunting, and standing guard duty)
- Ponchos and gaiters
- Mosquito repellent
- Subdued (red filter) flashlights and penlights
- Noise, light, and litter discipline
- Range cards and sector sketches

**Note:** If you live in the boonies, then piece together nine of the United States Geological Survey 15-minute maps, with your retreat property on the center map. Mount that map on an oversize map board. Draw in the property lines and owner names of all of your surrounding neighbors' parcels (in pencil) in at least a 5-mile radius. (Get boundary lines and current owner names from your county recorder's office.) Study and memorize both the terrain and the neighbors' names. Make a phone number/e-mail list that corresponds to all of the names marked on the map, plus city and county office contact numbers for quick reference, and tack it up right next to the map board. Cover the whole map sheet with a sheet of heavy-duty acetate.

# GLOSSARY

**10/22:** A semiautomatic .22 rimfire rifle made by Ruger

**24/7:** Twenty-four hours per day, seven days per week

## A

**AC:** Alternating current

**ACP:** Automatic Colt Pistol

**AD:** Anno Domini

**AI:** artificial intelligence

**AIDS:** Acquired immunodeficiency syndrome, caused by infection with the human immunodeficiency virus (HIV)

**AM:** Amplitude modulation

**American Redoubt:** A political migration movement first proposed in 2011 by JWR that designates three states in the northwestern United States (Idaho, Montana, Wyoming), and adjoining portions of two other states (eastern Oregon, eastern Washington) as a safe haven for conservative, libertarian-leaning religious people

**Ammo:** Slang for ammunition

**AR:** Depending on context, automatic rifle or ArmaLite rifle. This is the generic term for semi-auto variants of the ArmaLite family of rifles designed by Eugene Stoner (AR-10, AR-15, AR-180, etc.)

**AR-10:** The 7.62mm NATO predecessor of the M16 rifle, designed by Eugene Stoner. Modern-day AR-10s have about 40% interchangeability of parts with the smaller caliber AR-15 and M4. See also AR and AR-15

**AR-15:** The semi-automatic civilian variants of the U.S. Army M16 rifle

**ARRL:** Amateur Radio Relay League

**ASA:** Army Security Agency

**ATM:** Automated teller machine

## B

**Battle Rifle:** A military service rifle that is fed ammunition via a detachable magazine and fires a full-powered rifle cartridge

**BC:** Before Christ

**Biltong:** An Afrikaner style of jerky, made with various meats

**BSAP:** British South Africa Police

**Bug out:** In the context of this book, egressing to a place of refuge, just before or during a disaster

## C

**CB:** Citizens band radio, a VHF broadcasting band. No license is required for operation in the United States. Some desirable CB transceivers are capable of SSB operation. Originally twenty-three channels, Citizens band was later expanded to forty channels

**Centerfire Pistol:** A firearm whose cartridges have the primer in the center of the base

**CIA:** Central Intelligence Agency

**CO:** Carbon monoxide

**C-O-B:** Corn-oats-barley

**COG:** Continuity of Government

**COMSEC:** COMmunications SECurity. The measures used to protect both classified and unclassified traffic on military communications and computing networks

**COOP:** Continuity of Operations

**CSA:** Community supported agriculture

**CT:** Counterterrorism

## D

**DC:** Direct current

**DHS:** Department of Homeland Security

**DIA:** Defense Intelligence Agency, a U.S. government agency specializing in defense/military intelligence

**DIY:** Do-it-yourself

**DOD:** Depth of discharge

**DSL:** Digital Subscriber Line

## E

**EMP:** Electromagnetic pulse

## F

**FAL:** See FNFAL

**FEMA:** Federal Emergency Management Agency

**FBI:** Federal Bureau of Investigation

**FIFO:** First in, first out. A method of rotating perishable food and supplies

**FM:** Frequency modulation

**FN:** Fabrique Nationale, a Belgian arms maker

**FNFAL:** A 7.62mm NATO battle rifle originally made by the Belgian company Fabrique

Nationale (FN), issued to more than fifty countries in the 1960s and 1970s. Now made as semi-auto-only "clones" by a variety of makers including DSArms

**FRS:** Family Radio Service

# G

**Glock:** The popular polymer framestriker-fired pistol design by Gaston Glock of Austria

**G.O.O.D.:** Get out of Dodge. See also Bug out

# H

**Ham:** Slang for amateur radio operator.

**HDPE:** High-density polyethylene. A plastic often used in food and water containers. Note that not all HDPE is classified as "food grade"

**HEPA:** High-efficiency particulate air (filter)

**HIV:** Human immunodeficiency virus (HIV), the cause of AIDS

**HK:** Heckler und Koch, the German gun maker

**HKG3:** Heckler und Koch Model G3. A 7.62×51mm NATO, select-fire battle rifle

# I

**IDS:** Intrusion detection system. A security alarm system to detect unauthorized entry to a secure facility

**IRA:** Irish Republican Army

**ITAR:** International Traffic in Arms Regulations

# J

**JASBORR:** Jim's Amazing Secret Bunker of Redundant Redundancy

**JWR:** James Wesley, Rawles

# K

**Kg:** Kilogram

**$KIO_3$:** Potassium iodate

**KJV:** King James Version of the Bible

# L

**LED:** Light-emitting diode

**Long Rifle:** Commonly used rifles for hunting characterized by an unusually long barrel

**Lp/mm:** Line pairs per millimeter, a measure of resolution

**LP/OP:** Listening post/ observation post

# M

**M4:** The U.S. Army-issue 5.56mm NATO selective-fire carbine. (A shorter version of the M16, with a 14.5-inch barrel and collapsing stock.) Earlier-issue M16 carbine variants had designations such as XM177E2 and CAR-15

**M4gery:** A civilian semi-auto-only version of an M4 Carbine, typically with a 16-inch barrel instead of the military 14.5-inch barrel

**Mag-Lite:** A popular American brand of sturdy flashlights with a machined aluminum casing

**MERS:** Middle East respiratory syndrome

**MG:** Depending on context, milligrams or machine gun

**MI:** Military Intelligence

**MRE:** Meal, ready to eat

**MUPS:** Medically unexplained physical symptoms

**MURS:** Multi-use Radio Service. A VHF two-way radio service in the U.S. that does not require a license. See also FRS

# N

**NATO:** North Atlantic Treaty Organization

**NBC:** Nuclear, biological and chemical

**NEC:** National Electrical Code

**NFA-34:** National Firearms Act. The U.S. 1934 law that for the first time required registration of machine guns, short-barreled rifles, and short-barreled shotguns

**NiMH:** Nickel metal hydride (rechargeable battery)

**NRC:** Nuclear Regulatory Commission

**NVDs:** Night-vision devices

**NWO:** New world order.

# O

**OC:** Oleoresin capsicum, the active ingredient in most bear repellent sprays

**OPSEC:** OPerational SECurity. The systematic and proven process by which potential adversaries can be denied information about capabilities and intentions by identifying, controlling, and protecting generally unclassified evidence of the planning and execution of sensitive activities. The process involves five steps: identification of critical information, analysis of threats, analysis of vulnerabilities, assessment of risks, and application of appropriate countermeasures

## P

**PF:** Protection factor (nuclear shielding)

**PLA:** People's Liberation Army of China

**Pre-1899:** Guns made in or before 1899, which are classified as unrestricted "antiques," under U.S. law (outside of federal jurisdiction)

**Pre-1965:** U.S. silver coins with 1964 or earlier mint dates, usually with little or no numismatic value. They are sold for their 90 percent silver bullion content. Well-worn pre-1965 coins are sometimes derisively called "junk" silver by rare-coin dealers

**PV:** Photovoltaic (solar power conversion cell or array), used to convert solar power to DC electricity, typically for battery charging

## R

**R:** Rad or roentgen, unit of measurement

**RE:** Renewable energy

**Rebar:** Reinforcing bar, used primarily in concrete work

**Remington:** A popular U.S. arms manufacturer

**Retreat:** In the context of this book, a retreat is a place of refuge from disaster, usually in a lightly populated food-producing refuge

**Rimfire rifle:** A firearm whose firing pin strikes the cartridge's rim to ignite the primer

**RPG:** Rocket-propelled grenade

**Ruger:** A major U.S. firearms manufacturer

**Rule 308:** A joking term for law and order enforced only by private use of arms

## S

**S&W:** Smith & Wesson, a popular U.S. arms manufacturer

**SAM:** Surface-to-air missile

**SARS:** Severe acute respiratory syndrome

**SEC:** Securities and Exchange Commission

**SIG:** Schweizer Industrie Gesellschaft. A major Swiss conglomerate that was a gun maker until the 1980s

**SOC:** State of charge. See also DOD

**SOP:** Standard operating procedure

**SSB:** A single sideband transmission, a type of amplitude modulation in which the carrier wave and one sideband are suppressed in order to occupy less bandwidth

**SUV:** Sport utility vehicle

## T

**TEOTWAWKI:** The end of the world as we know it

**Terr/terrs:** Slang contraction for Rhodesian/Zimbabwean terrorist(s)

**Three K:** Jobs that are ***kitsui*** ("hard"), ***kitanai*** ("dirty"), and ***kiken*** ("dangerous")

**TSA:** Transportation Security Agency

## U

**UPS:** Uninterruptible power source

**USGI:** United States government issue

**USSR:** Union of Soviet Socialist Republics

## V

**VAC:** Volts, alternating current

**VDC:** Volts, direct current

**VHF:** Very high frequency

## W

**WD-1:** U.S. military-issue two-conductor insulated field telephone wire

**WiFi:** Wireless fidelity

**Winchester:** A popular U.S. arms manufacturer

## Z

**ZANU-PF:** Zimbabwe African National Union–Patriotic Front

# INDEX

# YOUR LISTS

# PICTURE CREDITS

The publishers would like to thank the following sources for their kind permission to reproduce the pictures in this book.

Page 5: Stokkete/Shutterstock; 11: Stokkete/Shutterstock; 12: Romolo Tavani/ Shutterstock; 15 (top): Andrey Lobachev/ Shutterstock; 15 (right): Robyn Mackenzie/ Shutterstock; 16: sunsinger/Shutterstock; 17 (top): Foto24/Herman Verwey/ Shutterstock; 18: Christian Roberts-Olsen/ Shutterstock; 19 (bottom): Real Window Creative/Shutterstock; 20 (top): Sk Hasan Ali/Shutterstock; 20 (left): Hanna Grzesik/ Shutterstock; 21 (bottom): Keystone Pictures USA/Shutterstock; 22 (bottom): Peter Liddiard; 24 (left): Roman Vanur/ Shutterstock; 24 (bottom): Jagoush/ Shutterstock; 25 (top): Godong/UIG/ Shutterstock; 26 (top): Daily Express/ Hulton Archive/Getty Images; 26 (bottom): Granger/Shutterstock; 27: Library of Congress Prints and Photographs; 28: Public Domain; 29 (bottom): Everett Historical/Shutterstock; 30: Daniel Irungu/ EPA-EFE/Shutterstock; 31 (bottom): Tinxi/ Shutterstock; 33: H. Christoph/ullstein bild/Getty Images; 34: Universal History Archive/Shutterstock; 35 (top): ZUMA Press Inc/Alamy Stock Photo; 36: vaalaa/ Shutterstock; 37 (top): Sipa/Shutterstock; 38: Victority/Shutterstock; 39 (bottom): Freaktography/Shutterstock; 41 (top): Sucharas Wongpeth/Shutterstock; 41 (bottom): Eleanor McDonie/Shutterstock; 42 (left): Uniden America Corporation; 42 (right): Peter Liddiard; 43 (both): Private Collection; 44 (bottom): Sergey Kamshylin/ Shutterstock; 45: Bulgac/Getty Images; 46 (top): BlurryMe/Shutterstock; 47 (top): Bloomberg/Getty Images; 49: Hugh Kinsella Cunningham/EPA-EFE/Shutterstock; 52: Barnes Ian/Shutterstock; 54: Rogelio Solis/AP/Shutterstock; 55: Kpa/Zuma/ Shutterstock; 56: DiamondGT/Shutterstock; 57 (top): smereka/Shutterstock; 57 (centre): Marina Varnava/Shutterstock; 57 (bottom): off5173/Shutterstock; 58: dimid_86/ Shutterstock; 59 (bottom): Raimundo79/ Shutterstock; 60: Kotkoa/Shutterstock; 62: S and S Imaging/Shutterstock; 63 (left): Ragemax/Shutterstock; 63 (right): digitalreflections/Shutterstock; 64 (bottom): MadamKaye/Shutterstock; 65: varandah/Shutterstock; 66: Militarist/ Shutterstock; 67 (top): Private Collection; 68 (top): Private Collection; 68 (bottom): Stokkete/Shutterstock; 69: Darryl Brooks/ Shutterstock; 70: Page Light Studios/ Shutterstock; 71: Freedomz/Shutterstock; 72: sima/Shutterstock; 75: chomplearn/ Shutterstock; 76 (left): Sam Wordley/ Shutterstock; 76 (bottom): Muhammed Muheisen/AP/Shutterstock; 77: Khalil Hamra/AP/Shutterstock; 78: Phototee/ Shutterstock; 80: Tippman98x/Shutterstock; 81 (top): Chere/Shutterstock; 81 (bottom): Peter Liddiard; 85 (top left): Peter Liddiard; 85 (top right): Private Collection; 85 (bottom left): AMV_80/Shutterstock; 85 (bottom right) Gute Reise Inc.; 86: Susse_n/ Shutterstock; 87: Peter Liddiard; 88: blojfo/ Shutterstock; 90: vubaz/Shutterstock; 91: Bondareva Elena/Shutterstock; 92: Peter Liddiard; 93 (top): vectorlight/Shutterstock; 93 (bottom): Mary Evans Picture Library; 94: Erik Pendzich/Shutterstock; 95 (top): Keith Homan/Shutterstock; 95 (bottom): Peter Liddiard; 96: Peter Liddiard; 98: Eleanor McDonie/Shutterstock; 100: Private Collection; 101 (both): Peter Liddiard; 102: Hortimages/Shutterstock; 103: ChiccoDodiFC/Shutterstock; 104: Muhamad Norairin Ngateni/Shutterstock; 105: Everett Collection/Shutterstock; 106: Surasak muangsuk/Shutterstock; 107 (top): Poogie/Shutterstock; 108 (top): Phil Darby/Shutterstock; 109 (bottom): Jiang Hongyan/Shutterstock; 110 (bottom): Public Domain; 111: SABIDA/Alamy Stock Photo; 112 (bottom): Yana Bo/Shutterstock; 113 (top): Nic Murray/Alamy Stock Photo; 113 (bottom): Hein Nouwens/Shutterstock; 114 (top): Morphart Creation/Shutterstock; 114 (bottom): Ruksutakarn studio/Shutterstock; 115: Alison Hancock/Shutterstock; 116: mamita/Shutterstock; 117: Sherry V Smith/ Shutterstock; 118: Dn Br/Shutterstock; 122: Wollertz/Shutterstock; 124 (top): Regine Poirier/Shutterstock; 125: W. Scott McGill/ Shutterstock; 126: Private Collection; 127: Rick Rycroft/AP/Shutterstock; 128 (top): Everett Historical/Shutterstock; 129: Everett Historical/Shutterstock; 130 (top left): DIAC images; 130 (bottom left): otsphoto/ Shutterstock; 130 (bottom right): Jim Tampin/Alamy Stock Photo; 131 (bottom right): Peter Liddiard; 132: Keystone Pictures USA/Keystone/Shutterstock; 133 (top): Public Domain; 133 (centre): Public Domain; 133 (bottom): Private Collection; 134: Krasula/Shutterstock; 135 (top): Laszlo66/Shutterstock; 135 (bottom): MyImages - Micha/ Shutterstock; 136: AlexandrMakedonskiy/ Shutterstock; 137 (top left): New Style Pictures/Shutterstock; 137 (top centre): Miroslav Hlavko/Shutterstock; 137 (top right): Rudmer Zwerver/Shutterstock; 137 (bottom left): Amee Cross/Shutterstock; 137 (bottom centre): Zdenek Machacek/ Shutterstock; 137 (bottom right): Derek R. Audette/Shutterstock; 138: K Steve Cope/ Shutterstock; 139 (both): Private Collection; 140: Private Collection; 141 (bottom): Mountains Hunter/Shutterstock; 142: Private Collection; 143 (bottom): Wikimedia Commons; 144 (left): Private Collection; 144 (bottom): P A/Shutterstock; 145 (top left): Liviu Gherman/Shutterstock; 145 (top centre): Marco.Warm/Shutterstock; 145 (top right): Lasse Jesper Pedersen/Shutterstock; 145 (left): Oleksii Borodachov/Shutterstock; 145 (centre): 2j architecture/Shutterstock; 145 (right): surasaki/Shutterstock; 145 (bottom): KDM Creative/Shutterstock; 146: Always_Sunshine/Shutterstock; 147 (top): Jurand/Shutterstock; 147 (bottom): Kritsada.S/Shutterstock; 148 (top): Mario Hoesel/Shutterstock; 149: Peter Liddiard; 150: ARTYuSTUDIO/Shutterstock; 151: Smith Collection/Gado/Getty Images; 152: Private Collection; 153: Image Point Fr/ Shutterstock; 154 (left): Private Collection; 154 (bottom): Peter Liddiard; 155: EyeEm/ Alamy Stock Photo; 156 (top left): Lifestyle Travel Photo/Shutterstock; 156 (top centre): 2happy/Shutterstock; 156 (top right): Laborant/Shutterstock; 156 (right): timages/Shutterstock; 157: Bobby Coutu/Getty Images; 158: KPG_Payless/ Shutterstock; 160 (both): Private Collection; 161: Aubord Dulac/Shutterstock; 162 (bottom): Private Collection; 163 (top left): STOCKFOLIO®/Alamy Stock Photo; 163 (top right): Private Collection; 165: Lutsenko_Oleksandr/Shutterstock; 166: Kent Sievers/Shutterstock; 168 (top): Private Collection; 171 (top): deryabinka/ Shutterstock; 172: Granger/Shutterstock; 173 (bottom): Osmancan Gurdogan/ Depo Photos/Zuma Wire/Shutterstock; 175: Jim Lo Scalzo/EPA-EFE/Shutterstock; 176: Patryk Kosmider/Shutterstock; 177: J Scott Applewhite/AP/Shutterstock; 179: Everett Historical/Shutterstock; 180: Louai Beshara/AFP/Getty Images; 182: B.Forenius/Shutterstock; 184: ullstein bild/Getty Images; 186: NASA images/ Shutterstock; 187: Natwick/Shutterstock; 188: Monica Garza 73/Shutterstock; 189 (top): Radovan1/Shutterstock; 190: Ryan DeBerardinis/Shutterstock; 192: Everett Historical/Shutterstock; 193: Peter Liddiard; 194: Nadezhda Kharitonova/Shutterstock; 196: Roschetzky Photography/Shutterstock; 197: Peter Liddiard; 198 (bottom): Vittee/ Shutterstock; 201: JodGy/Shutterstock; 202: Zern Liew/Shutterstock; 203 (top): stephtodds/Shutterstock; 204: vitec/ Shutterstock; 206: Peter Liddiard; 207 (bottom): streetphotog66/Shutterstock; 208 (top): Irina Fischer/Shutterstock; 208 (bottom left): Radowitz/Shutterstock; 208 (bottom centre): rblfmr/Shutterstock; 208 (bottom right): Trigub/Shutterstock; 209 (top): wavebreakmedia/Shutterstock; 210: Juan Barreto/AFP/Getty Images; 212: Ruben Alfonzo/Shutterstock; 214 (top): anasalhajj/Shutterstock; 214 (bottom): Libor Fousek/Shutterstock; 215: Patrick Jennings/ Shutterstock

All other backgrounds and icons are © Noun Project

Every effort has been made to acknowledge correctly and contact the source and/ or copyright holder of each picture. Any unintentional errors or omissions will be corrected in future editions of this book.